JAMES AND JOHN STUART MILL
PAPERS OF THE
CENTENARY CONFERENCE

JOHN M. ROBSON, co-editor of *The Mill News Letter* and General Editor of the Collected Works of John Stuart Mill, is principal of Victoria College, University of Toronto.
MICHAEL LAINE of Victoria College, co-editor of *The Mill News Letter*, is a member of the Department of English, University of Toronto.

These papers on key issues in intellectual history derive from those delivered at a conference held at the University of Toronto in May 1973 to honour the bicentenary of James Mill's birth and the centenary of John Stuart Mill's death.

Nine authorities – J.H. Burns, Karl W. Britton, J.B. Schneewind, George J. Stigler, Samuel Hollander, L.S. Feuer, Joseph Hamburger, Edward Alexander, and John M. Robson – were invited to discuss what they took to be significant aspects of the thought of the two Mills.

While history, philosophy, economics, social science, and the history of thought were the focal points for the conference, the contributors were free to choose their own topics and approaches. One of the most striking aspects of Mill scholarship that emerges in this volume is the applicability of their ideas to modern problems.

These papers are not final assessments; they are individual and independent contributions to Mill studies that clearly show the vitality of both Mills's thought and the certainty that it will continue to influence and change the ways in which we think about the human condition.

James and
John Stuart Mill /
Papers
of the Centenary
Conference

EDITED BY
JOHN M. ROBSON AND MICHAEL LAINE

UNIVERSITY OF TORONTO PRESS
TORONTO AND BUFFALO

© University of Toronto Press 1976
Toronto and Buffalo
Printed in Canada

Library of Congress Cataloging in Publication Data
Main entry under title:

James and John Stuart Mill.

'Held at the University of Toronto on 3–5 May 1973, honouring the bicentenary
of James Mill's birth and the centenary of John Stuart Mill's death.'
1. Mill, John Stuart, 1806–1873 – Congresses.
2. Mill, James, 1773–1836 – Congresses.
I. Robson, John M. II. Laine, Michael. III. University of Toronto.
B1607.J35   192   76-16117
ISBN 0-8020-5338-6

Contents

Preface

JOHN M. ROBSON
AND
MICHAEL LAINE

The papers in this volume derive from the conference held at the University of Toronto on 3–5 May 1973, honouring the bicentenary of James Mill's birth and the centenary of John Stuart Mill's death. In planning the conference, we were prompted in part by the suggestion of their biographer and disciple, Alexander Bain, who concluded his *John Stuart Mill* (1882) with the comment that the spring of 1973 would provide an appropriate occasion for finally summing up 'their conjoint influence.' Another possible treatment for the younger Mill is suggested by the series of notices in 1873 in the *Examiner*, a newspaper to which he had contributed extensively, on various aspects of his career and writings. (These, still worthy of attention, were collected by H.R. Fox Bourne, and published in 1873 as *John Stuart Mill: His Life and Works*.) Neither Bain's suggestion nor Fox Bourne's collection could, however, provide an exact model, and the planning committee decided to invite nine authorities to discuss what they took to be significant aspects of the thought of the two Mills.

Recognizing that all areas could not be covered in one conference, the committee chose certain emphases: history, philosophy, economics, social sciences, and history of thought. But the contributors were left free to choose their topics and approaches, the primary intent being to elicit individual and independent contributions to Mill studies. As a result, this volume has variety and, inevitably, some gaps; it also has, however, unity beyond that obviously supplied by concentration on the two Mills, a unity deriving from the attention all the papers pay to key issues in intellectual history. The variety results not only from the focus on different areas and on different topics within those areas, but also from the different approaches. Within the variety there is coherence of many and interesting kinds, at least partly revelatory of contemporary concerns. For example, attitudes to history, the theme of the paper by J.H. Burns, is also treated by Edward Alexander, and touched on by L.S. Feuer and Joseph Hamburger. Ethics, the central concern of J.B. Schneewind, is of importance in the discussions of Karl Britton, John M. Robson, and Feuer. Views of progress, a major issue for Alexander, are also significant for Burns, Feuer, Hamburger, and Robson. Questions of comparison with others, and of influence on and by the Mills, are raised by George J. Stigler, Samuel Hollander, Burns, Britton, Schneewind, Feuer, and Hamburger. And readers will find other common themes and concerns.

One of these merits special mention: six of the contributors (Burns, Britton, Schneewind, Stigler, Feuer, and Hamburger) explicitly bring out implications for our time of the ideas examined in their papers, and similar implications can be extracted from the other discussions. While only Hamburger pursues the matter at length, the consensus supports one of the most striking aspects of scholarship on the younger Mill, one that is particularly obvious in discussions of his social and political thought – the applicability of his ideas to modern problems. His relevance can, of course, be discussed crudely and unhistorically, by isolating particular notions and labelling them wise or foolish, exemplary or dangerous; more subtly, the discussion can be directed towards elucidation of the historical background to our cultural and intellectual condition.

Seen in the latter way, these essays can be viewed as an attempt to satisfy Bain's request for a summing-up of the conjoint influence of the Mills, even though the authors did not concentrate on influence. (Bain's requirement of a final judgment is, not regrettably, beyond our competence.) Evidently, James Mill's influence on contemporary opinion is minor – or else his time has not yet come – for, while he occupies a prominent place in Burns' argument, and captures some of the attention of Stigler and Robson and is mentioned more briefly by Britton, Schneewind, and Feuer, he clearly is seen by these critics as much less important than his son. (This unsurprising judgment is supported overwhelmingly by a canvass of the critical literature of the past 150 years.) As for John Stuart Mill, finality of judgment is further off. It will be noted that the essays are not as eulogistic as might be expected from the occasion: there is praise (for example, by Stigler, Hollander, and Feuer), and also dispraise (for example, by Burns and Hamburger), but there is more dispassionate analysis than either. There can be no question, however, that the contributors believe the issues raised by the younger Mill are of continuing significance, especially with reference to man's understanding of, and influence on, institutional and personal relations and the development of better ways of coping with the human condition. While his more abstract discussions are still seen to have value (as Hollander's paper, for instance, shows), it would appear, on the evidence of this volume, that his more general treatments of social, moral, and historical tendencies are thought to have special contemporary force.

Each reader will identify different gaps in the treatments, but a few may be mentioned. In the case of James Mill, perhaps most obvious is detailed reference to his place in the history of psychology. For both father and son, it might be argued, an assessment of their educational theories would be appropriate. With reference to John Stuart Mill, who expressed views on an extremely wide range of subjects, many omissions are necessary. Perhaps no one will miss a treatment of him as a botanist (a matter covered in the Fox Bourne volume), and only a few will regret the absence of a critique of his attitude to India, but it may appear surprising that, apart from some discussion of method by Feuer and Burns, logical matters are not an important issue. Undoubtedly, however, the most striking omission in the present age is that of a major treatment of sexual equality, which was of as great concern to Mill as it is in the mid-1970s. Defensively, we might urge that, like other gaps, this one (as well as the absence of a female contributor) is merely adventitious; in any case, the balance is being rectified by current literature (and practice).

All this having been said, we believe that the main value of the volume will be found in the individual contributions to an historical understanding of the thought of James and John Stuart Mill. As indicated, the papers are meant to be further, not final, assessments; the year 2073 will speak, if at all, in other tones and, most likely, on other matters.

Our thanks are due to all those who aided in the conference, particularly the other members of the planning committee, Dean Francess G. Halpenny, Professor F.E.L. Priestley, and Professor Clifford Leech. Only the generous support, for which we are deeply grateful, of the Canada Council and the University of Toronto made the conference feasible. Publication of this volume is now made possible by a grant from the Humanities Research Council of Canada, using funds provided by the Canada Council.

J M R
M L
Victoria College
University of Toronto

JAMES AND JOHN STUART MILL
PAPERS OF THE
CENTENARY CONFERENCE

The Light of Reason: Philosophical History in the Two Mills

J. H. BURNS

The role of history in the work of the Benthamite Utilitarians presents us with a paradox. On the one hand there is the common, almost commonplace observation that Bentham's theory of society is essentially ahistorical. Such gestures as he makes in the direction of recognizing an historical dimension in the problems with which he is concerned are at best perfunctory, at worst contemptuous. His 1782 *Essay on the Influence of Place and Time in Matters of Legislation* is in fact largely concerned with local rather than historical variations in the circumstances to which the legislator must attend.[1] Though his own historical reading was far from negligible, he developed an attitude of dismissive scorn towards history as a subject of study. He referred to it as essentially 'the history of times to which our own are happily as unlike as possible,'[2] and seems in general to have feared that any considerable attention to the historical record could only generate the 'Chinese fallacy' of judging social and political issues by references to 'the wisdom of our ancestors.'[3]

Yet two of Bentham's principal followers (I refrain from begging any questions by using Bentham's own favourite term, 'disciples') left histories as their most substantial single works. In the case of George Grote, the most

1 *The Works of Jeremy Bentham, published under the superintendence of his executor, John Bowring*, 11 vols. (Edinburgh 1838–43), I, 169–94. There the title of the essay is given with the word 'Time' before 'Place,' but the order used above is overwhelmingly commoner in the MSS and more accurately indicates the emphasis in Bentham's discussion.

2 Bentham MSS, University College London, cxlix, 71. From notes, c 1795, headed 'Diffusion of Knowledge'

3 *The Book of Fallacies* (1823), *Works*, II, 398–401

substantial was also by far the most distinguished and the most valuable: the *History of Greece* was a major contribution to historiography in its field and long retained a position of pre-eminence among works in English on the subject. And if James Mill's *History of British India* fell an earlier victim to corrective criticism and supersession, it was none the less an important, even an epoch-making, work in its day. In the 1840s Horace Hayman Wilson, though unsparingly critical of many aspects of Mill's *History* in his annotated and extended edition, still regarded it as 'the most valuable work upon the subject which has yet been published.'[4]

From John Stuart Mill we have, of course, no substantial work of an historical character. What we do have, however, is a conception of the relation between history and the science of society which surely belongs to a very different intellectual world from that in which we commonly locate the Benthamites. There is no need at this point to rehearse in detail that conception: some aspects of it will be central to later stages of this paper. It may suffice for the moment to recall one weighty sentence from the *System of Logic*: 'It has become the aim of really scientific thinkers to connect by theories the facts of universal history: it is acknowledged to be one of the requisites of a general system of social doctrine, that it should explain, so far as the data exist, the main facts of history; and a Philosophy of History is generally admitted to be at once the verification, and the initial form, of the Philosophy of the Progress of Society.'[5] This is a far cry, it seems, from Bentham's amused or angry contempt.

How far a cry is it, however, from the author of the *History of British India*? James Mill, as recent work on him has been reminding us, grew up and received his intellectual formation in the Scotland of Mr Duncan Forbes's 'scientific Whigs,' of those writers who have been emerging over recent decades as the founding fathers of historical sociology. Benthamite in some sense he may have become, but not, it may be thought, until he had absorbed the notion of philosophical history, directly or indirectly, from Adam Smith and Adam Ferguson, John Millar and Dugald Stewart. We may feel bound to agree with Wilson when he says of Mill's *History* that it 'is remarkable for ... opinions which are peculiar ... to the school of which he was a distinguished disciple'[6] – that school being the 'sect of utilitarians' of whose foundation Bentham was dreaming as early as the 1780s.[7] Yet we are surely not less bound to recognize that it was no mere Benthamite Utilitarian who published in

4 James Mill, *The History of British India*, 8 vols. (4th ed., with notes and continuation by Horace Hayman Wilson, London 1840–8), I, ix. (All subsequent references are to this edition.) Wilson (1786–1868) was professor of Sanskrit at Oxford from 1832, and librarian to the East India Company from 1836.

5 *Collected Works*, VIII (Toronto, 1974), 930 (VI, x, 8)

6 *History*, I, i

7 Bentham MSS, University College London, clxix, 79

1818 the work which was to make his reputation and to be instrumental in securing his permanent deliverance from the journalistic insecurity in which he had lived for so long. Indeed, it is well worth our while to remember that the *History of British India* was conceived and begun some two years before the author is known to have met Bentham and before there are any grounds for supposing that Bentham's ideas had any particular hold upon his mind.[8] The historian was and may be supposed to have remained a 'Scotch philosopher' who had little to learn from Bentham either in method or in self-confidence as he approached the task of writing the history of the British connection with a subcontinent which he had never visited and with none of whose languages he had the least acquaintance.

I come then, at last, to my title. The phrase with which it begins is taken from a remark by J.S. Mill in *Auguste Comte and Positivism* (1865), where he refers to his father as 'the historian who first threw the light of reason on Hindoo society.'[9] The questions raised in my mind by this filially pious comment were these: What, in the context of historical writing, did John Mill understand by 'the light of reason'? Why did he think that his father's *History* had brought that light to bear upon its subject? And finally, how substantial were his grounds for the claim he had made, in terms of his own understanding of the method and purpose of historical enquiry?

The order in which these questions have been posed makes it appropriate to begin with some consideration of the view of history in relation to social science to which John Mill's reflections led him in the 1830s and early 1840s. It is a familiar enough fact that these reflections were precipitated by the argument which had followed Macaulay's celebrated review in 1829 of James Mill's *Essay on Government*. Confronted, as he thought, with two alternative methodological approaches – the 'geometrical' or abstract method exemplified in the work of Bentham and his father, and Macaulay's version of 'the method of Induction,' with its explicit reference to 'assiduously studying the history of past ages' in quest of 'the evidence of facts' – Mill soon concluded that each was mistaken: 'I saw that Macaulay's conception of the logic of politics was erroneous; that he stood up for the empirical mode of treating political phenomena, against the philosophical ...' Yet at the same time he concluded 'that there was really something more fundamentally erroneous in my father's conception of philosophical Method, as applicable to politics, than I had hitherto supposed there was.'[10] It was in his attempt to identify this paternal mistake that Mill began to work towards his own eventual conception of the true historical method in social science.

---

8 Alexander Bain, *James Mill: A Biography* (London 1882), 61: 'The commencement of the *History of India* dates from the end of 1806.'
9 CW, X, 320
10 J.S. Mill, *Autobiography*, ed. J. Stillinger (Boston 1969), 95

In the first of what were later published as *Essays on Some Unsettled Questions of Political Economy* (1844), itself first published in the *London and Westminster Review* for October 1836, Mill was writing 'On the Definition of Political Economy; and on the Method of Investigation proper to it.' Here, writing in 1830 and revising in 1833, he argues, against Macaulay, that 'the social science ... presupposes the whole science of the nature of the individual mind,' so that 'Pure mental philosophy ... is an essential part, or preliminary, of political philosophy.'[11] He further asserts that the *a priori*, as opposed to the *a posteriori* or merely inductive method, is 'the only method by which truth can possibly be attained in any department of the social science.'[12] This is because the alternative *a posteriori* method is quite simply inapplicable in social science since we are there debarred from making contrived experiments. At the same time, however, Mill recognizes that the *a priori* conclusions reached by, for example, an economist will be abstract in relation to total social reality in the same way as the conclusions of geometry are abstract in relation to bodies and figures actually existing in space.[13] This is to recognize that concrete social effects are the product of a concurrence of causes,[14] but Mill does not at this stage seem to have drawn methodological conclusions for a general science of society. His interest is still concentrated upon specific sciences such as economics, where abstract conclusions deductively established are to be verified and modified by means of a careful comparison with the observed facts. Though we know that Saint-Simonian and, so to speak, pre-Comtean ideas were already at work in his mind, he had not yet arrived at a fully developed and architectonic notion of the science of society as such.

It is by no means easy to be sure what Mill in this essay understood and intended as to the nature and status of the science which is concerned with what (he acknowledges) may be called, 'though in a somewhat looser sense, *laws* of society.'[15] Even his nomenclature is unfixed; though seeming to prefer, in the passage just cited, the term 'social economy' (with 'speculative politics,' 'the *science* of politics,' and 'the natural history of society' as less eligible

11 CW, IV, 320. While there is no explicit reference to Macaulay in the essay, the example Mill chooses to illustrate his distinction (ibid., 324) between 'two kinds of reasoners' in social and political analysis – the question of the probable behaviour of absolute rulers – shows that the debate between Macaulay and his father was certainly in his mind. He there (ibid., 325) calls the two groups the 'practicals' and the 'theorists.'

12 Ibid., 326. It is perhaps worth remarking that in the 1836 text, rather than the phrase 'any department of the social sciences,' the reading is 'the moral sciences' (326^{t-t}). But Mill was already using the phrase 'department of the social science' in 1836. Compare ibid., 329, 'either in Political Economy or in any other department of the social science.'

13 Ibid., 325–7

14 Ibid., 322, 328

15 Ibid., 320

substitutes), he was already prepared, as noted above, to refer to a 'social science' of which such special sciences as political economy were branches or 'departments.'[16] What he does not seem to do at all at this stage is to indicate a methodology for this general science, while he insists with emphasis that only the *a priori* method is appropriate, and indeed available, for its branches. It is noteworthy that the 1836 text included a passage (significantly suppressed in 1844) referring to 'Knowledge of what is called history' as, in this context, 'useful only in the third degree.'[17] In 1844, on the other hand, an insertion in the paragraph which introduces the notion of 'social economy' as the general science of society adds to the list of its concerns 'the historical order' in which states of society 'tend to succeed one another.'[18]

These minor adjustments to the earlier essay are symptomatic of something of far wider and more profound importance – the influence on Mill's mind of Auguste Comte's *Cours de philosophie positive* as its successive volumes came to his notice in the late 1830s and early 40s is a point that needs no labouring. What is important here is to recall that it was 'the connected view of history' in Comte's fifth volume that excited Mill's most enthusiastic response; and that it was to Comte's notion of an inverse deductive or historical method in social science that Mill acknowledged his most direct indebtedness.[19] Philosophical history for John Mill, then, was to mean historical investigation which employs this method for the establishment and verification of general laws of society.

It may be useful to follow Mill briefly in the order of exposition which he adopts at this stage in the *Logic*, beginning with his recapitulation and elaboration of the case for rejecting alike 'the Chemical, or Experimental, Method' professed by the self-styled 'true Baconians'[20] and the 'Geometrical, or Abstract Method' adopted by Hobbes and in 'the interest-philosophy of the Bentham school.'[21] Both in their different ways neglect the cardinal point that 'In social phenomena the Composition of Causes is the universal law.'[22] As a result the pseudo-Baconians treat 'political facts in as directly experimental a method as chemical facts,' as though men in society were 'converted into another kind of substance.' In fact, Mill maintains, 'Human beings in society have no properties but those which are derived from, and may be resolved into, the laws of the nature of individual man.'[23] But the Hobbesian or Benthamite geometricians, fully aware as they are of the fundamental relevance of the laws of individual psychology, neglect the 'Composition of

---

16 Compare n 12 above. Towards the end of the essay (334, 335) Mill shows some inclination to use the term 'social Philosophy.'
17 Ibid., 333ᵘ
18 Ibid., 320
19 *Autobiography*, 125–6
20 cw, viii, 880 (vi, vii, 1)
21 cw, viii, 890 (vi, viii, 3)
22 cw, viii, 879 (vi, vii, 1)
23 Ibid.

Causes' in their own fashion by grossly oversimplifying the operation of these laws, and by neglecting in their analyses the influence of such factors as 'the habitual sentiments and feelings, the general modes of thinking and acting, which prevail throughout the community of which they' – in this case, rulers – 'are members; as well as ... the feelings, habits, and modes of thought which characterize the particular class in that community to which they themselves belong.'[24]

The deductive method, then, which Mill holds essential to any science worthy of the name, must in social as in physical science be concrete, not abstract: it must proceed 'by deduction from many, not from one or a very few, original premises; considering each effect as (what it really is) an aggregate result of many causes, operating sometimes through the same, sometimes through different mental agencies, or laws of human nature.'[25] Such indeed is the complexity of social phenomena that this 'Physical' method in which deduction is followed by verification *a posteriori* has to give way in crucially important areas to the Comtean inverse deductive or historical method. But Mill dissents from Comte's view insofar as that view reduces all sociological investigation to verification by reference to the laws of human nature of what are essentially and originally generalizations from history. For him – else there had been no *Principles of Political Economy* to follow the *System of Logic* – there are important aspects of social life in which the facts 'though influenced like the rest by all sociological agents, are under the *immediate* influence, principally at least, of a few only.'[26] Economics afforded one instance; another was the 'hypothetical or abstract' science of 'Political Ethology, or the theory of the causes which determine the type of character belonging to a people or to an age.'[27] But we shall vainly search even the Toronto edition of Mill's works for his 'Principles of Political Ethology': it may challenge Lord Acton's 'History of Freedom' for the title of 'the greatest book that never was written.'

And in the end the Comtean view prevails even if it does not monopolize. In the 'general science of society,' where the full range of the compound and complex causal factors is to be grasped, there is no hope for direct deduction to be followed by verification: 'nothing of a really scientific character is here possible, except by the inverse deductive method.' Nor must it be supposed that sociology in this comprehensive sense is for Mill a mere decorative pinnacle or even a coping-stone. It is the true keystone of the arch he is describing, and the special sciences such as economics can assert only conditional conclusions 'subject to the paramount control of the laws of the general science.'[28]

These laws are in some sense historical laws, for whether they relate to what Mill, following Comte, calls social statics – 'the theory of the mutual actions

24 CW, VIII, 891 (VI, viii, 3)   25 Ibid., 894
26 CW, VIII, 900 (VI, ix, 2)   27 CW, VIII, 904–5 (VI, ix, 4)
28 Ibid., 906–71

and reactions of contemporaneous social phenomena'[29] – or to social dynamics – 'of which the aim is to observe and explain the sequences of social conditions'[30] – they derive from a process of investigation in which the data of historical observation are the necessary point of departure. Mill is as dubious as ever about the status and value of what are sometimes presented as historical generalizations. The establishing of a deductive connection between the facts of history and the laws of ethology and psychology is the only way in which we can advance from superficial empiricism to scientific understanding. Yet the historical process is fundamental to our social experience and to any understanding of it: 'what we now are and do, is in a very small degree the result of the universal circumstances of the human race, or even of our own circumstances acting through the original qualities of our species, but mainly of the qualities produced in us by the whole previous history of humanity.'[31] That history, Mill is convinced, is progressive, not cyclical in character even though we can have no absolute assurance that progress will mean improvement.[32] It is a process characterized by a complex 'filiation' between successive 'states of society,' and there would be little hope, even by the true historical method of inverse deduction, of reaching 'the real scientific derivative law of the development of humanity and human affairs' if we could not identify some 'prime element' in the process. But this, Mill believes, is what we can in fact do. The 'central chain,' to which all the other chains of uniformity in historical succession can be related, is provided, he argues, by 'the state of the speculative faculties of mankind' in successive ages and in different societies.[33] And the law of development governing the state of men's speculative faculties is indicated by Comte's 'great generalization' concerning the three stages – theological, metaphysical, and positive – of knowledge.[34] It is ultimately on this kind of basis that Mill looks forward to the development of 'a sociological system widely removed from the vague and conjectural character of all former attempts, and worthy to take its place, at last, among the sciences.'[35]

John Mill published his *System of Logic*, its sixth book culminating triumphantly in the concept of social science just outlined, in 1843, a quarter of a century after the publication of his father's attempt to 'throw the light of reason on Hindoo society.' What is the relation between the father's notion of history and the son's vision of 'a Philosophy of History ... directed and controlled by ... sociological evidence'?[36] We are not, of course, to expect a close correspondence

29 cw, viii, 918 (vi, x, 5)   30 cw, viii, 924 (vi, x, 6)
31 cw, viii, 915–16 (vi, x, 4)   32 See cw, viii, 913 (vi, x, 3)
33 cw, viii, 924–6 (vi, x, 6–7)
34 cw, viii, 928–9 & n (vi, x, 8). It is in the long footnote dealing with criticisms of
   Comte, by Whewell in particular, that Mill refers to 'This great generalization ...'
35 Ibid., 930
36 Ibid.

or a startling anticipation. The *History of British India* was, after all, a good deal less than fully systematic in its approach; the author himself referred to it as 'a motley kind of production.'[37] John Mill, moreover, had, as we have seen, moved towards his own conclusions as to historical and sociological method by way of some considerable degree of reaction against his father's ideas. Besides, he was profoundly convinced that the kind of historical insight he found in the Continental writers of his own generation was an essentially new intellectual departure, a major element in that 'reaction against the eighteenth century' which in the *Autobiography* he mentions in the context of the final assessment of his father as 'the last of the eighteenth century.'[38] And one of the characteristics of the *philosophes* of the Enlightenment to whose position and attitudes he so clearly assimilates those of his father was, needless to say, the disrespect for history to which Mill refers in the 1840 essay on Coleridge.[39] That essay is indeed a crucial document in the present context and it is significant that Mill thought fit to quote so extensively from it in the account of historical method in the *Logic*.[40] Where Coleridge had apparently led, it was not to be supposed that James Mill would have followed. In any case his son was far from convinced that even in the 1840s and even on the continent of Europe (England being 'usually the last to enter into the general movement of the European mind')[41] the essential point had been securely grasped, except by Comte.[42] Comte himself, for that matter, was not beyond suspicion, and certainly in some of his applications of and deductions from his principles was already showing signs of those tendencies that were in the end to alienate Mill completely from his later thought.[43] It is in a sense to a highly esoteric truth that Mill introduces his readers in 1843, and one therefore hardly likely to have been accessible to his father during the intermittent labours that produced the *History of British India* in 1818.

Yet it was hardly a mere rhetorical flourish or a supererogatory deference to the maxim *De mortuis nil nisi bonum* that led John Mill, another twenty-

---

37 James Mill to David Ricardo, 6 Oct. 1816, *The Works and Correspondence of David Ricardo*, VII, ed. P. Sraffa (Cambridge 1952), 75

38 *Autobiography*, 122–3

39 'The disrespect in which history was held by the *philosophes* is notorious ...' (CW, X, 139).

40 CW, VIII, 921–4 (VI, X, 5)

41 CW, VIII, 930 (VI, X, 8)

42 CW, VIII, 913–15 (VI, X, 3). See esp. 915: 'M. Comte alone, among the new historical school, has seen the necessity of thus connecting all our generalizations from history with the laws of human nature.'

43 *Autobiography*, 126–7; and compare *Logic*, CW, VIII, 928 (VI, X, 8), where Mill says he will not discuss 'the worth of his [Comte's] conclusions, and especially of his predictions and recommendations with respect to the Future of society, which appear to me greatly inferior in value to his appreciation of the Past ...'

two years later, to use the phrase with which my enquiry began. His father's *History*, whatever its defects in system, was no mere compilation. Few writers excel James Mill in their capacity to give the impression of a mind energetically, relentlessly, at work. The results may be attractive or otherwise, but they nearly always seem to be the intended effects of a forceful and resolute intellect. It was, to repeat, an intellect schooled in a particular fashion, a fashion to which the concept of philosophical history had made a substantial contribution. The *History of British India* may be something of a patchwork, but if it has a pattern, it may be expected to be a philosophical one. What kind of philosophy is the question still to be explored.

In a book which must for sheer intellectual quality and excitement rank very high among modern studies of Utilitarianism, Eric Stokes has argued that Mill's *History* was 'principally an attempt to make a philosophical analysis of Indian society and assess its place in the "scale of civilisation." '[44] Stokes further recalls that its author conceived of its having perhaps an even broader and more general purpose. Writing to Ricardo in the years immediately before its publication, Mill argued that despite its 'motley' character, the book might 'make no bad introduction to the study of civil society in general'; and indeed that it might exhibit 'the principles and laws of the social order in almost all its most remarkable states, from the most crude to the most perfect with which we are yet acquainted.'[45] Now this is certainly the language of philosophical history as the Scottish Enlightenment understood that discipline, though it is by no means specific enough to allow us as yet to identify the precise position Mill adopts in his approach to the writing of history. Perhaps the presumably more studied indications given in the author's preface to the work can help us forward. There, Mill follows his depreciatory account of what advantages might accrue from the opportunities he had lacked of assembling at first hand data of observation for his work, by an examination of 'certain ... endowments, which the discharge of the highest duties of the historian imperiously demands.' These duties require the historian to exhibit not merely 'the obvious outside of things,' but 'just ideas of great measures'; and so he must have 'A clear discernment ... of their causes; a clear discernment of their consequences; a clear discernment of their natural tendencies; and of the circumstances likely to operate either in combination with these natural tendencies, or in opposition to them.' A fair enough account, no doubt, of the ideal historian's equipment: *O si sic omnes!* What matters here, however, is Mill's more precise analysis of the kinds of knowledge presupposed by such 'discernment.'

44 Eric Stokes, *The English Utilitarians and India* (Oxford, 1959), 53
45 James Mill to David Ricardo, 19 Oct. 1817, *Works and Correspondence of Ricardo*, VII, 195–6

'It is plain,' we are told, that the historian

needs the most profound knowledge of the laws of human nature, which is the end, as well as instrument, of every thing. It is plain, that he requires the most perfect comprehension of the principles of human society; or the course, into which the laws of human nature impel the human being, in his gregarious state, or when formed into a complex body along with others of his kind. The historian requires a clear comprehension of the practical play of the machinery of government; for, in like manner as the general laws of motion are counteracted and modified by friction, the power of which may yet be accurately ascertained and provided for, so it is necessary for the historian correctly to apprehend the counteraction which the more general laws of human nature may receive from individual or specific varieties, and that allowance for it with which his anticipations and conclusions ought to be formed. In short, the whole field of human nature, the whole field of legislation, the whole field of judicature, the whole field of administration, down to war, commerce, and diplomacy, ought to be familiar to his mind.[46]

One may think, wryly, of Rousseau's remark that 'it would take gods to give men laws,' but if Mill's godlike historian is avowedly only a pattern laid up in the heavens it is a pattern with great significance for what Mill was trying to achieve in terrestrial historiography. Some points are at once obvious and of evident importance. The final frame of reference for history is to be provided by a science of human nature of which the laws correspond in the moral and social world to the laws of motion in the physical world. From these laws of human nature derive the principles of human society, and in determining the precise way in which the derivation operates in particular instances the functioning of government is of essential importance. This seems to be because it is 'the practical play' of governmental machinery which fills the role of counteractive and modifying friction in the social world and produces thereby those variations in the actual operation of the laws of human nature for which the historian must make due allowance.[47]

Such a view of the relation between government, society, and human nature seems characteristic of what Eric Stokes describes as 'the immense and indefinite influence which the Utilitarians allowed to the power of law and government.'[48] It may remind us too of Alexander Bain's remark that in Book II of the *History of British India* – certainly the part most relevant to the present

46 *History*, I, xxvi–xxvii
47 It may be worth noticing that John Mill, in the essay on the definition of political economy, mentions the frequency with which the comparison had been made between friction in mechanics and the effect of 'disturbing causes' in social science (cw, IV, 320).
48 Stokes, *Utilitarians*, 55

discussion – 'The best ideas of the sociological writers of the eighteenth century were combined with the Bentham philosophy of law ...'[49] In fact, of course, Mill's approach is more than Benthamite here, more even than Utilitarian in any narrowly defined use of the term. The image of human society in which the fundamental laws of human nature are modified and can be controlled in their operation by the manipulation of laws and institutions is central to the whole notion of a science of legislation which represents one major strand in the social theory of the Enlightenment during its later phases. Condillac's *Traité des systèmes* is only one – though a notable one – of many sources for this way of thinking. There is no doubt that the Utilitarian, and specifically the Benthamite theory of law and government is focussed to a great extent upon the notion of the legislator as Condillac's *machiniste* or social engineer.[50]

Neither Condillac nor Bentham, however, reflected what Bain thought of as 'the best ideas of the sociological writers of the eighteenth century'; and if those ideas are indeed prominently present in the more 'philosophical' aspects of Mill's *History*, the approach adopted by its author may have been less simple and unilinear than Stokes suggests. In Stokes's view, Mill in the *History* 'aimed at the same simplicity of analysis as his *Essay on Government* ... Above all he strove to deduce the Indian problem and its solution from a single principle ... and to reason with the logic of his "abstract or geometrical method." ' Bad government was the source of Indian, as of other human ills, and the remedy for those ills 'lay simply in a reconstruction of the machine of government.'[51] In a sense, no doubt, and in the context of the problems with which *The English Utilitarians and India* is explicitly concerned, this is a legitimate view. It does serve to define accurately the distinctive approach of the Utilitarians and those who were influenced by them to the problems of Indian society. Is it acceptable, however, as an account of Mill's historical approach in a book written, after all, before he had any reason to think that he would ever have more than an observant citizen's interest in those problems?

No one can doubt that the influence of the form of government and the closely associated effects of the legal system and the system of taxation are of central importance in Mill's analysis of Indian society. They significantly precede, for instance, in his order of discussion, the topics of religion and manners. Yet even government is not the first factor to which Mill attends.

49 Bain, *James Mill*, 177
50 Etienne Bonnot de Condillac, *Traité des systèmes* (1749) in *Œuvres complètes*, 23 vols. (Paris 1798), II. Compare for example, 375–6: 'Un peuple est un corps artificiel, c'est au magistrat ... d'entretenir l'harmonie et la force, dans tous ses membres. Il est le machiniste qui doit rétablir les ressorts, et remonter toute la machine aussi souvent que les circonstances le demandent.'
51 Stokes, *Utilitarians*, 66

In his account of the Hindus in Book II, the sceptical examination in the first chapter of their ancient history and chronology is followed not immediately by the discussion of government but by a chapter devoted to the 'Classification and Distribution of the People.' This chapter, moreover, opens with an explicit reference to the evolution of society towards a specific form of government: 'The transition from the state of tribes to the more regulated and artificial system of a monarchy and laws is not sudden; it is the result of a gradual preparation and improvement.' And 'slow is the progress made by the human understanding, in its rude and ignorant state.' But there is a catalyst in the case. It need cause us no surprise to find that for James Mill, as doubtless for his son, this was because 'In every society there are superior spirits, capable of seizing the best ideas of their times, and if they are not opposed by circumstances, of accelerating the progress of the community to which they belong.'[52] What is perhaps a little surprising, and even amusing, is to discover the figure of the Legislator advancing onto the stage, with Lycurgus among others in the wings – or at least in a footnote. We had been prepared, it seemed, for the gradual evolution of a caste system, which now proves to have been the work, in origin at least, of 'the Hindu legislator.'[53] Wilson was as quick to detect the contradiction as he was to point out that Mill's account of the supposed lawgiver and his activities was in fact without any foundation in the Hindu tradition.[54] This is conjectural history indeed, and with a vengeance.

Nonetheless, dubious as Mill's account may be, it remains an interesting and important point that he begins his analysis of Hindu society with an examination of its structure in terms of classes and functional groupings. Nor does any conviction grow, as we proceed through the ensuing chapters, that we are dealing here with quite the kind of geometrical or abstract analysis we might expect from Stokes's discussion of the book. There is, needless to say, Benthamism in plenty. However great the extent to which Mill's mind had been moulded before his association with Bentham began, no one can doubt that, for instance, the account of 'The qualities desirable in a BODY OF LAW' is Bain's 'Bentham philosophy' in its purest form.[55] Or that the analogous account of 'two primary qualities desirable in a system of taxation' in which 'every thing is included' is equally of Benthamic inspiration.[56] And it is doubtless true enough that the defects Mill found in Indian law and fiscal methods

---

52 *History*, I, 177–8
53 'The first legislator of the Hindus ...' (ibid., 179) and 'the author of the Hindu laws ... the Hindu legislator' (ibid., 182). Compare also ibid., 181: 'When the Hindus were lingering in this uneasy situation, it would appear that there arose among them one of those superior men, who are capable of accelerating the improvement of society.'
54 Ibid., 180 nn1, 2
55 Ibid., 282–3
56 Ibid., 291–4

were for him the inevitable consequences of the more basic and radical defects in the system of government; for 'the political establishment' is at once 'the great circumstance by which' the people's 'condition, character, and operations are determined,' and 'the system of actions by which the social order is preserved.'[57] These phrases occur at the opening of the chapter on 'The Form of Government' in Book II. But the chapter as a whole is surely a profound disappointment. Not only is it on certain crucial points merely conjectural. 'We may conjecture what we please,' Wilson drily comments, 'of a stage of society of which we know nothing, but it is conjecture only, and little calculated to extend real knowledge.'[58] From our present viewpoint this might have mattered less than it did from Wilson's. Mill's conjectural views about the development and character of Indian government might have been of considerable interest here. In fact they fall, it seems to me, far short of the level of interest one might have expected because they are so unsystematic, so uncoordinated, and indeed so contradictory.

The chapter on 'the political establishment,' then, is ill-fitted to provide us with a key to unlock the argument as a whole. True, there are distinct enough traces in it of the view of political motivation which made so celebrated a figure, only a year or two later, in the *Essay on Government*.[59] And it is interesting to find Wilson, in a note drawing attention to the contradiction in Mill's simultaneous assertion of virtual monarchical absolutism and virtual priestly despotism, remarking that in any case neither assertion would be strictly true since 'Hindu princes and Brahmans [sic] are held in check by many considerations.'[60] This had been the kind of critique of the analysis in the *Essay* deployed in turn by Macaulay and, in a modified form at least, by Mill's own son. We have thus been brought close to an essential question: How far is it justifiable to take the argumentative and polemical method of James Mill's *Essay on Government* as reflecting accurately his concept of the nature and appropriate method of the science of society?

Macaulay and John Mill, for all their differences, would presumably have given an affirmative answer to this question, and to their voices must be added that of Eric Stokes in our own time. I have already quoted his explicit assertion that James Mill used the 'geometrical or abstract method' in his analysis of Indian problems, and he goes on to develop the point by equally explicit reference to the *Essay on Government* considered as 'a summary exposition of the whole Utilitarian doctrine.'[61] Now this is not the only occasion on which

57 Ibid., 202
58 Ibid., 212n
59 Compare the 'short analysis,' ibid., 217–22
60 Ibid., 222n. Compare also Wilson's critique of Mill's analysis of the motives of the Brahmin class, 220n
61 Stokes, *Utilitarians*, 66

we may derive a corrective from the shrewd and canny mind of Alexander Bain. It will be recalled that Bain concludes his discussion of the *Essay on Government* with an account of 'John Mill's criticism of his father's Method of Politics' and with a counter-critique. In this he argued that the son was mistaken in regarding the *Essay* 'as a nearly pure specimen of *a priori* reasoning':

His father knew as much history as any man of his time; he had pondered its lessons, and would not have published any doctrine at variance therewith. But in such a very synoptical article, the citation of historical instances would have been impossible, or, if possible, illusory. What was wanted was a formal and exhaustive setting forth of the generalizations of historical facts, widely examined, sifted, and compared; a process that John Mill would have been the first to do homage to, as the only complete and satisfactory supplement to his deductive positions.[62]

With the adequacy of this as a rejoinder to John Mill's critique I need not here concern myself. I cite it only to indicate that a knowledgeable commentator found it possible to argue that the *Essay on Government* can itself be read as a highly concentrated distillation of certain 'lessons of history.' The conclusions were indeed connected to universal laws of human nature; but John Mill himself demanded no less if the use of history was not to stop short at the level of superficial empiricism. Bain's view, for what it is worth, presents us with an intriguing inversion of Stokes's argument. Stokes claims in effect that Mill wrote history in terms of the abstract theory of the *Essay on Government*; Bain seems to be saying that the *Essay on Government* is the essential oil pressed from its author's extensive historical knowledge. Neither interpretation may be entirely plausible as it stands, yet each may serve to correct some degree of imbalance in the other.

The question of James Mill's governing intentions as an historian is less than adequately answered, and it is natural to hope that the chapter of 'General Reflections' with which he closes the protracted discussion of Hindu society in Book II should throw light on the problem. Such hopes seem to be confirmed by the kind of point Mill makes early in the chapter. It is here, for instance, that he says: 'No scheme of government can happily conduce to the ends of government, unless it is adapted to the state of the people for whose use it is intended.' The remark is made, moreover, in the immediate context of Mill's explicit indication that his object has been the ascertaining of 'the true state of the Hindus in the scale of civilization.'[63] A little further on, the following critically important paragraph occurs:

62 Bain, *James Mill*, 232–3
63 *History*, II, 152

It is not easy to describe the characteristics of the different stages of social progress. It is not from one feature, or from two, that a just conclusion can be drawn. In these it sometimes happens that nations resemble which are placed at stages considerably remote. It is from a joint view of all the great circumstances taken together, that their progress can be ascertained; and it is from an accurate comparison, grounded on these general views, that a scale of civilization can be formed, in which the relative position of nations may be accurately marked.[64]

When we find that this is immediately succeeded by a reference to 'all that modern philosophy had performed for the elucidation of history' by the latter part of the eighteenth century, though (Mill adds) 'very little had been attempted in this great department'; and when we further find, appended at this point, a lengthy footnote discussing the work of 'Mr. Miller [sic] of Glasgow,' we may well feel that we are on a track of considerable significance.[65] This is perhaps the clearest evidence of Mill's conscious identification of his enterprise with those of the philosophical historians of the Scottish Enlightenment. It is something more. It involves the assertion that John Millar's pioneering work had not been followed up: 'the subject, great as its importance is, has not been resumed.' And this leads in turn to the declaration that 'One of the ends which has at least been in view during the scrutiny conducted in these pages, has been to contribute something to the progress of so important an investigation. It is hoped that the materials which are here collected will be regarded as going far to elucidate the state of society in all the leading nations of Asia.'[66]

The hope, however, proves to be more than a little delusive. One reason for the disappointment is, incidentally, a feature common to the *History* and the compact *Essay on Government*. The feature is polemic. One does not have to read far in the chapter we are now considering to appreciate the strength and vehemence of Mill's controversial purposes. It is 'the tone of eulogy adopted with regard to the Hindus,'[67] and more generally with regard to Asian cultures as a whole that he is concerned to dispel and the sources of which he wishes to eradicate. In its way the attack is, as Eric Stokes says, a *tour de force*,[68] reaching its climax, perhaps, in the paragraph on the characters of the Indian and Chinese peoples which it is impossible not to follow Stokes in quoting at large:

Even in manners, and in the leading parts of the moral character, the lines of resemblance are strong. Both nations are to nearly an equal degree tainted with the vices of insincerity; dissembling, treacherous, mendacious, to an excess which surpasses even

---

64 Ibid., 156
66 Ibid., 157n
68 Stokes, *Utilitarians*, 53

65 Ibid., 156, 156 n2
67 Ibid., 159, and compare generally 153ff

the usual measure of uncultivated society. Both are disposed to excessive exaggeration with regard to every thing relating to themselves. Both are cowardly and unfeeling. Both are in the highest degree conceited of themselves, and full of affected contempt for others. Both are, in the physical sense, disgustingly unclean in their persons and houses.[69]

We are to remember, too, that the Hindus 'are in a state of civilization very nearly the same with that of ... the Persians, and the Arabians,' as well as the Chinese; while 'the subordinate nations, the Japanese, Cochin-Chinese, Siamese, Burmese, and even Malays and Tibetians' are to be regarded as subordinate branches of the same cultural system.[70]

Now the effrontery of all this might be palliated, the almost blood-curdling arrogance of Mill's cultural chauvinism might be in some measure extenuated, in several ways. The splendid felicities of Gibbon's style, for instance, may reconcile many readers who do not wholly share his opinions on the historical role of Christianity. And if we are not to look for that kind of felicity in Mill, he himself has taught us to expect a range and rigour of philosophical analysis which might redeem the method even though it had been misapplied. If, by the unfortunate Sir William Jones, 'The term of civilization was ..., as by most men, attached to no fixed and definite assemblage of ideas,'[71] Mill has given us every reason to look for a different state of affairs in his own work. We do not find it. Not only has Mill failed, as Wilson pointed out, to define fully the standard of civilization he is applying.[72] Still more serious is the absence from his analysis of any clearly articulated method. At point after point one is reminded, it seem to me, of the censure Mill directed against those he was attacking: 'This was a theory invented to preserve as much as actual observation would allow to be preserved, of a pre-established and favourite creed. It was a gratuitous assumption. It preceded inquiry, and no inquiry was welcome, but that which yielded matter for its support.'[73] One must speak as one finds; and I must confess to finding Mill's practice as an historian in those aspects of his work to which I have been able here to give an admittedly cursory examination disturbingly distant from the principles he himself professed.

Yet, after all, we may, any of us, be grateful at times for being judged in accordance with our principles rather than our practice; and if there is, as I suspect, a good deal more of the journalist than of the genius in Mill's *History of British India*, there may still be interest and even value in his conception of what philosophical genius could achieve in historical investigation. Certainly it is still worth reverting to the questions which, I suggested, were raised by John Mill's laudatory reference to his father as historian.

69 *History*, II, 220
71 Ibid., 156
73 Ibid., 162

70 Ibid., 213–14
72 Compare ibid., 232 n2

The first of these questions, then, was that of the meaning to be attached to the phrase 'the light of reason'; and it seems clear that in regard to history this must for John Mill have meant some attempt to treat historical data philosophically or scientifically, in a fashion fundamentally different from the kind of misconception he condemned, for instance, in his critique of Sedgwick in 1835.[74] It must, that is to say, be something quite other than the facile attempt to treat the historical record as a laboratory in which experiments could be observed and conclusions reached by an imperfect and misconceived process of induction. If James Mill had indeed brought this rational, philosophical, scientific light to bear upon his subject – here we pass to my second question – it could only be, for his son, because the *History of British India* had endeavoured to establish a properly deductive relation between the facts of history and the laws of human nature. Imperfections in the achievement need not deprive the author of the merit of the attempt; he was, we are being told, the first, but only the first, to focus this kind of analytical scrutiny upon Indian history and society. Pioneers may be working on the right lines even if their equipment is in some respects crude and undeveloped.

Thus the light of reason will not here include the illumination to be derived from the science of political ethology. If it is difficult to envisage exactly what John Mill would have expected from that science, it is easy to conclude that he must have hoped for something better than his father's broad-brushed caricature of national character in Hindustan and beyond. Was there not, however, a more radical fault, even a vice in the method of the *History*? If it exemplifies, as Stokes for one seems to hold, the same essential structure of analysis and argument as the *Essay on Government*, but on a grander scale, then it must fall victim to the criticism of that method which John Mill had begun to develop, however hesitantly as early as 1830. My impression, however, for what little it is worth, is that this criticism fails. Unless I have skimmed so near the surface of the *History of British India* as to miss its true character completely, its defects – and there are certainly substantial defects – are not those of unilinear, 'geometrical' reasoning from restricted premises to abstract conclusions. The faults are rather those of an imperfectly realized conception of philosophical history in which the object is indeed to relate social phenomena to 'the laws of human nature,' but in which it is recognized that such phenomena, and the development of society, can be understood only by way of 'a joint view of all the great circumstances taken together.' This may be a programme that James Mill lacked the capacity, as he certainly seems to have lacked sufficient time and resources and perhaps also an adequately strong motive, to fulfil. But, as a programme, it might legitimately enough command

74 cw, x, 44–5. As with the essay on the definition of political economy, some minor but significant changes were made in the text of the essay as it was incorporated, in 1859, into *Dissertations and Discussions*; see 44[a-a]

his son's support. If the verdict of 1865 was more than a casual and perfunctory one, its substance presumably lay in some such understanding of what the *History of British India* might have been and at times gestured towards being.

Three further remarks occur to me by way of conclusion. First, to the extent that the shape of philosophical history as John Mill understood it in the 1840s shows, however indistinctly, in his father's work a generation earlier, one sees, as so often in the history of ideas, the blunting and blurring of a once sharp distinction. No doubt there was, in the second quarter of the nineteenth century, a radical transformation taking place in the nature and role of history in European thought. But in finding this transformation primarily in such writers as the Saint-Simonians and Comte, John Mill may have been missing the essential point and finding instead one of those areas where the continuity of 'progressive' thought in his own generation with the world of the Enlightenment is most marked. Second, it is at least arguable that in their various ways the two Mills and Auguste Comte himself all exemplify the poverty of at least one kind of historicism. The price of gaining the whole world of sociological laws may be too high if it costs the historian his saving grasp of the concrete and the specific. The question must in the end be bluntly asked, whether the kind of history to which these concepts lead is either possible or useful. Third and last, what strikes me most about those aspects of James Mill's *History of British India* on which I have been commenting is not the light of reason shining from the page, but the dogmatism and the passionate prejudice which give most of its vigour to the author's pen. Like it or loathe it, this is surely what breathes life into those arid and outdated pages. It may have more to do with rationalism than with reason: certainly it has much to do with the radicalism which has been part of the modern world's inheritance from the Enlightenment.

John Stuart Mill on Christianity

KARL W. BRITTON

John Stuart Mill tells us that he regarded the religion of the English in much the same way as the religion of the Ancient Greeks: as something that neither surprised nor concerned him. I wish to consider how it came about that religion did concern John Stuart Mill and occupied his thoughts from time to time throughout his adult life. In this context it is desirable to distinguish three different aspects of religion, and, it is important to note, Mill insisted that we can have religion without one or other of these aspects.

There is first of all religion viewed as a matter of metaphysical belief. Such beliefs may be true or false. There is absolutely no question of accepting anything as revealed truth. Views about the origin of the world, its constitution, its remote future are to be considered from the point of view of science.[1] Mill does not seem to have rejected the very notion of the transcendent: what he asked for was some reason for adopting one view rather than another. In his examination of religion in his *Three Essays*, he often has this metaphysical view of religion in mind.

The second notion of religion which Mill introduces into his discussions is simply that to have a religion is to have an object of self-devotion which provides a dominant aim for a life-time. It is the notion of vocation; but a 'calling' need not suggest a call from God: one is called by being born into a world in which some most excellent thing is lacking and might be achieved. Mill says that anyone who has such an object has a religion, while recognizing

I am greatly indebted to the editors of the *Collected Works* and to my colleague Martin Hughes with whom I have discussed the questions raised in this paper.

1 'Theism,' *Three Essays on Religion, Collected Works*, x (Toronto 1969), 434

that this may not be the usual sense of the word. So he says that when at the age of sixteen he read some of Bentham's major works, he came to have 'in one (and the best) sense of the word, a religion.'[2] He uses as near-synonyms the expressions, a creed, a doctrine, a philosophy. He also remarks that such a doctrine or religion would be regularly appealed to in making conscientious decisions; it was, indeed, a most serious concern, a supreme object by reference to which all our actions were to be judged. Mill of course saw the improvement and the happiness of mankind as one such aim; if this devotion *alone* constituted a religion we should have to say that Mill and his father and Jeremy Bentham all shared the same religion. But in fact Mill never does say this. He came to see that something very important was missing in his father and in Bentham – something that he commonly regarded as an *essential* element in religion.

This is the third aspect of religion which Mill first came to acknowledge after his mental crisis of 1826. To this time belongs the idea of something more than devotion to a practical aim, one day perhaps to be achieved by human purpose. That 'something more' is a matter of having now, and enjoying now, a strong imaginative picture of what human perfection would be and of perfections beyond the powers of man. This implies a pure, noble, and intense feeling for 'the good' and for those in whom it is partly realized. In this we can certainly see Mill's attachment to new friends and new leaders: to John Sterling, Coleridge, Wordsworth, and Maurice. No doubt all these men shared some religious belief – whether Christian or near-Christian. What they all had for Mill was a certain grace in their lives that was for him a new experience – they had something now. It is easy to see that this notion of religion as something *now* connects with Mill's well-known introspective account of the effect of Wordsworth's poetry on him during his recovery from his mental crisis. In this poetry, he wrote, 'I seemed to draw from a source of inward joy, of sympathetic and imaginative pleasure, which could be shared in by all human beings; which had no connection with struggle or imperfection ...'[3] Mill's own religion *had* a connection with struggle and imperfection, but there was more to it, and that 'more' was for Mill a discovery.

Mill considered it possible to have a religion (devotion to a high cause, the present imaginative grasp of the good) without any transcendental beliefs. How would such a religion compare with Christianity? We must of course take Christianity to be a set of beliefs and something more than a set of beliefs. It involves 'graces of character' and practical moral aims: it involves, in fact, all three religious aspects distinguished above. We may notice that some agnostics have higher ideals and nobler thoughts than some Christians. Mill

2 *The Early Draft of John Stuart Mill's Autobiography*, ed. Jack Stillinger (Urbana, Ill. 1961), 75–6
3 *Autobiography*, ed. Jack Stillinger (Boston 1969), 89

says in the *Autobiography* that Christianity and the religion of humanity are to be judged principally by the ideal they present of a Perfect Being who is a guide to conscience.[4] That would mean that the most striking difference between them – the presence and absence of transcendental beliefs – is not the principal ground for deciding between them. If, like Mill himself in his boyhood, we thought of the story of the Gospels as being a story of the same sort as the descent of Orpheus, we should of course have to look for some other ground for deciding between them. (Mill, in his boyhood, did not make any attempt to decide between them.) Behind this remark we may see the view of Harriet, Mill's wife, as stated in a letter of 1854:[5] Christianity offers consolation for the suffering, a hope of heaven for the selfish, the love of God for the tender and grateful; and *all these* are to be superseded by morality. This is very much what Mill attempted in the first two essays written at this time. (To the years 1854–6 belong the first two of the *Three Essays on Religion* and the early draft of the main part of the *Autobiography*.) But after Harriet's death, in the essay on 'Theism,' Mill reconsiders the relation between transcendental metaphysical beliefs (of God, immortality, creation) and moral ideals. He notices that in fact the Humanist ideal (or the local version of it) is very largely derived from the Gospels. Mill then goes on to ask whether those who cannot accept any transcendental beliefs can nevertheless have all that is of real value in Christianity. It might seem obvious that they cannot. But Mill hits on the notion that those who cannot believe can still *hope*. 'Religion in the region of mere hope' is John Stuart Mill's distinctive contribution to philosophical theology. Can such a hope do for men what actual belief can do? This is the question asked and answered in the final pages of Mill's last work. In what follows I shall consider the views of this terminal essay and, where it seems desirable, the views of the first two essays, 'On Nature' and 'On the Utility of Religion.'

In asking us to look at religion 'not from the point of view of reverence but from that of science,'[6] Mill proposes an examination of religion from the outside: the tests of truth and of morality are not to be themselves dependent upon religious beliefs. I think his enquiry is on the same basis as Locke's, Butler's, and Hume's. In each case we have an empirically-minded philosopher trying to assess the validity of religious beliefs and the value of religious practices by principles accepted independently of religion. Mill's basic presupposition is that there is one and only one *system* of knowledge. This rests upon observation and induction, and it embraces physics, biology, sociology, and all the branches of pure and applied mathematics. Even history is systematic

4 Ibid., 29
5 See cw, x, cxxviii.
6 'Theism,' cw, x, 434

knowledge only in so far as it yields general laws. Of course not all knowledge is systematic; we all know particular matters of fact which have no relation to any system and which may, for instance, be inexplicable by any general laws we know. But we suppose that they might be explained. Where general propositions have the fullest evidence, we can claim knowledge of laws of nature. Therefore whatever anyone claims to know on religious grounds, or by intuition, testimony, or even by observation, can properly be tested by science. Mill holds that anything that conflicts with science will have to be rejected: 'the legitimate conclusions of science are entitled to prevail over all opinions, however widely held, which conflict with them, and .... the canons of scientific evidence which the successes and failures of two thousand years have established, are applicable to all subjects on which knowledge is attainable ...'[7] A very downright statement: but Mill, like Locke, is very much aware of the limitations of our knowledge. Nature shows us separable chains of causes and effects. Some seem to be linked to produce a complicated result; but even if every event has a cause, it is not clear that all these sequences are connected in any intelligible way. Again we know nothing much about the origin of the world or its prospects, and we do not know what man's place in the whole scheme is. This Mill regards as 'an obvious want of the human mind.'[8] He says: 'Who would not desire this more ardently than any other conceivable knowledge, so long as there appeared the slightest hope of attaining it.'[9] And surely there are many of whom this assertion is still true.

I think Mill had another question also. On what ultimate principles do the uniformities we know rest? He considers seriously whether we could have some guarantee of uniformity in nature, if we knew that the regularities we observe were the work of one God. We ourselves are familiar with the confidence that arises from knowing that something is intended, and it is arguable that in some cases this confidence is independent of induction. Mill asks, in effect, whether belief in God would logically strengthen our assurance of inductive argument and scientific proof. This question is a test of religion in that we are considering matters of proof and argument: we are asking whether the idea of God, manifestly itself a religious notion, can be incorporated into scientific knowledge and actually fill some of the logical gaps in that knowledge.

Mill thinks that it can (and so, after all, did David Hume). He holds that the very idea of gods arises from speculation about the causes of natural events. Religion, he thinks, begins in questions and explanations; it does not begin with hopes or fears, or with practices. He dismisses the notion – which is the basis of Hume's *Natural History of Religion* – that the gods begin in feelings and in imagination. Mill says that 'Belief in Gods had, I conceive,

7 Ibid., 431
8 Ibid., 433
9 'Utility of Religion,' ibid., 419

even in the rudest minds, a more honourable origin.'[10] The gods are conceived as the causes of self-moving things in nature. Can the scientist make
use of this concept? Primitive minds want explanations of what is random and
unusual, but what really needs explaining is the regularity and order in the
universe. It is possible to see this as the work of a god – but not an almighty
god. The laws of nature show a sustained attempt to contrive a certain result –
the seeing eye, for example. This contriving is a sure mark of an incomplete
power. The Almighty does not contrive.

The scope and unity of design suggests one god, but the frequent break-
downs of the design could suggest an anti-god who can sometimes defeat
God's purposes. This is a natural and primitive explanation of defeat. The
farmer sowed good seed in his field. 'Whence then hath it tares? An enemy
hath done this.' Mill does not like this kind of argument – it puts up an *ad hoc*
hypothesis with no independent verification. He would prefer (as Hume did)
to look for 'the secret operation of contrary causes.' But of course these regular
processes, which here defeat the orderly plan, might be designed and contrived
by an anti-god. Could the order we discover, with apparent defeats and break-
downs, result from a kind of *stasis* between warring gods? Could the Mani-
chaeans be right after all?

I think this view had great attraction for Mill. He mentions that it was
James Mill's alternative hypothesis, free from the incoherence of Christianity.
And Mill himself often wrote of the struggle between good and evil. In his
Inaugural Address to the students of St Andrews University, he told them
that an unremitting conflict is going on. Everything any of us does is a part of
this conflict: none of us can avoid taking part; none of us can escape the
responsibility for his share. Mill did not say to whom we are responsible, nor
exactly for whom it is we are fighting. Against whom are we fighting? No doubt
the Evil One was a very familiar figure to the students of St Andrews – he certainly has many picturesque names in Scotland. But this formulation is not
that of the Manichaean heresy.

Mill remarks ("Theism," 454) that we cannot expect a perpetual struggle
between hostile powers to establish firm and reliable frontiers. What we wish
to explain is (or is at this stage) the regularity and order in the world. In war
the frontiers are always changing. So we revert to the notion of one intelligence
at work. God is trying to produce order; we do not need to posit a second god
to explain disorders. But then what exactly is God struggling against? Does
God struggle with the nature of matter? This after all is what a workman or
an artist does. But if we take this view of God it follows not only that he is not
the cause of all things, but that he is not the cause of all the *order* in the world.
I think this is a very unsatisfactory conclusion to an argument from the appearance of design. Perhaps God struggles not against any order, but against

10 Ibid., 418

disorder – the unlimited. For the moment let us look at Mill's conclusion that order could be explained by reference to a finite contriving God, a single plan.

In his third essay Mill claims that there is a straight-forward inductive argument to the existence of a divine intelligence, but it is not a conclusive argument. And he goes on to say that the evidence for design would be 'greatly attenuated' if Darwin's hypothesis of natural selection were accepted. We see then that Mill is using God as a scientific term and his proposition is a scientific hypothesis, and Darwin's theory may prove to be a better explanation of the formation of species. We are familiar enough, from nineteenth-century history and fiction, with those who read Darwin and threw up their religion. To think of belief in God and belief in Natural Selection as rival scientific theories is not so common.[11] Mill's God is an object in the world, discrete and separable from other objects and other minds: 'one cause at work' – that is the hypothesis.

If, for the moment, we *accept* this argument, can we go on to infer that there must be greater order in the world than we have ever come across? David Hume insisted that an *a posteriori* argument cannot endow God with any properties not already apparent in nature.[12] Mill does not accept this restriction. God is the efficient cause of the seeing eye – but he is inevitably more than that. He is intelligence and will. God brings about this regularity because that is his aim, and it is not absurd to suppose that God is of such a character as to strive to produce all kinds of order in the inaccessible regions of the universe. So a kind of extrapolation is theoretically proper. And this depends upon our ascribing a character to God. Were there, as Hume insisted, no extrapolation at all, we should have to conclude that what matters to us is simply the way God works in that corner of nature we know, and no clues would be provided as to God's remoter aims and achievements if there are any. This is Hume's view: what matters to us is still the world we come across, as it would appear whether we believed in God or not. God's character contributes nothing. In other words, Hume says that the world we live in matters to us – a magnificent truism. Mill does not acquiesce: he thinks that if we can know anything of God's character, we can from this basis make inferences about things that never have come within the range of our observations and never will. The discussion of God's character is therefore of practical and theoretical importance. Mill is already (as Hume would put it) moving out 'beyond the present course of things,' and the God proposed as a scientific hypothesis has to be provided with a character.

God is limited in power; the world is extremely imperfect. Are we to say that God has low aims, lacks goodness, cares little; or that the imperfection is

11 See *Logic*, cw, vii, 498–9ᵛ (iii, xiv, 5n), added in 1862; and letters to H.C. Watson, 24 Feb. 1869, cw, xvii, 1567, and to Bain, 11 April 1860, cw, xv, 695.
12 *Dialogues*, ii

something God cannot avoid? Mill argues for a God of great power and intelligence, of great, perhaps unlimited, goodness, facing great difficulties. That
God cares for us is shown in the workings of pleasure and pain: a familiar
argument no doubt taken from Locke's *Essay*.[13] But on what grounds are we
to suppose that God is morally transcendent? In the detached examination to
which Mill is committed, it seems to him proper to put the best possible moral
construction on religious claims. I think that the reason for this view is that
Mill wants to consider whether we have grounds for believing in a God who
can properly be worshipped, with whom one might, in one's highest moments,
be in communion.[14] Mill believes that God may be worshipped even if his
power is limited – perhaps even if his wisdom is not unlimited – but not, of
course, if his moral character is questionable. Can we then justify the claim,
which all the great religions always make, that God is good?

Mill does not take this claim for granted. He cannot accept any religious
claim unexamined. And to reach a decision we have to have a concept of
goodness that is fully intelligible outside the sphere of religion. In the two
earlier essays, Mill considers and rejects two well-known views of what goodness is. (I am not here giving a full account of these essays: I am simply remarking that in fact in each essay he considers and rejects a notion of what
makes good things good.)

In the essay on the utility of religion, Mill considers the view that goodness itself is a religious notion and that it must be self-contradictory to deny
that God is good. He says this may seem to be the case because morality is a
tradition and it comes to us in our society through the church – comes to us
represented as God's will. But as we grow away from our childhood teachers
we learn to make up our own minds about good and bad, and we could very
well reach the conclusion that God as presented in orthodox belief is not good.
So Mill claims that we do not *derive* our notion of goodness simply from
religion. He remarks that if our notion of goodness derived from our notion
of God's will we should have to say that whatever God might will would then
become good, but in fact what we mean when we say that God is good is
(amongst other things) that he wills things *because* they are good. The opposite view is in Mill's opinion a naïve confusion more often imputed than
committed. (As Bain remarks, Mill scarcely ever read a theological book.)[15]

If our notion of good is a tradition, where does it start from? In the essay
on Nature, Mill considers the view that our notions of good and evil are derived from nature, that to live well is to live in accordance with nature. This
is a moral point of view: it is naturalistic but avoids committing the naturalistic fallacy, as Mill makes very clear: 'Those who set up Nature as a standard

13 II, vii
14 Letter to Henry Jones, 13 June 1868, CW, XVI, 1414
15 Alexander Bain, *John Stuart Mill, a Criticism* (London 1888), 139

of action do not intend a merely verbal proposition ... they think they are giving some information as to what the standard of action really is. Those who say that we ought to act according to Nature do not mean the mere identical proposition that we ought to do what we ought to do.'[16] Here then is a view of a criterion of goodness and some hint as to how we come by it – by observing and understanding the workings of nature and imitating them.

Mill deals thoroughly with all the confusions that such a proposal rests on and tends to generate. In the end he considers the view that virtue consists in conforming freely to a certain order that also obtains in nature outside man. This view can only apply to certain limited aspects of nature: how are these aspects selected? We are not (presumably) to kill our own food and eat it in the raw, nor are we to blame for concealing ourselves behind man-made fibres. Mill takes it that the doctrine means us to live in accordance with our instincts in certain respects. And he clearly shows that instinct does not select for us the kind of conduct we call good. On the contrary, our notions of living well are largely based on intelligence and on educated feeling – on imagination and insight. Mill speaks here as a single-minded intellectual: 'The truth is that there is hardly a single point of excellence belonging to human character, which is not decidedly repugnant to the untutored feelings of human nature.'[17] So Mill rejects also this second account of what we means by goodness. Both views have had heavy theological backing: those who think it desirable to imitate nature take it for granted that nature is God's handiwork, and also that God is good. Mill does not take it for granted that God is good. We have to decide this question by examining and judging the world God made. And to judge, we must have a prior notion of what goodness is. As we all know, Mill puts forward a notion of right action and a rather lame notion of moral goodness. All I want to notice here is that when Mill asks: What goodness can we reasonably apply to a finite God? what he has in mind is always moral goodness, the 'artificially perfected nature of the best and noblest human beings.'[18] This may seem a topsy-turvy procedure, but Mill took it very seriously, as we can gather from his controversy with Dean Mansel about the meaning of good as applied to God.[19]

If we have a notion of goodness, what evidence can we find that God is good or not good? The world includes every kind of evil – suffering, failure, privation, decay, loss, death, depravity. Mill distinguishes sharply between those features of the world which excite awe – the vast scale of the cosmic forces – and those which could excite admiration. We are not to confuse these two: 'Those in whom awe produces admiration may be aesthetically developed,

16 'Nature,' cw, x, 377. I doubt that G.E. Moore ever came across this passage.
17 Ibid., 393
18 Ibid., 396–7
19 Letter to Bain, 7 Jan. 1863, cw, xv, 817

but they are morally uncultivated.'[20] The power of God (as we may infer it from the world) is one thing; God's goodness quite another thing. God is good (in Mill's view) if we can properly ascribe to God our human notion of moral goodness. What of the evidence? All living things are ordered by God – that is the hypothesis Mill is considering: Do the arrangements of the animal kingdom, apart from man, show God's moral goodness? That the 'entire existence of the lower animals, [may be] divided, with scarcely an exception, into devourers and devoured,'[21] seems almost to be a matter of regret. (Animals do not even keep themselves clean, Mill says.) We begin to wonder just what God can have in common with animals – or with vulgar instinctual man: '[N]early every respectable attribute of humanity is a result, not of instinct, but of a victory over instinct ...'[22] Man alone makes the effort to be respectable and so is a possible ally of God's. As for the rest of nature, we may only conclude that God cannot do better with it yet.

The final result is to divide God from nature and to divide God from man. God and men share many faculties and they share moral aims, but Mill writes of man's actions and efforts as if they were entirely distinct from God's. God is an object in the world; he has great but limited power over other objects. We must struggle against most of the powers of nature and of our own natures. God maintains the whole universe (good, bad, and indifferent) in some kind of stable order. But God has to contrive and adapt: God has to struggle.

Is the existence of the world connected with the ethical? To this great question, Wittgenstein is reported to have replied: It is said that God the Father created Nature. God the Son, who proceeded from the Father, is the ethical. In this way men first divided and then reunited the Godhead.[23] Mill fails to reunite the Godhead.

Mill next considers two other doctrines characteristic of Christianity: a divine revelation in history and a life after death.

Locke had said that the only way in which God could get through to the unlettered, labouring man was by sending a messenger. And the only way of convincing everyone that this was God's messenger was by external signs – that is, miracles. Mill thinks it not unreasonable that God might send his angel or messenger, but absolutely denies miracles would serve to authenticate the messenger, or indeed anything else. So the messenger must be revealed in his life and teaching taken together. Mill considers that Jesus of Nazareth claimed to have been such a messenger and may really have been: 'religion cannot be said to have made a bad choice in pitching on this man as the ideal repre-

20 'Nature,' cw, x, 384
21 Ibid., 399
22 Ibid., 393
23 Friedrich Waisman, 'Notes on Talks with Wittgenstein,' *Philosophical Review*, cxxiv, 1965, 16

sentative and guide of humanity ...'[24] Mill sharply rebukes those who suggest that the whole story of Jesus is a fiction. Who could have invented it? Not the fishermen of Galilee, at all events. Yet Mill is prepared to accept a carpenter of Galilee and to ascribe the Gospel message to the peculiar mental and moral endowment of one man. If there is a God, he may have sent Jesus; and if this argument is not sufficient we need not look for another.

On the question of a life after death, Mill was well known to have strong feelings. The separation of friends at death was for him one of the great griefs and privations of human life. The hope of a reunion could rest only in God, and it would be a boon worthy of God and promised by Jesus. Mill tries to show that an endless disembodied existence is possible. We may be destined to live other lives. And Mill adds the typical common-sense remark that no doubt our position and starting point in a next life would depend on our behaviour in this.[25]

All that Mill says about these two momentous doctrines is that they are compatible with the notion of a world ordered by God. They are not to be inferred from this notion, if only because the religious concept of Divine Goodness, on which they in part depend, is itself only one of the many versions of the nature of God. Are we then to believe that God exists, is good, has sent his messenger, has prepared for us a life after death?

For the first proposition there is (or was before Darwin wrote) strong evidence of a straight-forward inductive kind. But not conclusive evidence. It is in fact not enough to justify the assertion that there must be a God. This proposition is not more than a hypothesis having a certain probability. The remaining propositions are not rendered probable by evidence proper to them, but are not impossible if there is a God. We can indeed *hope* that God exists and has all the goodness we can imagine, that he is able and willing to grant us immortality, that Jesus Christ was his messenger. And so the matter is concluded: 'The whole domain of the supernatural is thus removed from the region of Belief into that of simple Hope; and in that, for anything we can see, it is likely always to remain ...'[26]

What can Mill mean by religion in the region of mere hope? That it is of value to contemplate imaginatively the highest notion of moral goodness we can conceive? This effort is part of the cultivation of the imagination, a theme to which Mill recurs so often. He now says that there is a very important principle that ought to govern the imagination: where things are within our power we must of course consider them as they are before we decide what we want them to become. To begin by taking them to be other than they are is irrational and absurd. (As he says in his essay on nature, to study and heed the properties of things is the very definition of intelligent action.)[27] But we

24 'Theism,' cw, x, 488

25 Ibid., 466

26 Ibid., 483

27 'Nature,' ibid., 379–80

can know, or have sufficient assurance, that many of the important things in our lives are not knowable by us, and so not alterable by any planned action of ours. Mill thinks it is nevertheless proper and valuable to consider what we would wish these things to be. A life after death is an example. We can do nothing to secure it. There may be an after-life and there may not – and we cannot know which of these possibilities is true. But the possibility that there is an after-life seems to some people very much more attractive than the other. It is then desirable to dwell on the more attractive one, and to hope that it is true. And of all our hopes, those which have regard to the government of the universe and the destiny of man after death are the most important. Here we should strive to imagine the best and hope for it. 'The beneficial effect of such a hope is far from trifling. It makes life and human nature a far greater thing to the feelings, and gives greater strength as well as greater solemnity to all the sentiments which are awakened in us by our fellow-creatures and by mankind at large.'[28]

Mill claims for imaginative hope that it will do what all the great religions claim to do: it will enlarge the scale of our feelings and relieve us of a sense of the insignificance of human life; it will enable us to escape from 'the disastrous feeling of "not worth while." ' Here at all events Mill is talking about something he has known, something from which he escaped slowly and painfully by the help of Wordsworth's poetry. That Christianity has done this for many people seems incontestable; it has prevented the feeling which Nietzsche described as 'weightlessness,' the 'weightlessness of all things.'[29] This account is a restatement of the conclusions of the 1820s, as described by Mill in his *Autobiography*: 'I had now learnt by experience that the passive susceptibilities needed to be cultivated as well as the active capacities, and required to be nourished and enriched as well as guided.'[30]

How is hope related to imagination? In the second of his *Three Essays*, Mill writes of the origin of our world, the present government, the future fate: 'What would not one give for any credible tidings from that mysterious region ...?' But we can penetrate it in imagination only. 'Religion and poetry address themselves, at least in one of their aspects, to the same part of the human constitution [here Mill is quoting Harriet's very words used in a letter to him]: they both supply the same want, that of ideal conceptions grander and more beautiful than we see realised in the prose of human life.'[31]

But religion is a search after what is true. Imagination is poetical construction and contemplation. Mill says this may be accompanied by hope. Does the

28 'Theism,' ibid., 485
29 Cited by Lionel Trilling, *Sincerity and Authenticity* (Cambridge, Mass. 1972), 156, 166
30 *Autobiography*, 86
31 'Utility of Religion,' cw, x, 419

doctrine of God in the region of hope amount to a religion? I do not want this question to turn on a matter of definitions. We know that Mill uses 'religion' in at least two senses, but he does not always confuse them. At the end of the essay on theism Mill says that a picture alone cannot have the power over men that an actual transcendental belief would have. The passage I quote is very clumsy indeed; no doubt Mill would have put it into better shape in a final revision had he lived: 'And, it cannot be questioned that the undoubting belief of the real existence of a Being who realises our own best ideas of perfection, and of our being in the hands of that Being as the ruler of the universe, gives an increase of force to these feelings beyond what they can receive from reference to a merely ideal conception.'[32] He at once goes on to say that such a belief is not possible for rational minds, so he asks us to accept the picture instead: 'Impressions ... not in themselves amounting to what can properly be called a religion,'[33] that is, not a transcendental religion.

That we can be bewitched by a picture we all know. We have an imaginative picture of life after death, a reunion with long-lost friends. Is the imaginative picture to be accompanied by hope? In his second essay Mill had virtually excluded this hope from the religion of humanity. He there argued reasonably enough that we can never have any direct evidence for or against another life – evidence, that is, available in this life. Is this argument a way of excluding the notion of immortality from the region of hope? But so long as it is regarded as desirable, must we not (on Mill's view) hope for it? So it reappears in the last of the essays. To deny that we can now have any evidence for it is, on Mill's final account, irrelevant to what we may *hope*.

And here is the real difficulty: Is it, after all, irrelevant? Hope evidently requires some basis in belief. (Aristotle says that we can *wish* for the impossible, but wishing is not what Mill has in mind.) I cannot hope to become young again because I cannot believe it is possible. Can we hope for a life after death simply because we do not believe it to be impossible? Perhaps we can. Thomas Hardy, in his well-known Christmas poem about the oxen, asks himself what he would do if someone invited him to go to see the oxen kneel at midnight:

'I should go with him in the gloom
   Hoping it might be so.'

Hardy (who was a disciple of Mill's) does not of course mean 'wishing it might be so,' but something more like 'hoping it was so but knowing it was not so.' Perhaps this is exactly what Mill had in mind, but I think not. I think he wants us to hope for something that we do see to be possible. And if so, I

32 'Theism,' ibid., 486
33 Ibid., 488

think there is a real gap in the argument. How, on this interpretation, can we hope for something that altogether transcends experience, unless we have some beliefs that altogether transcend experience? What else could show us that it was possible? Scientific knowledge (or scientific theories) may not contradict these 'possibilities,' but perhaps simply because they say nothing for or against them – are not in any sense *about* them. Can we make sense of the *hope* that there is a God, a divine revelation, a life after death? The question is whether the propositions of science – in Mill's view the only system of knowledge – relate to these things. Or rather, do they relate to them in such a way as to show that they are not impossible? It seems to me that Mill needs to show, and fails to, that the propositions of science relate to these beliefs in the particular logical fashion he takes for granted.

As his early letters to Carlyle reveal, Mill of course meditated upon the Gospels. In this, I think, he is very Victorian and very English: a Bible-reader. Although invited by his father to regard Jesus as one of a long succession of spurious gods or misguided prophets, in fact, as we have seen, the teaching of Jesus and His life and death had a central place in Mill's later meditation on religion. He once remarked that for Coleridge the very fact that any doctrine had been believed by thoughtful men and received by whole generations or nations of mankind was a problem to be solved, a phenomenon to be accounted for, and that he regarded the long duration of a belief as proof of an adaptation in it to some portion or other of the human mind.[34] Of course for Coleridge these facts were the salient facts of life, while for Mill they were a puzzle he could not solve and would not abandon.

It has to be admitted that Mill's discussion of religion was always uphill for him. He may have been (as Elie Halévy said) religious by nature, but he lacked the language and lacked the *Speilraum* to give an account of a possible God who would command reverence and love. And for the existence of this possible God there is said to be some but not enough evidence. Could anything be less satisfactory? We are bidden to hope, but Mill does not go on to any kind of commitment. He does not consider whether it might be reasonable to accept and act on a proposition for which there is inadequate evidence.

Of course in many practical affairs it clearly is reasonable to make up our minds on a matter which cannot be decisively settled by the evidence – make up our minds and act accordingly. On particular practical matters it is unreasonable to be too rational, and drowning men are not necessarily unreasonable when they cling to straws. 'To be indecisive and reluctant to act, because we have not evidence of a perfectly conclusive character to act on, is a defect sometimes incident to scientific minds, but which, wherever it exists, renders them unfit for practical emergencies.'[35] The question is whether it could ever

34 'Coleridge,' ibid., 120
35 *Logic*, cw, vii, 592 (iii, xxiii, 2)

be reasonable to accept metaphysical propositions on such grounds. Mill thinks it would not be reasonable. No exigencies of action, it seemed to him, required us to come to a decision about the existence of God, a last judgment, an after-life. Since in every case the evidence is indecisive, we cannot go wrong in suspending judgment – although to hope is profitable.

Such a view is tenable only if it is clear that the kind of life we are to live now in no way depends upon whether there is a God or not, a last judgment, another life. This implication was quite clear to Mill and his friends, and the contrary was of course quite clear to most of Mill's thinking and unthinking contemporaries in Christendom. Mill's view might now be called the Autonomy of Morals. (The good will needs no rewards and fears no punishment or discouragements.) I am inclined to think this is an *a priori* simplification. In my experience – and in Mill's own experience as he so plainly tells – the good will may need every encouragement; the will to go on living at all may need encouragement; the disastrous feeling of 'not worth while' faces us all. And for some it can be overcome only by the kind of encouragement that reflection on this world cannot provide – a man may need that which *by nature* he cannot have.

Within this life, hopes and fears and half-beliefs help to decide our choices and actions. If, after all, hope must have some basis in belief there are many who will make up their minds even on metaphysical matters as they make up their minds in any tight corner: life, they will argue, is a tight corner.

Concerning some Criticisms of Mill's Utilitarianism, 1861-76

J. B. SCHNEEWIND

As *Utilitarianism* was appearing in parts in *Fraser's Magazine* during 1861, John Stuart Mill wrote to the French translator of his *Representative Government* to correct a misapprehension:

Like many of the French, you appear to be of the opinion that the *idea of Utility* is in England *the dominant Philosophy*. It is nothing of the sort. I understand that one might see in that doctrine a certain analogy with the spirit of the English nation. But in fact it is, and it has almost always been, very unpopular there. Most English writers do not only deny it, they insult it: and the school of Bentham has always been regarded (I say it with regret) as an insignificant minority.[1]

Mill was, I believe, correct, at least as far as the standing of utilitarianism among British philosophers is concerned, but within fifteen years a philosopher of the stature of F.H. Bradley could suggest that 'modern Utilitarianism' might 'be called ... our most fashionable philosophy.'[2] Certainly utilitarianism has been a permanent matter of serious philosophical consideration since Bradley's time; in recent years writing about it by philosophers has reached epidemic proportions, and no one could say today that the descendants of the school of Bentham are an insignificant minority. It is a matter of some interest,

Portions of this paper have been used in the author's *Sidgwick's Ethics and Victorian Moral Philosophy*, Oxford University Press, forthcoming.

1 Letter to Charles Dupont-White, 10 Oct. 1861, *Collected Works*, xv (Toronto 1972), 745. In French, my translation.
2 F.H. Bradley, *Ethical Studies* (Oxford 1876; reprinted 1935), 103

and of no little difficulty, to assess the part played in this change by Mill's book. I propose to look at the early critical reception of *Utilitarianism*, hoping that it will shed some light not only on the extent of Mill's immediate influence but also on the particular direction which his work helped to give to philosophical discussion of the theory he was attempting to propagate.

There is one small but significant preliminary matter to note. At the time Mill's work was written, there was no readily available systematic exposition of the secular utilitarian point of view. This is a fact to which it is perhaps hard to give full weight today, when there are innumerable reprints of classics, new expositions, textbook presentations, and critical discussions of every sort of view. The facts, however, are clear. Most of the earlier eighteenth-century utilitarians held theological versions of the view and would not have served Mill's purpose even if their works had been in print. Paley, of course, was in print, but he was so conservative, in addition to being a religious writer, that he simply did not figure as a possible vehicle for Mill's views. While there were two works by theological utilitarians which Mill admired, neither was available. One was John Austin's *Province of Jurisprudence Determined*. It was published in 1832 but never reached a wide audience; because of Austin's diffidence it was not reprinted until 1861, after his death. The other was William Smith's *Discourse on Ethics of the School of Paley*, published in 1839. Although Mill in 1842 thought it 'one of the best extant defences of utilitarianism,'[3] it seems never to have been reprinted and to have left no traces on the literature.

The secular utilitarians had nothing much more suitable to offer. Mill had a variety of reasons for not appealing to Hume as a fellow-moralist, but even if he had wished to, he could not have sent large numbers of readers to him. For there was no collected edition of Hume's works between 1825 and 1860; the *Treatise* was not reprinted separately between 1817 and 1888; and the *Enquiry* had to wait until 1894 for a separate modern edition.[4] That wellspring of utilitarianism, Bentham's *Introduction*, was not reprinted separately between 1823 and 1876, and the format of Bowring's edition in the *Works* (part issue beginning in 1838) did not invite wide readership. The posthumous *Deontology* (1834) was unsystematic as well as unreadable, and has, I believe, never been reprinted. The writings of James Mill provided no useful substitute. His discussions of morality in the *Analysis of the Phenomena of the Human Mind* (1829) were too perfunctory to be serviceable. His articles and encyclopaedia essays do not offer a systematic defence of the ethics underlying his position. The *Fragment on Mackintosh* (1835), surely one of the most irascible and most irritating books ever written, contains no systematic treatment of the issues; and though James Mill's scattered comments are

3 Letter to Albany Fonblanque, 5 April 1842, CW, XIII, 511
4 See T.E. Jessop, *A Bibliography of Hume and Scottish Philosophy* (London 1938).

often good, they are not readily extractable. There was an anonymous *Utilitarian Catechism* published in 1830, but it was philosophically extremely weak, and it seems to have vanished unnoticed.

Little help could be expected from other sources. The universities in Scotland were dominated by anti-utilitarians. Dr Whewell reigned at Cambridge and had supplanted even Paley with his own, drastically anti-utilitarian treatise. Oxford was busy with its movement and with recovering from its movement; and although Mark Pattison tells us that Mill's *Logic* dominated Oxford for the quarter century following its appearance,[5] there is no evidence to suggest that there was any teaching of utilitarian ethics to accompany it. None of these centres of learning was producing reliable accounts of a view they all detested, and neither were other writers. Such histories of philosophy or of ethics as there were – by Mackintosh, Blakey, Whewell, Morell – were all written by anti-utilitarians who did not trouble to suppress their antipathies when they presented the views of Bentham. There do not even seem to have been the now commonplace aids to students, aside from innumerable annotated editions of Butler and Paley. Other than Stewart's very brief *Outlines of Moral Philosophy*, first published in 1793 and frequently reprinted, the only handbook of ethics published prior to the appearance of Mill's work, so far as I know, is the *Manual of Moral Philosophy*, first brought out in 1860, by William Fleming, DD, of Glasgow University. It is an unabashedly anti-utilitarian jumble of miscellaneous information and assorted, but not connected, argument. Finally, Herbert Spencer's *Social Statics* came out in 1850. We may think of him now as a close philosophical relative of the utilitarians, but at the time his book was taken, for quite good reasons, as being opposed to utilitarianism, and it was not until considerably later that the kinship of his view to theirs became clear.

Quite aside from the sheer shortage of presentations, Mill had long felt that existing versions of utilitarianism were unsatisfactory. (His criticisms of Bentham, as well as of other moralists, have been studied several times, and need not be reviewed here.)[6] We know that in his early days he thought his countrymen were passing through what the Saint-Simonians called a 'critical period,' in which the old moral outlook had lost its power as a cohesive social force. To replace it a new morality was needed, one which would draw, as the Benthamites had signally failed to do, on the traditional wisdom and the insights of poets as well as on the strengths of a variety of opposing philosophical camps. These different points of view had to be brought together into a unified outlook which would prove convincing to the leaders of opinion, and through them, come to be accepted by the masses.[7] Himself neither poet nor

5 Mark Pattison, *Memoirs* (London 1885), 166
6 See, eg, the Introduction by F.E.L. Priestley, CW, x.
7 See the Introduction to my collection of *Mill's Ethical Writings* (New York 1965).

prophet, Mill held that philosophy provided the proper mode of articulating such a morality. In later years Mill may have ceased to use the Saint-Simonian vocabulary, but he did not cease to think that a good philosophical ethic was a vitally needed tool of social improvement. Thus in 1847 he urged John Austin to write 'a systematic treatise on morals,' saying that 'until it is done we cannot expect much improvement in the common standard of moral judgments & sentiments.'[8] Nor did he cease to think earlier versions of utilitarianism philosophically inadequate: we can find him in 1854, when he had already begun writing his own treatise, telling an enquirer that 'ethics as a branch of philosophy is still to be created.'[9] His presentation of utilitarianism was undoubtedly meant in part to remove popular antipathy to and suspicion about the doctrine, but it was at least as important to him to convince the philosophical community of the soundness of the position. For acceptance by the philosophers – not just those at universities – Mill thought, was needed for a broad-based and enduring acceptance of his doctrine by the general public. What, then, was the immediate response?

The early criticisms and reviews of Mill's *Utilitarianism* cover a wide range of topics, and it will be impossible to deal with all of them in the present paper.[10] I shall begin by giving a brief chronological and impressionistic sketch of the critical response, and then go on to a discussion of some of the chief themes.

Alexander Bain, after reminding his readers that *Utilitarianism* first appeared as essays in a magazine, adds 'I am not aware that any change was made in reprinting it as a volume, notwithstanding that it had its full share of hostile criticism as it came out in *Fraser*.'[11] Bain may be correct about the 'full share of hostile criticism,' but if so the criticisms were not printed in the usual places. I have failed to find any responses to *Utilitarianism* in the *Edinburgh*, the *Quarterly*, the *Westminster*, *Macmillan's*, *Fraser's* itself, or any

8 cw, xiii, 712

9 cw, xiv, 235

10 I append a checklist of writings about Mill's *Utilitarianism* published between 1861 and 1876. Future references to any of this material in the footnotes as well as in the text will be abbreviated.

In compiling the checklist I have been greatly aided by the 'Mill Bibliography' by John M. Robson and Dudley Hascall published in various issues of *The Mill News Letter*. The two volumes of Walter Houghton's magnificent *Wellesley Index to Victorian Periodicals* have been of inestimable assistance in enabling me to supplement the Robson-Hascall bibliography, in attributing authorship, and in finding out about the non-existence of relevant publications. My knowledge of the R.H. Hutton article comes from 'The Writings of Richard Holt Hutton' by Robert H. Tener, *Victorian Periodicals Newsletter*, no 17, Sept. 1972.

I should like particularly to thank the staff of the Reference Room of the Carnegie Library of Pittsburgh for their patient and skilful assistance in obtaining the journals I needed for this study.

11 Alexander Bain, *John Stuart Mill* (London 1882), 112

other journal or book during 1861 or 1862. In fact, the first general impression one gets is that very little notice was taken in print of the work for seven or eight years. In 1863 an anonymous reviewer praised it unreservedly in the *Westminster*, and T. Cliffe Leslie, the economist, attacked its view of the highest good in *Macmillan's*. During the following year there appeared an eccentric anonymous volume, *Utilitarianism Explained and Exemplified in Moral and Political Government*, attacking Mill from a religious point of view but not achieving any great degree of clarity. In 1865 the journalist William Brightly Rands published two pseudonymous volumes attributed to, and entitled, *Henry Holbeach, Student in Life and Philosophy*. The second volume contains a 'Controversial Letter' to Mill, subtitled 'The Sphere of Law.' Rands is remarkable as being a self-avowed disciple of William Wollaston, but little philosophical acumen is displayed in his criticisms. The first American notice of *Utilitarianism* came out during this year in the *North American Review* as part of a review of an edition of *Dissertations and Discussions* which included it, and James McCosh published his first criticisms of *Utilitarianism*. Appearing as a very brief appendix to a reprint of Stewart's student handbook, they were expanded somewhat in the following year, when McCosh's *Examination of Mill's Philosophy* appeared: its twentieth chapter was devoted to attacking Mill's ethics. In 1866 another American notice appeared, in the *Bibliotheca Sacra*, and Mansel denounced 'Utility as a Ground of Moral Obligation' in a lecture at Oxford, which was not published until 1873. In 1867 the only pertinent publication is a long article in the *North British Review* by J.C. Shairp. It deals with Mill only incidentally and sees Austin as a far better expositor of utilitarianism. 1868 is notable for two historical studies which include Mill. Bain's dry compendium for students, *Mental and Moral Science*, gives him more pages than anyone except Aristotle, Hobbes, Hutcheson, and Kant; and S.S. Laurie, in *Notes Expository and Critical on Certain British Theories of Morals*, gives him more pages than he gives anyone else – not, however, very meaty pages. History did not entirely replace controversy that year: on 3 April the Rev Robert Watts of Belfast read a vituperative sermon attacking 'Utilitarianism Expounded by J. Stuart Mill, Alexander Bain, and Others,' and published two editions of it.

The year 1869 gives us a good idea of what 'a full share of hostile criticism' looked like in Victorian journals. What Mill did not get, the historian W.E.H. Lecky certainly did. His *History of European Morals* was reviewed in every major journal and many minor ones, and some of them carried more than one discussion of it. Most of the reviewers discussed his elephantine first chapter, which was a vehement, if not a careful, critical survey of the two great positions in Victorian philosophical ethics – the intuitional and the utilitarian. Lecky was strongly opposed to utilitarianism, and his chapter called forth the wrath of John Morley and Fitzjames Stephen, while it was defended – not altogether whole-heartedly – by Henry Reeve, Henry Calderwood, and R.H.

Hutton. There was not this much discussion of utilitarianism in the Victorian journals in any later year. Mill figured in a good part of it, but not quite as centrally as might have been expected. For Lecky's chapter is notable because, among other things, it practically fails to mention Mill, and certainly does not discuss his version of the doctrine in any detail. Even the reviewers who sympathized with Lecky's own stance felt somewhat impatient with him on account of his carelessness, and a large element in their impatience was due to his failure to come to grips with the best version of the theory he was attacking – and plainly the best version was felt to be Mill's. The Lecky controversy seems to me, in fact, to mark the point at which it became generally clear that to deal with utilitarianism one had to deal with Mill's version of it.

The following year, in which the Lecky controversy continued, was mainly notable for the publication of what Bain called 'the best hostile criticism of Utilitarianism that I am acquainted with,'[12] the *Examination of the Utilitarian Philosophy*, by John Grote, a younger brother, by some twenty years, of George Grote. John Grote had been Knightbridge Professor of Moral Philosophy at Cambridge, and had written much of his *Examination* in 1861, as Mill's essays were appearing in *Fraser's*. He had had it set up for publication after the appearance of Mill's essays in book form, but he lacked confidence in its value, did not publish it, kept adding to it, and left a tangled mass of manuscripts to his editor, who finally brought it out four years after his death. The book was not widely reviewed and seems to have made little public impression, but I agree with Bain's estimate of its value and shall discuss some of its points in detail. Incidentally, the review of it in the *Westminster* in 1871 gives to certain attacks on Mill, for the first time in print, some of the kinds of rebuttals that have now become quite familiar, and is one of the very few published defences of Mill during the early period.

The other publications in 1870 and 1871 are not of much value: a brief and rather ineffectual attack by W.T. Thornton in the *Fortnightly*, a few remarks in an article on Epicureanism by F.W. Newman, and a set of pompous, pious lectures by J.S. Blackie, originally delivered in 1869. 1872 saw the appearance of a brilliant article by William George Ward in the *Dublin Review*, a few comments in a Scottish professor's jurisprudence text, and Calderwood's *Handbook of Moral Philosophy*, which was a great improvement over Fleming's. It is worth noting that although Calderwood thinks that Mill's 'is now the accredited type of Utilitarianism,'[13] two Oxford philosophers as late as 1875 could speak of Mill, in the historical review they planned as an introduction to a systematic treatise on ethics, as 'not yet [having] acquired historical importance.'[14] In 1873 the *New Englander* printed B.P. Bowne's long article

12 Ibid., 115
13 Calderwood, *Handbook of Moral Philosophy* (London, 1872), 130
14 M. Wilson and T. Fowler, *Principles of Morals* (Oxford 1875), 112; cf Preface, vii

trying to effect a reconciliation between Mill's utilitarianism and intuitionism; and one Henry Bleckly published a book attacking Lecky's first chapter. It is of interest here solely because it contains not only no references to Mill but no views which are clearly due to his influence, although it seems to try to defend a vaguely utilitarian view.

Three final publications close out our period. In 1874 T.R. Birks, Grote's successor at Cambridge, published his lectures on *Modern Utilitarianism*. He surveys Bentham and Paley as well as Mill, discusses Mill's strictures on them, and criticises Mill's version of the doctrine at length. Owing most of his specific criticisms to Grote, he includes also a good deal of religio-moralistic preaching against utilitarianism. He is perhaps the last of the critics of this style. In the same year Henry Sidgwick published *The Methods of Ethics*. It is primarily an analytic, not a critical or historical treatise, but it contains objections to two or three of Mill's central contentions. F.H. Bradley's dazzling chapter on 'Pleasure for Pleasure's Sake,' in *Ethical Studies* (1876), by contrast, makes Mill the central individual target in a broad attack on hedonism and utilitarianism. These latter two works show Mill firmly ensconced as a target of criticism along with other classical philosophers, and may therefore be taken to mark the end of the early response to his *Utilitarianism*.

Philisophical discussion of Mill's *Utilitarianism* during the first fifteen years was, then, almost wholly occupied with attacking it. Almost every criticism that has since been developed was made in at least rudimentary, and usually in fairly sophisticated, form during this early period, while a number of criticisms were made that have since dropped out of sight. I shall discuss the objections offered to four of Mill's points: his views on the derivability of moral notions from non-moral ones; his so-called 'proof' of the principle of utility; his distinction between higher and lower pleasures; and his claim that the rules of common-sense morality may be taken as the middle axioms of a utilitarian ethic.

McCosh in 1865 offers the first objection to Mill's account of the derivation of 'the ideas involved in the words *ought, obligation, merit, demerit*,'[15] but has no argument to show it mistaken. At least the rudiments of argument were supplied in 1866 by two writers. The Rev John Bascom points out that 'when ... it is said that what is useful is right, the assertion is not a disguised truism. There is something added to the judgment of utility by that of right.' He means this as an argument to show that a theoretical account of human faculties must allow for a faculty of intuition, since no derivation of moral ideas from non-moral ideas is possible.[16] In defence of the same point, Mansel suggests the same argument (and, following Prior, I shall call it 'the argument from

15 James McCosh, *Outlines of Moral Philosophy by Dugald Stewart* (London 1865), 142; cf *Examination of Mill's Philosophy* (London 1866), 385–90
16 John Bascom, 'Utilitarianism,' *Bibliotheca Sacra*, XXIII, 1866, 442–3; cf 435 ff

trivialisation').[17] Taking a commonplace maxim as an illustration of moral judgments in general, he says: 'The proverb "honesty is the best policy", if it is anything more than the bare truism that policy is policy, testifies to the natural conviction of men that the *idea* of honesty is one thing and the *idea* of policy is another.'[18] Lecky makes a related critical remark to the effect that all languages and all peoples distinguish between 'the ideas of interest and utility on the one hand and of virtue on the other';[19] but a fuller articulation of the points these various writers suggest was presented by John Grote.

It is a general thesis of Grote's moral philosophy that no true ethical view can be constructed which does not recognize the sharp and clear distinction between the ideal and the actual, between what ought to be and what is. As one way of showing this, he asks whether the utilitarian principle, that promotiveness of happiness makes an action right, can be held to be true in virtue of the meaning of the word 'right.' If this were so, Grote says, then it would be hard to see why there are separate words for 'right' and its synonyms; moreover, the utilitarian principle would not really be a proposition since it would not really join two separate ideas.[20] These two remarks are meant to bring out the weakness of the view that the utilitarian principle is true just because 'right' means 'promotive of happiness.' That view, Grote thinks, amounts to the claim that language would be more truthful if actions were only distinguished in terms of their relation to happiness: moral terms do not explicitly do so and could be eliminated. But the consequences of eliminating them are, Grote insists, unacceptable. For we should then not be able to say why action promotive of happiness 'should be recommended rather than that which is not so: there is no other idea of rightness, goodness, valuableness, than that which belongs to itself.'[21] That is, without a moral vocabulary, we could neither praise nor give reasons for recommending certain actions. We could only say of actions that they are what they are. But, Grote asks, 'if felicific action is better than that which is not felicific, *why* is it better?' It must be, he says, because it has more goodness than that which is compared with it, 'and this quality of goodness ... cannot be itself: what is it then?' There must, Grote thinks, be 'a moral preferableness of one sort of action to another,' which might coincide with promotiveness of happiness 'but is not, in the notion of it, the same thing.'[22]

In other works Grote makes it clearer than he does in the *Examination* that his insistence on an 'ideal' which is not just 'actual,' and on a correlative distinction in thought and language, is part of a broad philosophical view which

17 Arthur Prior, *Logic and the Basis of Ethics* (Oxford 1949), 100
18 Henry L. Mansel, *Letters, Lectures and Reviews* (London 1873), 364–5
19 W.E.H. Lecky, *History of European Morals* (London 1869), 34
20 John Grote, *An Examination of the Utilitarian Philosophy* (Cambridge 1870), 267–8
21 Ibid., 268   22 Ibid., 268–9; cf 275–6

serves to defend a religious outlook. The same animus, this time in defence of Catholicism, is behind the essay published in 1872 by William George Ward. The first aim of the essay[23] is to show that the idea of moral goodness is not 'complex and resolvable ... into simpler elements' but simple. If Mill disagrees, Ward says, then he must take it that 'morally good' means neither more nor less than 'conducive to general enjoyment.' Now ideas of moral goodness and its 'correlatives' are familiar to us all. If we simply consider any of the innumerable commonplace moral propositions in which such ideas figure, we will immediately see that Mill's definition must be wrong. If someone says that man is bound to do what God commands, it is plain that he does not *mean* that man's obedience would minister to general enjoyment, even though this might also be true: the latter is simply a different proposition. 'If [Mill's] theory were true, it would be a simply tautologous proposition to say, that "conduct, known by the agent as adverse to general enjoyment, is morally evil" ... Now ... the contradictory of a tautologous proposition is simply unmeaning.' But Mill himself would not hold that it is meaningless to say that 'some conduct, known by the agent to be adverse to general enjoyment, may be morally good'; and plainly that proposition is not meaningless. Ward goes on to point out, as did Grote, that this is a general result: 'Arguments entirely similar to those which we have here given would equally suffice to disprove any *other* analysis which might be attempted, of the idea "morally good"; and we conclude, therefore, that this idea is simple and incapable of analysis.' The second step in Ward's argument is predictable. If 'morally good' is a simple idea, then it cannot be contained in the conclusion of a syllogism unless it is expressly included in one of the premises. Hence it cannot be the case – as Mill says it is – that all moral judgments are inferential. For if a moral judgment is a conclusion, somewhere its premises must contain the simple idea of goodness. The premise containing that idea cannot be known inferentially but must be known intuitively; for if not, we are off on an infinite regress which would force us to conclude that there is no moral knowledge. But Mill holds that some moral judgments are known to be true. Hence he must admit that there are some intuitively known moral propositions.

In his 1870 review of Grote's *Examination*, the Rev. Llewellyn Davies remarks that 'the difficulty of obtaining an adequate sense for the word "ought" – of extracting the imperativeness which we associate with the idea of duty – out of the elements of the Utilitarian creed, is so obvious and familiar that no hostile critic could fail to insist upon it.'[24] The writings cited above should show that there is at least a considerable portion of truth in this remark. And if there is, we must revise not only G.E. Moore's extremely naïve view of history,

23 All the quotations in this paragraph are from W.G. Ward, 'Mr. Mill on the Foundation of Morality,' *Dublin Review*, LXX, 1872, 80–7
24 J.L. Davies, 'Professor Grote on Utilitarianism,' *Contemporary Review*, XV, 1870, 91

according to which Sidgwick was the only philosopher prior to Moore himself to have noticed the irreducibility of 'good':[25] more significantly, we must revise Arthur Prior's much more knowledgeable version of history. Prior traces the claim of irreducibility back to the controversies with Hobbes. He sees Archbishop Whately as the Victorian transmitter of the insight underlying the arguments for irreducibility, the one thinker prior to Sidgwick to use and appreciate the argument from trivialization. Now it is true that Sidgwick thinks some moral concepts are *sui generis* and irreducible. He does not develop the point specifically against Mill, and it is not clear that in the first edition of the *Methods* he uses the trivialization argument. This observation is not itself a criticism of Prior, nor is it terribly important to point out that there were several thinkers between Whately and Sidgwick who appreciated the trivialization argument. Prior's interpretation of the Whately-Sidgwick agreement on irreducibility, however, does call for criticism. Prior thinks of Sidgwick, 'with Huxley the agnostic beside him and Whately the Archbishop behind him,' as keeping alive a 'tradition of sanity and logical rigor.'[26] I fear this comment misses two points. First, the tradition kept alive by Whately and the numerous other Victorian intuitionists was the tradition which holds that it is only through our unique moral insight, attested to by the empirically inexplicable moral concepts, that we have firm evidence of our spiritual nature and of the divine government of the universe. That this philosophical commitment of the intuitionists seemed unbreakable was one of the reasons for Mill's determined resistance to their arguments. Second, Sidgwick's originality here lies in breaking with precisely this aspect of the intuitional tradition, and in becoming the first Victorian philosopher to see how to give a rationalistic account of the irreducibility of moral notions which nonetheless gives no special support to any religious view.[27]

Because Mill refused to appeal to any moral intuitions, and because he wanted to justify using the utilitarian principle to reform common-sense morality, he thought he needed some sort of rational basis for the principle which did not depend on the truth of common-sense moral beliefs. This basis he tried to supply in the fourth chapter of *Utilitarianism*. Those of his early critics who deal with the considerations meant to determine their intellects to assent to the principle unanimously find them unconvincing. Some of the now standard difficulties are noted in quite early writings. The anonymous objector of 1864

---

25 G.E. Moore, *Principia Ethica* (Cambridge 1903; reprinted 1951), 17
26 Prior, *Logic*, 107; compare cf 36
27 It is interesting that J. Llewellyn Davies does not seem to care about the irreducibility of moral notions and also does not think we must rely on morality for our main evidence of the divine governance. He is happy to take morality simply as obedience to God's will, and to see evidence of God's existence everywhere in the universe. See especially his 'Universal Morality and the Christian Theory of Duty.'

points out – for what is, I believe, the first time in print – the disanalogy be-tween 'visible' and 'desirable,' and suggests, not very clearly, that there is a 'fallacy of speech' involved in the argument.[28] The brief review in the *North American Review* in 1865 says that the 'proof' fails since it 'shows nothing more than that each man desires *his own* happiness,' and, not showing that anyone in fact desires the general happiness, gives no reason for saying that the general happiness is desirable. Nor is evidence given, the reviewer writes, that 'happiness' and 'desirable' are synonymous.[29] McCosh adverts obscurely to a 'gap ... which utilitarianism cannot fill up' between pursuing one's own good and the obligation to pursue the good of others;[30] but he does not further explain the problem. Of the Lecky controversialists, only R. H. Hutton touches on Mill's 'proof.' His concern is that no basis is given for saying that equal amounts of happiness are equally desirable, regardless of who enjoys them: since each man seeks his own happiness, 'to whom is A's happiness as desirable as an equal lot of B's?'[31] The other writers up to 1870 do not discuss Mill's 'proof,' and so Grote's criticism is the first full discussion of it to be published, as it was the first to be written.

Mill's general endeavour, Grote says, is in this matter as in others to base the ideal on the 'ground of experience and observation.' Hence Mill tries to present his main premise as a factual one. The premise is that each man desires what is pleasant to him, and this, Grote remarks, Mill 'gravely speaks of as a fact which we might possibly doubt.' The general problem with Mill's rationale for the principle is then this: 'Mr. Mill has to prove that "happiness," as the ideal *summum bonum* of man, is the one thing which ought to regulate his conduct ...: this is not a thing that *any* observation can prove, and it is quite a vain proceeding to set observation ... to warrant a truism, and then to say that in doing so it proves a point entirely different.'[32] Observation cannot show that man desires the desirable 'if by the desirable we mean the *ideally desirable*'; and the truism that each desires what he actually desires (and this is all that Mill's allegedly factual premise comes to, in Grote's view) will not help prove any moral theory.[33] Moreover, even supposing that because each desires his own happiness, his own happiness is a good to him, we can hardly conclude that the happiness of the aggregate is a good to the aggregate, for the conclu-sion is 'unmeaning' unless the aggregate can desire or act. And if Mill had really shown that in the same way each man's happiness is his own end, 'the

28 Anonymous, *Utilitarianism Explained and Exemplified* (London 1864), 63–4
29 J.B. Thayer, 'Mill's Dissertations and Discussions,' *North American Review*, C, 1865, 263
30 McCosh, *Stewart*, 143–4; *Examination*, 403–4
31 R.H. Hutton, 'The Latest Phase of the Utilitarian Controversy,' *British Quarterly Review*, L, 1869, 71, where Mill is not explicitly mentioned.
32 Grote, *Utilitarian Philosophy*, 63–4
33 Ibid., 65

aggregate happiness is an end to *each individual*,' much of his philosophizing would have been unnecessary.[34] Grote is aware, unlike some of the later critics, that Mill does not mean to give a logically conclusive proof. Hence he does not give further technical consideration of the details of Mill's argument. Most of his chapter is given over to broader considerations of the inadequacies of Mill's treatment of the issue, considerations resting in large part on Grote's view that human nature is as essentially active as it is sentient, so that a view of the highest good which takes account only of the sentient aspect of it will necessarily be incomplete. But Grote's editor, J.B. Mayor, with a tidier if less perceptive mind than his author, puts into footnotes two technical points. First, there is a formal failure of analogy between 'visible' and 'desirable'; second, Mill commits in addition to formal fallacy of composition in his attempt to move from what is desired *by each* to what is desirable *for all*.[35]

We can be brief about the remaining early criticisms of the proof, as they have little new to add. Birks leans heavily on Grote: he quotes extensively and dignifies as text what had been editor's notes, but seems to have nothing of his own with which to supplement the attack.[36] Sidgwick is admirably concise. He hints at the mistaken analogy between 'visible' and 'desirable,' and he points out that from the fact that each man desires his own happiness the natural inference – if one were to be allowed – would be, not to universalistic hedonism but to egoistic hedonism. He adds a new point, however, because he rejects Mill's psychology. It is not true, he argues, that each man desires only his own happiness; and if it is not, then yet another step in Mill's argument is lacking, the step that would show that a hedonistic interpretation of the moral end or good is correct.[37] Even Bradley is brief concerning the 'proof.' The distinctive point about his remarks, aside from their famous rhetoric, is that Bradley, unlike Grote and Sidgwick, seems to treat Mill as if he were trying to offer a conclusive argument. But Bradley has no new substantive objections to offer.[38]

Mill's views on the derivability of our moral concepts from our non-moral ideas, and his attempt to find a basis for the utilitarian principle in universal human desires, are continuations of traditional utilitarian positions. I turn now to criticisms of two points on which Mill departed from the tradition. The first is his notorious belief that there are distinctions of quality as well as of quantity among pleasures, and that moral decisions may be justified not only by appeal to amounts of pleasure but by showing that the pleasures to be produced are 'higher' regardless of amount. The original *Westminster*

---

34 Ibid., 70–1   35 Ibid., 65n, 70n

36 T.R. Birks, *Modern Utilitarianism* (London 1874), 200–1

37 H. Sidgwick, *The Methods of Ethics* (London 1874), 364–6. All references to Sidgwick are to the first edition.

38 Bradley, *Ethical Studies*, 112–15

reviewer avoids the topic altogether, but the critics attack it from the very beginning. Cliffe Leslie raised questions about it;[39] Rands hints that Mill is inconsistent for asserting it;[40] Mansel explicitly points out that to admit a distinction of kind among pleasures is to admit an independent, non-hedonistic standard;[41] Laurie 'gladly notes' that this move takes Mill away from pure utilitarianism;[42] Lecky finds Mill's view 'completely incompatible with utilitarian theory,'[43] and Hutton, one of Lecky's half-sympathetic, half-critical reviewers, here agrees with him.[44] There were others prior to the publication of Grote's *Examination* to point out Mill's failings on this topic, but Grote's chapter on the subject still deserves notice. Grote, like all the others, holds that this admission of a qualitative distinction introduces a basic incompatibility into utilitarianism. He also raises some acute questions as to the possibility of separating pleasures out as objects of comparison from the activities in the course of which they occur,[45] thus anticipating later idealist objections. Sidgwick put the basic criticism in another light. He holds that if a pure and consistent utilitarian method of resolving moral questions is to be developed, 'all qualitative comparison of pleasures must really resolve itself into quantitative.' Otherwise a non-hedonistic ground of preference is admitted into a method that claims to be purely hedonistic.[46] Only John Morley was bold enough to defend Mill on this point. He fails to see any inconsistency in admitting qualitative distinctions of pleasure.[47] The *Westminster* reviewer of Grote, while anxious to defend Mill, was not so brave. He says first that it would be 'premature' to hold that difference in the quality of two pleasures is unresolvable into difference in quantity, 'until it is shown that the apparent difference in quality is not due to the difference of the accompanying mental state'; and then he says that recognition of qualitative superiorities 'has nothing in it necessarily contradicting the Utilitarian formula' – without, however, making out a case for this claim in any detail.[48] By the time Bradley thought

39 T.E.C. Leslie, 'Utilitarianism and the Common Good,' *Macmillan's Magazine*, VIII, 1863, 157–8

40 W.B. Rands, *Henry Holbeach, Student in Life and Philosophy* (London 1865), II, 23–4

41 Mansel, *Letters*, 374

42 S.S. Laurie, *Notes Expository and Critical on Certain British Theories of Morals* (London 1868), 102–3

43 Lecky, *History*, 90n

44 Hutton, 'Utilitarian Controversy,' 79–83

45 Grote, *Utilitarian Philosophy*, see Chapter III. See also Birks, *Modern Utilitarianism*, 224ff, 232ff.

46 Sidgwick, *Methods*, 77–8

47 John Morley, 'Mr. Lecky's First Chapter,' *Fortnightly Review*, XXIX, 1869, Morley, 535–6

48 Anonymous, review of Grote's *Utilitarian Philosophy*, *Westminster Review*, XCV, 1871, 20–1

it necessary to devote six condescending pages to trouncing Mill on this subject, the matter had really been fairly thoroughly brought to the public's attention.[49]

The second of Mill's innovations which I shall discuss is not quite so marked a break with the utilitarian tradition as his position concerning higher and lower pleasures, but is far more significant. This is his claim that the existing rules of common-sense morality may be taken to represent the insight and experience of generations of men in estimating the consequences of actions and so may be used for utilitarian moral guidance. While both John Austin and James Mill had suggested a point like this in response to the objection that there is not time, prior to each action, to carry out the complex calculations utilitarianism requires, they each were far more explicit about the criticism that ordinary morality needs than about the wisdom it carries.[50] J.S. Mill, by contrast, though not in any way wishing to suggest that ordinary morality did not need criticism, put the emphasis on the considerable positive utility of following its rules, and his general authoritativeness as spokesman for the utilitarians meant that this shift of emphasis would be taken quite seriously. Before discussing the general response to this change, we should note a technical criticism of it.

Explicit consideration of the philosophical problem involved in Mill's attempt to co-opt ordinary morality for utilitarianism does not, I believe, occur prior to the *Methods of Ethics* in 1874. Sidgwick points out that popularly accepted moral beliefs are not held as beliefs about the best ways of achieving general happiness: 'They present themselves as the expression of an immediate preference for certain kinds of conduct: and we have no more right to interpret the moral preferences of any society into current opinions as to what promotes general happiness, than we have to identify the appetites, tastes, and inclinations of an individual with his opinions as to what is best for his health.'[51] There is in other words a logical or categorical difference of type between beliefs about means to a given end and beliefs about what is to be done as immediately preferable. Since ordinary moral beliefs are of the latter kind, Mill has – so Sidgwick concludes – no warrant for treating them as being of the former kind. On factual grounds, Sidgwick continues, Mill is also mistaken in thinking these rules to be the outcome of a 'consensus of competent judges, up to the present time, as to the kind of conduct which is likely to produce the greatest amount of happiness.'[52] It is interesting that F.H. Bradley seems to be making the same categorical criticism as Sidgwick, though Bradley's remarks

49 Bradley, *Ethical Studies*, 116ff
50 For Austin's views, see *The Province of Jurisprudence Determined* (1832; reprinted London 1954), esp. 47–53, 73–81. For James Mill, see *A Fragment on Mackintosh* (London 1835; reprinted 1870), 163, 249–65.
51 Sidgwick, *Methods*, 430
52 Ibid., 435

are a little difficult to interpret. Moral laws, he says, are not guides which we may or may not choose to follow. They bind us, in a much stronger way than such guides do. Obedience to the rules of a 'moral almanac' is not part of the end itself: obedience to true moral laws, presumably, is.[53] If following the almanac's rules does not help in achieving the end in a given case, we are free to abandon the rule. And this is a serious objection to Mill's theory: 'the moral consciousness is the touchstone of moral theories, and that moral consciousness ... has laws which are a great deal more than rules. To that consciousness, "Do not commit adultery" is a law to be obeyed; it is not the prescription of a more or less questionable policy.'[54]

Bradley's remarks are important for a further reason. He is plainly prepared to treat utilitarianism as a moral theory attempting to explain the convictions to be found in the ordinary 'moral consciousness' and supporting its principle by the argument that that principle is the 'one and only possible account' of the moral consciousness.[55] In this attitude Bradley is at one with a surprisingly large number of Mill's critics. Although there is very little technical comment on Mill's adoption of the rules of ordinary morality into the utilitarian system, the considerable part of the critical response to Mill that concerns itself with the *moral substance* of utilitarianism is in fact directed to this claim. It is well known that critics of utilitarianism prior to Mill's version of it made much of the viciousness, lowness, and immorality of the doctrine, and some post-Millian critics took up the same old war-cries. McCosh and Lecky and Birks are tempted in this direction; the Rev Robert Watts thinks utilitarianism is 'morally pernicious,' says that its main positions are 'subversive of morality, as they are irreconcilable with the central doctrine of Christianity,'[56] and argues at length that Mill's particular theory concerning the morality of intentions is exactly the same as that of – the Jesuits;[57] and Henry Reeve blames utilitarianism for the increase of political corruption, the decline of commercial good faith, the loss of the integrity of manufacturers, the extinction of respect for parental authority in America, the reckless rush to ruin of 'multitudes of young men of the upper classes,' and the decay of female decorum.[58] But by and large this is quite strikingly *not* the tone of the critics. They are not willing to accept Mill's view that the principles of common-sense morality may be read in a utilitarian sense. They are certainly not willing to accept the rather stronger claim made by Mill's enthusiastic *Westminster* reviewer of 1863 that 'utility is even already accepted as the only test' of human conduct,

53 Bradley, *Ethical Studies*, 105–6
54 Ibid., 110
55 Ibid., 88
56 R. Watts, *Utilitarianism as Expounded by J. Stuart Mill, Alex. Bain and Others* (Belfast 1868), 37, 24
57 Ibid., 34–7
58 H. Reeve, review of Lecky's *History*, *Edinburgh Review*, cxxx, 1869, 21

and who explains how 'it almost always happens in the progress of human society, that a certain principle of actions comes into general practical application long before people have the thoughtfulness or the courage to recognise it as a principle. So it is with the Utilitarian creed. It is at present the practical inspiration of all civilized society.'[59] But the critics are prepared to debate the matter, not as opponents in a political battle, not as separated by an impassable moral chasm, but as fellow philosophers, working together to develop an adequate ethical theory.

Perhaps the change may be described in this way: criticisms initially made as charges of immorality, angrily levelled against the utilitarian view, come to be simply complaints that utilitarianism fails to give a sound account of the central moral convictions which we all hold in common – 'we' being philosophers as well as plain men – before we begin to philosophize. For this change of attitude on the part of the majority of the critics, I think Mill must take whatever credit is due. The chief instrument of the change is Mill's theory concerning the status of common-sense morality, and this is aided by the much-mocked theory of higher and lower pleasures. The reason why is not hard to see.

Victorian intuitional moralists give many different accounts of the nature and role of intuition, but there is at least one point on which they are fairly closely united. Ordinary morality, the accepted rules of common sense, cannot be wholly erroneous or even far removed from the truth. To say that the moral beliefs of the majority could be completely, or very seriously, mistaken would be to weaken fatally the claim that every normal human being has the ability to intuit essential moral truth. The pre-Millian utilitarians were so critical of the accepted morality that even the Austin-James Mill concession about its utility did not convince the intuitionists that it was being taken seriously. John Stuart Mill did convince them. His views on higher and lower pleasures, although they caused his critics to doubt his logical abilities, persuaded them of what Thayer in 1865 calls his 'noble qualities of mind.'[60] The usual explanation of his inconsistency about pleasure, in fact, is that he shares with every decent man certain intuitions that are incompatible with the older hedonism, and is trying to adapt his theory to take account of them. Thus reassured that J.S. Mill and they have a wide range of pre-philosophical convictions in common, the intuitionists see that Mill is in earnest about allowing greater cognitive weight to common-sense morality. This move did not, of course, suffice to bring about a complete rapprochement concerning all the moral points that still divided the two schools. But it surely helped in encouraging the intuitionists to treat utilitarianism as a serious philosophical theory. For

59 Anonymous, review of Mill's *Utilitarianism, Westminster Review*, XXIII, 1863, 63
60 Thayer, 'Mill's Dissertations,' 266; compare J.S. Blackie, *Four Phases of Morals* (London 1871), 329

now, in addition to breathing a moral spirit more nearly recognizable as akin to their own, utilitarianism offered an alternative account of one of the central points of their own theory of moral knowledge. On both accounts, therefore, it called for a far more careful philosophical examination than it had hitherto, in their eyes, deserved.

Utilitarianism was one of Mill's major attempts to exemplify his belief that an adequate philosophy would have to incorporate the insights of previously opposed thinkers. It appeared at a time when this reconciliationist attitude was growing among the anti-utilitarians as well. We can see this in some of the early critics. Dr Bascom, for instance, is confident that 'right action, under God's government, will ultimately attain the highest pleasure; that is, will perfectly coincide with utility.'[61] Hutton and Bowne, both of them followers of Martineau, are insistent that a utilitarian element is a necessary part of a complete moral theory. Leslie Stephen, reviewing Lecky, points out that Lecky is much closer to Mill than he seems to realize, and suggests yet further possibilities of agreement.[62] This approach to ethics is particularly striking in Grote – so striking, indeed, that Grote's *Westminster* reviewer felt compelled to comment: 'Mr. Lecky took up the Utilitarian formula in all its varieties, and sought to show that its legitimate deductions must lead to immorality; that the great duties of veracity, chastity, &c., could never be based on their utility ... Mr. Grote, on the other hand, makes scarcely an attempt to prove a grave discrepancy between the Utilitarian standard and acknowledged obligations.'[63] Though this fails to note the many moral deficiencies Grote attributes to utilitarianism – its inability to supply a principle for the distribution of good or to allow for the intrinsic value of virtue, to mention just two[64] – it does focus on an important part of Grote's thought. He holds that although moral good and natural good or pleasure are different in kind, there must be a harmony of goods in the universe. Hence he thinks that although it is important to point out the deficiencies of utilitarianism, it is more important to see what its positive contribution to a complete theory might be than to castigate it for its failings. For its insistence on making means-ends calculations the core of moral thinking is a reflection of the complex structure of the ideal, and if it is partial, it is also not wholly untrue. This reconciling attitude, which reaches back, at Cambridge, at least to Coleridge, finds its greatest expression in the work of Sidgwick. Something like it, though with different roots, is present in Bradley. His view of 'the Utilitarian monster' is 'that its heart is *in*

61 Bascom, 'Utilitarianism,' 442
62 Leslie Stephen, 'Mr. Lecky's *History of European Morals*,' *Fraser's Magazine*, LXXX, 1869, 274–6, and compare Blackie, *Four Phases*, 334
63 Anonymous, review of Grote's *Utilitarian Philosophy*, 20
64 Other critics had dealt with both these themes before Grote, and the second point in particular was extensively criticized.

the right place, but the brain is wanting'[65] – it has many good aims and principles, but like Kant's theory, and like simple intuitional theories, it is one-sided and incomplete. No doubt its results must be taken up in any complete view; only as it stands, it will not 'justify to the inquiring mind those moral beliefs which it is not prepared for the sake of any theory to relinquish.'[66]

Mill achieved the aim of obtaining for utilitarianism an honoured place among philosophers. 'In presenting justice as fairness,' writes Professor Rawls, 'I shall contrast it with utilitarianism. I do this ... partly because the several variants of the utilitarian view have long dominated our philosophical tradition and continue to do so.'[67] Mill's reconciliationist efforts, exemplified in his views on higher and lower pleasures, and more importantly in his theory of the role of common-sense morality, made it both possible and necessary for anti-utilitarians to take utilitarianism seriously. But it was the failure, as everyone viewed it, of Mill's attempt to give rational support for the utilitarian principle, and the associated failure to demonstrate the derivability of moral from non-moral concepts, that helped give direction to the future philosophical development of utilitarianism. Given those failures – and if Mill failed, who might hope to succeed? – it seemed that the most sensible path to take was that of showing that the utilitarian principle *could* 'justify to the inquiring mind those moral beliefs which it is not prepared for the sake of any theory to relinquish.'

If Mill obtained respectability among the philosophers for his moral outlook, however, he paid a price to get it; and I shall conclude by noting John Grote's far-sighted comment on the price Mill paid. Grote speaks of the 'conserving or reforming' tone which a philosophical ethic may take.

If it is looked upon as a serious thing ... which is to give to man, not only the guards and restraints of his action, but also the principles and initiatives of it ... if, consequently it considers its task in relation to human feelings and society to be mainly one of correction and regeneration; – it has then what I mean by a reforming character. If on the other hand, it looks upon itself as a sort of second thought ... as what no state of human society could really owe its existence to ... if it contents itself, in the main, scientifically with describing human society, and practically with reinforcing and strengthening it; – it has then what I mean by a conservative character.[68]

Bentham's utilitarianism is of a reforming character, according to Grote, but Mill, to answer charges against that style of utilitarianism, defends a version of the theory which is of a conservative cast. And yet, Grote remarks, 'it is the

65 Bradley, *Ethical Studies*, 114–15
66 Ibid., 124–5
67 John Rawls, *A Theory of Justice* (Cambridge 1971), 52
68 Grote, *Utilitarian Philosophy*, 225–6

former with which he identifies himself; in other words ... the special charm of utilitarianism to him is ... the idea that by means of this a great reform may be brought about in the beliefs and customs and feelings of men.'[69] The subsequent history of ethics does not altogether refute the suggestion that Grote seems here to be making: that in trying to use philosophy to accomplish his reforming aims, Mill, quite *without* intending to, gave his moral philosophy and that which descended from it a conservative character.

CHECKLIST: PUBLICATIONS CONCERNING MILL'S UTILITARIANISM, 1861–76

Anonymous. Review of Grote's *Examination of the Utilitarian Philosophy, Westminster Review*, xcv, 1871, 41–53 (20–6 of the American edition, to which references are made)
– Review of Mill's *Utilitarianism, Westminster Review*, xxiii, 1863
– *Utilitarianism Explained and Exemplified in Moral and Political Government* (London 1864; attributed by Harvard Library to Charles Tennant, fl 1860)
Bain, Alexander. *Mental and Moral Science* (London 1868)
Bascom, Rev John. 'Utilitarianism,' *Bibliotheca Sacra*, xxiii, 1866, 435–52
Birks, Thomas Rawson. *Modern Utilitarianism* (London 1874)
Blackie, John Stuart. *Four Phases of Morals* (London 1871)
Bleckly, Henry. *A Colloquy on the Utilitarian Theory of Morals* (London 1873)
Bowne, Borden P. 'Moral Intuition vs. Utilitarianism,' *New Englander*, xxxii, 1873, 217–42
Bradley, F.H. *Ethical Studies* (London 1876; 2nd ed., Oxford 1935)
Bryce, James. Review of Lecky's *History of European Morals, Quarterly Review*, cxxviii, 1870, 49–81
Calderwood, Henry. *Handbook of Moral Philosophy* (London 1872)
Church, R.W. Review of Lecky's *History of European Morals, Macmillan's Magazine*, xx, 1869, 76–88
Davies, Rev J. Llewellyn. 'Professor Grote on Utilitarianism,' *Contemporary Review*, xv, 1870, 80–96
– 'Universal Morality and the Christian Theory of Duty,' *Fortnightly Review*, vi, 1869, 1–12
Grote, John. *An Examination of the Utilitarian Philosophy*, ed. J.B. Mayor (Cambridge 1870)
Hutton, R.H. 'The Latest Phase of the Utilitarian Controversy,' *British Quarterly Review*, L, 1869, 68–91
Laurie, Simon S. *Notes Expository and Critical on Certain British Theories of Morals* (London 1868)
Lecky, W.E.H. *History of European Morals* (London 1869; 3rd ed. 1877 [repr. 1920])
Leslie, T.E. Cliffe. 'Utilitarianism and the Common Good,' *Macmillan's Magazine*, viii, 1863, 152–60
Lorimer, James. *The Institutes of Law* (Edinburgh 1872; 2nd ed. 1880)

---

69 Ibid., 231–2. Birk's *Modern Utilitarianism*, 86ff, repeats Grote's criticism on this point, as on so many others.

Mansel, Henry L. *Letters, Lectures and Reviews,* ed. Chandler (London 1873)

McCosh, James. *Outlines of Moral Philosophy by Dugald Stewart, with ... a supplement by James McCosh* (London 1865)

– *Examination of Mill's Philosophy* (London 1866)

Morley, John. 'Mr. Lecky's First Chapter,' *Fortnightly Review,* XXIX, 1869, 519–38

Newman, F.W. 'Epicureanism Ancient and Modern,' *Fraser's Magazine,* LXXXIV (ns 4), 1871, 606–17

Rands, William Brighty. *Henry Holbeach, Student in Life and Philosophy,* Vol. II (London 1865)

Reeve, Henry. Review of Lecky's *History of European Morals, Edinburgh Review,* CXXX, 1869, 36–56 (references to American edition)

Shairp, J.C. 'Moral Theories and Christian Ethics,' *North British Review,* ns VIII, 1867, 1–46

Sidgwick, Henry. *The Methods of Ethics* (London 1874)

Stephen, James Fitzjames. 'Utilitarianism,' *Pall Mall Gazette,* 1869. Reprinted in *Liberty, Equality, Fraternity* (London 1873)

Stephen, Leslie [?]. 'Mr. Lecky's *History of European Morals,' Fraser's Magazine,* LXXX, 1869, 273–84. [Houghton attribution uncertain]

Thayer, J.B. 'Mill's Dissertations and Discussions,' *North American Review,* C, 1865, 259–66

Thornton, W.T. 'Anti-Utilitarianism,' *Fortnightly Review,* XIV, 1870, 314–37

Ward, William George. 'Mr. Mill on the Foundation of Morality,' *Dublin Review,* LXX, 1872. Reprinted in *Essays on the Philosophy of Theism,* ed. Wilfrid Ward, 1884, Vol. I, from which quotations are taken.

Watts, Robert. *Utilitarianism as Expounded by J. Stuart Mill, Alex. Bain, and Others.* 2nd rev. ed. (Belfast [1868])

Williams, Robert. 'A Few Words on Utilitarianism,' *Fraser's Magazine,* LXXX, 1869, 248–56

Wilson, John Matthias and Thomas Fowler. *Principles of Morals (Introductory Chapters)* (Oxford 1886; originally printed in 1875)

The Scientific Uses of Scientific Biography, with Special Reference to J. S. Mill

GEORGE J. STIGLER

The development of science is increasingly being viewed as a scientific problem in its own right: How do sciences evolve, and why? Do sciences admit of large and basic changes only by the revolutionary process which Thomas Kuhn has made famous? Are scientific discoveries almost always made independently by several scholars, as Robert Merton argues? Questions such as these suggest correctly that the evolution of a science is a fascinating area for study: subtle, complex, but surely obeying laws which eventually can be discovered.

One small or large problem of scientific evolution is: does the study of the lives of scientists provide useful knowledge of how sciences evolve? If we knew only that a Mr M, otherwise unidentifiable, had written a *Principles of Political Economy* in 1848 and revised it six times thereafter, would we be any less able to understand its contents and scientific role? Indeed, if we were uncertain that Mr M had survived the revolutions of 1848, so possibly the revisions had been made by a clever impostor, would we be less able to comprehend the work?

The answer to our question, one is tempted to assert, is at hand: more information is always better than less, hence biographical information must add to our understanding of science. But as Marshall said of economics, all short answers are wrong: our problem is not a trivial non-problem. The cost of information is never zero, so less information may be better than more. More specifically, an immense number of biographies of science has been written: suppose they have yielded no understanding or even additional misunderstanding of the evolution of science? We need to examine the problem more closely.

CUSTOMARY PRACTICE

The customary use of biography in explaining scientific work is, to be quite blunt, shocking. There is no other area which is remotely scientific in its pretensions which shows half the facility and even the popularity in the use of The Hand-picked Example, The Implicit Absurdity, the Abhorrence of Evidence. These are harsh words, but I propose to document them from the actual uses made of Mill's life to explain his economic theories. This choice of illustration, I can assure you, is dictated not by some special penchant in the literature for the careless use of Mill's biography, but simply by this felicitous occasion commemorating the resurrection of his scientific stature a century after his death.

The simplest scientific use of biography is presented in the form: to understand Mill's *Principles* 'requires some familiarity with the author's *Autobiography*.'[1] Unfortunately the contribution of biographical knowledge to understanding is not specified: perhaps one must know the historian's – in this case, Cossa's – life to comprehend what he meant. So much for *The Abhorrence of Evidence*.

Leslie Stephen provided an early example of the Implicit Absurdity when he wrote: 'The speed with which the book [*Political Economy*] was written shows that it did not imply any revision of first principles.'[2] The doctrine that the originality or heterodoxy of a volume is proportional to (or some increasing function of) the length of time the author has devoted to its *composition* (or, for that matter, its excogitation) would indeed be a wonderful hypothesis, if only it were not naked nonsense. Leslie Stephen had previously remarked that Mill's *Logic* took a substantial time to write: beginnings were made in 1830 and the book on the syllogism was written perhaps as early as 1832, but the manuscript was not completed until 1842. Does Stephen say that this work, whose writing covered more than a decade as compared to the two years for the *Political Economy*, was six times as original? Alas, no: 'The coincidence with its predecessors remains far closer than the divergence. The fundamental tenets are developed rather than withdrawn.'[3] Since this is what is asserted also of the *Political Economy*, Stephen should have inferred only that Mill had taken a course in speed writing sometime after 1842 and before 1847.

A less precise but no less definite association of time of preparation with results was presented by Alfred Marshall: 'A critic of Mill's writings may not ignore the following facts. In the small leisure that was left to him free from

---

1 L. Cossa, *An Introduction to the Study of Political Economy* (London 1893), 330. Other historians of thought have made the same statement, for example L.H. Haney, *History of Economic Thought* (3rd ed., New York 1936), 443.
2 *The English Utilitarians* (London 1900), III, 161
3 Ibid., 75

official work, Mill wrote on a wide variety of questions which had already been discussed by great thinkers. On almost every one of these questions his thoughts, whatever faults they contained, were in some respect new. Therefore he had not much time for elaborating the explanations of his thoughts.'[4] Putting aside the error of the assertion that Mill had small leisure, and the temptation to say that Marshall was advancing (in 1876, when the essay on Mill appeared) an apology for his own subsequent unbelievable procrastination in publishing work, one must insist that in one sense Mill had plenty of time. Between the first and last editions of the *Principles* lie twenty-three years, sufficient time to correct imprecisely expressed views. Marshall was defending Mill against lesser critics, a task that must frequently be resumed, but the defence does not require the exoneration of Mill's analytical shortcomings on so implausible a ground.[5] (The number of third, fourth, and lower-class economists who complain about Mill's lack of consistency, as if they could judge it, is too extensive and painful to enumerate.)

François Trevou, a French editor of Mill's work, found Mill's view on Malthusian doctrine to be incomprehensible unless one were acquainted with his personal life. Island dwellers, said Trevou, naturally fear overpopulation, and Mill's father drilled the same fear into him. In addition, 'the presence of 9 children in the house demonstrated to him the inconveniences rather than the pleasures of large families.'[6] 'Naturally he did not have children.'[7]

If we can explain a view of John's by its possession by James, then we should find all doctrines of the *Elements of Political Economy* reproduced in the son's *Principles*. In fact there are important departures, which will be discussed later, so the task of determining which doctrines were inherited is unfaced. If James Mill strongly believed in the Malthusian doctrine and had nine children, why should his son's similar belief (and larger income) lead to none? (James Mill was quite familiar with the famous *Essay on Population* by 20 August 1805, the date on which, as I calculate, Stuart was conceived.)[8] Yet I must give Trevou his due: Thomas Robert Malthus had one brother and six sisters – I would conjecture that he would have produced his theory several years earlier if he had instead had six brothers and one sister.

Overton H. Taylor has found in one episode, which can be viewed as

4 *Memorials of Alfred Marshall* (London 1925), 120
5 Others have given the same interpretation to the *Principles* – for example, F.W. Taussig, *Wages and Capital* (New York 1899), 217. Taussig's attribution of the wages-fund recantation in part to friendship for Thornton is too far-fetched to discuss (ibid., 248).
6 *Stuart Mill (Textes choisis et Préface)* (Paris 1953), 30
7 Ibid., 31
8 He had reviewed the second edition in *The Literary Journal*, Dec. 1803; see D.N. Winch, *James Mill* (Edinburgh 1966), 447.

either intellectual or biographical – the two obviously overlap, as we shall argue – the explanation for an important trend in Mill's *Principles* through the various editions:

It is of interest that in the successive editions of his *Principles* Mill lengthened and increasingly stressed the favorable parts of his comments on 'socialism.' No doubt he did so because his views were developing further in that direction, but perhaps also in part because he had disliked the misdirected praise of the first edition by a conservative reviewer. This reviewer took the work as a whole to be a sound, orthodox demonstration of the merits of the existing English economy and social order, and of *laissez faire*, and the chapters on 'socialism' to be intended simply to condemn and refute it. In an angry reply and objection to that review, in the journal which had published it, Mill avowed his opposition to the views or attitudes the reviewer had imparted to him ...[9]

One need not dispute (1) Mill's increasingly more favourable treatment of socialism, or the interpretation of (2) the reviewer and (3) Mill's rejoinder, although in all three respects Taylor's statement is subject to severe criticism.[10] How peculiar, even with these concessions, is the proposed sequence: one review leads Mill to make several successive revisions of his treatise. Surely Mill – and Taylor – should have looked at the reactions of all reviewers and readers: if mostly they thought Mill favoured socialism more than he actually did, he should have revised the text to a more critical view of socialism.

Of course not all uses of Mill's life have been so irresponsible, and I now move on to respectable – but unsatisfactory – biographical explanations. Let

9 *A History of Economic Thought* (New York 1960), 254–5
10 On the latter two points, I can be brief:
    (a) The 'review,' 'Associative Progress,' *The Leader*, 27 July 1850, 416, is a two-paragraph comment, signed 'ION,' with a passing reference to Mill's book (without mention of the author) : 'That recent work on Political Economy, which was first to admit the feasibility of associative views, yet foreshadowed the inanity and monotony which must supervene when the spur of animal want was conquered and withdrawn.' ION had enquired concerning wealthy people driven by boredom to the 'shoemaker's last,' and found none.
    (b) Mill's reply, 'Constraints of Communism,' *The Leader*, 3 Aug. 1850, 447, consisted of one long paragraph and was signed 'D.' It simply *corrected* the reason given for his doubts about co-operative societies: 'Now, it is this bondage which I am afraid of in the coöperative communities. I fear that the yoke of conformity would be made heavier instead of lighter; that people would be compelled to live as it pleased others, not as it pleased themselves; that their lives would be placed under rules, the same for all, prescribed by the majority; and that there would be no escape, no independence of action left to any one, since all must be members of one or another community. It is this which, as is contended in the "Political Economy," would make life monotonous; not freedom from want, which is a good in every sense of the word ...'

us begin with Edwin Cannan, who had a sharp mind well-stocked with accurate knowledge of the classical economics: '[From 1830 to 1844] Mill's
mind was extremely active, but it does not seem to have been directed towards scientific economics. When a man has been giving study and thought
to a subject, he does not take rejected manuscripts which have lain fourteen
years in his drawer, and print them "with a few merely verbal alterations." '[11]
This allusion to *Unsettled Questions in Political Economy* greatly oversimpli-
fies the problem. The five essays cover only a tiny part of economics, and give
no evidence on Mill's work elsewhere. Moreover, if one has a finished manuscript, he may well publish it without reworking its exposition if its substance
is still what he believes; indeed it becomes difficult to make any choice except
trivial or wholesale revision.[12]

Mill's rebellion against his 'dour and magerful' father has received emphasis from so learned a man as Viner.[13] In a curious essay whose ostensible occasion was the centenary of Mill's *Principles* but whose theme was a defence
of Bentham, Viner explained Mill's writings on Bentham with an eye to the
death of his father in 1836. The explanation may well be correct – it is one
used by Mill himself[14] – but it is valueless. Unless one systematically characterizes the views of James Mill which were respected by his son – who assur-
edly did not share his father's view on a variety of subjects, including Harriet
Taylor – one simply has not explained anything. If John's solicitude for
James' feelings made random appearances, a tossed coin would be equally
helpful in explaining John's tergiversations.

My final example of the misuses of biography is John Stuart Mill himself.
I shall not rely upon his most famous improbability: the assessment of the
influence of Harriet Taylor upon himself and his work.[15] The example I
choose is the benefits of his service in the East India Company:

I am disposed to agree with what has been surmised by others, that the opportunity
which my official position gave me of learning by personal observation the necessary

11 *Production and Distribution Theories*, 3rd ed. (London 1924), 390
12 Thus, Milton Friedman began an important article: 'This article was written in
    1935 ... I planned to do further work on the problem but I never did and so the
    paper remained buried in my files.' 'A method of Comparing Incomes of Families
    Differing in Composition,' *Studies in Income and Wealth*, xv (National Bureau of
    Economic Research 1952). Friedman had nevertheless given some 'study and
    thought' to economics in the intervening seventeen years.
13 'Bentham and J.S. Mill: The Utilitarian Background,' *American Economic Review*,
    March 1949. Reprinted in *The Long View and the Short* (Glencoe 1958), 321.
    Others may have experienced my difficulty with 'magerful': the *Oxford English
    Dictionary* makes 'mager' a variant of 'maugre,' none of whose meanings (ill-will,
    basically) seems appropriate.
14 *Autobiography*, ed. Jack Stillinger (Boston 1969), 123
15 Ibid., 145–50

conditions of the practical conduct of public affairs, has been of considerable value to me as a theoretical reformer of the opinions and institutions of my time. Not, indeed, that public business transacted on paper, to take effect on the other side of the globe, was of itself calculated to give much practical knowledge of life. But the occupation accustomed me to see and hear the difficulties of every course, and the means of obviating them, stated and discussed deliberately, with a view to execution; it gave me opportunities of perceiving when public measures, and other political facts, did not produce the effects which had been expected of them, and from what causes ... I was thus in a good position for finding out by practice the mode of putting a thought which gives it easiest admittance into minds not prepared for it by habit; while I became practically conversant with the difficulties of moving bodies of men, the necessities of compromise, the art of sacrificing the non-essential to preserve the essential.[16]

If Mill is correct, he was an unusually successful speculative reformer because of this experience. There is no evidence, so far as I know, to justify – or contradict – the claim. If he had shown how *his* case for land nationalization, for limited liability companies, or other policies differed from the cases presented by other economists with different backgrounds, we might have some test of his view. As it stands, the claim is vacuous.

THE PROBLEM

What is biography and how may it be distinguished from scientific development? The writers of high and low science are sentient beings, and they cannot completely exclude from their scientific work their hopes and anxieties, their friendships and vendettas, their dyspepsia and their liquor – even if they tried to do so more strenuously than often they appear to do. Yet the web of mortality that ties them to their time and place is *not* science: science consists of the arguments and the evidence that lead *other* men to accept or reject scientific views. Science is a social enterprise, and those parts of a man's life which do not affect the relationships between that man and his fellow scientists are simply extra-scientific. When we are told that we must study a man's life to understand what he really meant, we are being invited to abandon science. What Mill's contemporaries did not know about his personal life – and it is well known that he was a man of few friends and few social activities – could not affect their interpretation of his words, and if we are to understand nineteenth-century economics the details of his personal life should not affect our interpretation of his words. The recipients of a scientific message are the people who determine what that message is, and no flight of genius which does not reach the recipients will ever reach and affect the science.

Even on this view of scientific interchange, some elements of a man's milieu

16 Ibid., 52-3

must be known to understand him: in particular, words undergo changes of meaning, and we should also know whether a Mr Smith is Adam, or, say, Sydney. In short, we should seek to understand a scientist as his contemporaries understood. That understanding normally involves very little biographical information: men write for wider audiences than their neighbours and cronies, and indeed one of the lessons almost every adult learns is how remarkably few are the people who are interested in his personal affairs.

I therefore firmly disagree with the gracious, attractive statement of the contrary position presented by one of the most distinguished of historians of economics, William Jaffé.[17] When he complains about those who 'disdain the plodding labors required for understanding what Ricardo or Marx intended to say,'[18] I reply that if the labours involve biography, these scholars do right if they seek to understand the *scientific* role these men played in the evolution of economic theory: that role was played with the words they wrote, not with the ideas they intended to express.

Even if every syllable of what I have said is accepted, nothing should be inferred about the proper role of biography in the study of science. This is not a simple contradiction to the previous remarks – rather it draws a distinction between understanding a man's scientific work as it appeared to his contemporaries and understanding the evolution of science. After the sentence I have quoted, Jaffé continues: 'Nor are they [who "dabble in the history of economics"] at all interested in probing the question of how or why Ricardo or Marx came to formulate their theories. And they are still more indifferent to the question of how and why a given theory was received or rejected at the time it was first enunciated.' Perhaps there are dabblers subject to these absurd beliefs, but the beliefs do not follow from the view that detailed biographical knowledge is irrelevant to the interpretation of an individual's scientific work.

The science of science (the so-called sociology of science) is concerned precisely with such questions: why some discoveries are absorbed quickly and others never; why the science of economics flourished in England and languished in France; why and when innovators need be thoroughly trained in the received tradition; and so forth without limit. There, and not in the scientific content of the work, must we look for a possible role in the study of biography.

Biography is information, but it is not the kind of information, if indeed, any information is of that kind, which speaks for itself. Enough emphasis, I hope, has already been given to the essential deception involved in hand-picking congruencies between a man's life and his ideas.

The study of collections of biographies has reached that high level of achievement in which it has a special name – prosopography. Relatively few

17 'Biography and Economic Analysis,' *Western Economic Journal*, III, 1965
18 Ibid., 225

interesting applications of this technique to the history of science have come to my notice, however.[19] I made modest use of biographical data to date the shift of economics to the university,[20] and no doubt other examples exist.

Certainly it is easy to propose a list of comparative biographical studies whose length and variety are limited only by one's imagination. The effects of economic incentives on the work of scholars, for example, requires a comparative biographical approach. The effects of the choice of graduate school upon one's intellectual convictions and even academic career are capable of study, and indeed I am presently in the midst of precisely this topic.

Rather than continue with this shopping list, however, I propose to devote the remainder of this paper to the task of examining the problem of the systematic use of a single man's biography.

THE TWO MILLS

It has been a common belief that the elder Mill indoctrinated the younger in Ricardian–Smithian economics and that his heritage was a major obstacle to the son in striking out toward a new and better economics. At a much more specific level we have already encountered the belief that after James' death in 1836 John openly abandoned some of these inherited beliefs which previously he had been unwilling to disavow publicly.

The general charge of indoctrination is an extraordinarily unperceptive one, and for two very different reasons. The first is that John was taught the best economics of his time if he was taught Ricardo and Smith. Unless one is prepared to argue that a scientist is handicapped in his future work by a thorough training in the best scientific knowledge of his time – and despite the popularity of this view I consider it unbelievable – Mill was qualified to make contributions, not disqualified from doing so. This is not to say that all of the sound economics of 1817 could be found in Smith, Malthus, and Ricardo. In particular J.B. Say had a spacious, modern vision of the circular flow and general equilibrium that he lacked the power to push to an analytical level. But both contemporaries and modern economists must concede that John Mill was trained in *the* leading economics of his time.

The charge of indoctrination is unperceptive for a second reason. James Mill was wholly devoted to Truth and Logic, and would never teach anyone –

19 See Lawrence Stone, 'Prosopography,' *Daedalus*, winter 1971. One of the earliest applications of the method to science is R.K. Merton's *Science, Technology and Society in Seventeenth Century England, Osiris*, IV (Bruges 1938). See also J. Ben-David and R. Collins, 'Social Factors in the Origins of a New Science,' *American Sociological Review*, 1966, and H. Zuckerman and R.K. Merton, "Age, Ageing, and Age Structure in Science," in *Ageing and Society*, Volume 3 of *A Sociology of Age Stratification*, ed. M.W. Riley, M. Johnson, and A. Foner (New York 1972).

20 See my *Essays in the History of Economics* (Chicago 1965), and 'The Adoption of the Marginal Utility Theory,' *History of Political Economy*, IV, fall 1972.

let alone an undemonstratively beloved son – anything of which these stern masters would disapprove. Of course, the next sentence must begin, James Mill not only adhered to the truth, but believed that the devotion was reciprocated, and in this he differs from us ordinary mortals only in the intensity of this mutual esteem. Recall this passage from the *Autobiography*: 'My father never permitted anything which I learnt, to degenerate into a mere exercise of memory. He strove to make the understanding not only go along with every step of the teaching, but if possible, precede it. Anything which could be found out by thinking, I never was told, until I had exhausted my efforts to find it out for myself.'[21] It would no doubt be bitter-sweet for James to observe his son refute a parental theory, but the sweet, I suspect, would be of the approximate intensity of the bitter.

In ascertaining the influence of James Mill on his son's economics, then, we should distinguish two levels of possible influence. There are, first, those doctrines peculiar to James Mill – extensions or departures from Ricardian economics – where the father's net influence is most easily determined. There are, second, those doctrines common to the Ricardian school, where John Stuart Mill's departures are both more fundamental scientifically and less personal.

In his *Elements of Political Economy* (3d. ed., 1826), James Mill presented a stark, pseudo-rigorous, unattractive exposition of the ruling theory, with significant differences and several improvements.[22] Although the intellectual debts to Ricardo, Malthus, and Smith were admittedly very large ('I profess to have made no discovery'), there are a number of significant departures:

1 Mill argues on essentially *a priori* grounds that capital cannot grow as rapidly as population. The argument is uninteresting: either the rich have all non-subsistence income, and *they* have no inducement to save, or many people have such a surplus, and they see the real lack of need to save (ibid., 52ff). (Mill deserves credit, at least, for facing a problem most classical economists ignored: Why should capital grow less rapidly than population?)

2 Relative values of goods are governed exclusively by relative quantities of labour used, directly or indirectly (through capital), in their production (ibid., 96ff). The profits necessary to justify the aging of wine are really measures of labour. Mill's argument is nonsense or a tautology.

21 *Autobiography*, 20
22 Ricardo's own list of disagreements with the *Elements* was sent to Mill (*Works and Correspondence of David Ricardo*, ix, 126–33). Putting aside details and exposition, Ricardo notes my differences number 1, 2, 5, and 6. I neglect some minor innovations in Mill, such as an excellent discussion of regional price levels (*Elements*, 174–6).

3 Mill favours free competition in the issue of bank notes (ibid., 152ff). Ricardo was not hostile to the idea, but did not support it with Mill's enthusiasm.

4 Mill proposes a distinction between productive and unproductive *consumption*, which bears a closer verbal than substantive resemblance to productive and unproductive labour (ibid., 220ff). Productive consumption is that which is necessary to maintain a man's productive capacity, unproductive consumption any surplus beyond that level.

5 Mill has two versions of Say's law, of which he may have been an independent discoverer.[23] In *Commerce Defended* he proposed the proposition: total output, if properly composed of various goods, could always be sold. If he had added 'at prices equal to costs' this would have been an equilibrium proposition. In the *Elements* he presents (as Say usually did) a simple arithmetical identity. A man's supply is defined as what he does not consume, and supply is the 'instrument' of demand, so for each man (and hence for the nation) supply equals demand (ibid., 228ff). Mill proceeds to reintroduce price movements to equate supply and demand for individual commodities and effect changes in the pattern of production (ibid., 233ff), improving upon his earlier version – so it closely approximates Ricardo's version. Hence it is uncertain whether Mill's view on this topic was that of Ricardo,[24] or of Say.

6 Mill favoured the socialization, or at least the heavy taxation, of future increments in land rents (ibid., 248ff). This was a revenue source which on his simplistic theory of rent had no allocational effects; the values were created independent of any efforts of the landlord.

7 More durable income sources (eg, rent) should be taxed more heavily than equal incomes of shorter duration (eg, salaries). The income taxation should in effect be based upon capital values (ibid., 270ff).

John Stuart ignored the first and rejected the second of these innovations: neither in the *Essays on Unsettled Questions* nor in the *Principles* is the pure labour theory of value or the ambiguous *a priori* argument on savings adopted.[25] The free competition of banks in note issue was endorsed with substan-

---

23 See my 'Sraffa's Ricardo,' reprinted in *Essays in the History of Economics* (Chicago 1965).

24 Some differences in detail surely existed. Thus Ricardo admitted the possibility of a glut if everyone consumed only necessaries, whereas Mill denied a glut in this case ibid., 236). For Ricardo's concession, see *Principles of Political Economy*, in *Works and Correspondence of David Ricardo*, 1 (Cambridge 1951), ed. P. Sraffa, 292–3. On this point I side with Mill.

25 Essay IV of *Essays on Some Unsettled Questions* (*Collected Works*, IV (Toronto 1967), 293ff; *Principles of Political Economy*, CW, III, 477ff (III, iv)

tial modifications.[26] The distinction between productive and unproductive consumption was given a tolerant defence.[27] The son was much clearer on the distinction between tautology and theorem in dealing with Say's Law, and superior to both Ricardo and his father.[28] The rent increment socialization plan was fervently embraced in Mill's later years,[29] and the differential taxation of nondurable incomes was also accepted (and is commonly and, as we have seen, erroneously credited to the son).[30] With one exception, these were the correct positions for John Stuart to take in the light of the general level of economic theory of the time. The one unequivocal mistake was the socialization of land rent increments: both Mills believed that legitimate current investments in land should not be taxed more heavily than alternate incomes or property, and if the market in land was working efficiently (and hence predicting without bias the average future increments of rent), there would be nothing left to tax.

The treatment by John Stuart of James Mill's own innovations is difficult to interpret in any terms except of intellectual merits: there is neither systematic acceptance nor rejection, and it is easier to explain the departures of the son by a preference for superior theory than by some psychological relationship. It should be added that James Mill made revisions of his treatment of international trade and of profits in the third edition of the *Elements* in response to his son's criticisms.[31] At this stage I am prepared to argue that all one can say is that the son treated the father's views with courtesy but not with deference. It will be interesting to see if the same conclusion holds in the other main topics (psychology, government, and India) on which both wrote extensively.

The question of the existence of an uncritical devotion of John Stuart to the Smith-Ricardian economics can be disposed of summarily. In an earlier essay I claimed for Mill unusual creativity in economic theory, and listed six substantial contributions.[32] I should have added several other contributions, of which I shall name only two:

1   In a prodigious essay on 'Corn Laws,' written at the age of eighteen, Mill invented the compensation principle, that pillar of welfare economics.
2   In the early *Essays on Some Unsettled Questions*, he invented the theory of

26 *Principles*, cw, iii, 682ff (iv, xxiv, 5)   27 Essay iii of *Essays*, cw, iv, esp. 283ff
28 Essay ii of *Essays*, ibid., esp. 263ff
29 See especially the essay on land tenure reform in *Essays on Economics and Society*, cw, v, 689ff.
30 *Principles*, cw, iii, 813ff (v, ii, 4). There is an explicit disagreement with his father on one detail, ibid., 818n.
31 *Autobiography*, 108
32 'The Nature and Role of Originality in Scientific Progress,' reprinted in my *Essays in the History of Economics*

reciprocal demand in international trade theory, a fundamental part of that theory.[33]

There have been only a tiny handful of enormously fertile theoretical innovators in the history of economics, and Mill has full rights to membership in this regal circle along with Smith, Marshall, and Edgeworth.

CONCLUSION

The primary task of scientific history is to become scientific: to subject hypotheses to objective tests which the hypotheses are capable of failing. I wish I could claim that the foregoing paper constitutes much more than a sermon on methodology, because I have a singularly low estimate of the scientific value of sermons on methodology. But even if it is limited to this humble role, I hope that it will serve to remind all of us how easily illustration can be confused with evidence.

33 Numerous lesser contributions, especially to the theory of comparative cost, are discussed by Jacob Viner, *Studies in the Theory of International Trade* (New York 1937).

Ricardianism, J. S. Mill, and the Neo-classical Challenge

SAMUEL HOLLANDER

It was J.A. Schumpeter's firm conviction that J.S. Mill was not really a Ricardian economist and must be excluded from that group which constitutes Ricardo's 'school,' namely James Mill, McCulloch, and De Quincey.[1] 'From Marshall's *Principles*,' he wrote, 'Ricardianism can be removed without being missed at all. From Mill's *Principles*, it could be dropped without being missed very greatly.'[2] This evaluation, although expressed with particular insistence by Schumpeter, is considerably more widespread than is commonly believed and is characteristic of Marxist interpreters. It is my intention to subject the argument to a detailed analysis. Clearly, much depends upon what is meant by 'Ricardianism' and I shall pay particular attention to this matter to avoid a mere terminological debate. I shall try to show that, in fact, Ricardo's economics, in the strict sense adopted by Schumpeter, was accepted by Mill and indeed was formulated vigorously not only in the *Essays on Some Unsettled Questions* and the *Principles* but also in the celebrated *Fortnightly Review* article (1869) in which Mill (apparently) abandoned the wages-fund theory.

THE NEW POLITICAL ECONOMY
Let me say at the outset that I do not take issue with Schumpeter's account of the content of Ricardo's economics insofar as he emphasizes the key role played by the so-called absolute standard of value – a commodity produced by a constant quantity of labour – in the derivation of the proposition that profits de-

1 *History of Economic Analysis* (New York 1954), 476
2 Ibid., 529

pend upon wages, both conceived as proportionate shares in an output of constant value.[3] But to clear the ground I should like to formulate more explicitly my own conception of the core of Ricardian economics.

Ricardo, I believe, was concerned basically with the *rate of return on capital* as distinct from the aggregative shares strictly speaking, although the rate of return was envisaged as a function of the share of profits in net output minus rent. He identified an increase in wages in terms of his 'gold' measure of value – which reduces to a labour-embodied unit – with an increase in the proportionate share of wages in the output to be divided between labourers and capitalists. But Schumpeter, who based himself upon Cannan's authority, is I believe wrong in stating that the identification lacks generality since all depends upon a presumed constancy of *aggregate* value, that is, of the total labour force.[4] Ricardo's attention in the first instance was not, in fact, upon the labour value of aggregate wages and output but rather upon that of *per capita* wages and output; an increase in *per capita* 'gold' wages necessarily implies an increase in the share of wages in *per capita* output, which is of constant 'value' whatever may happen to total value.[5] The entire Ricardian scheme is thus designed to relate the rate of return on capital to changes in the value of wages *per capita*.

Profits appear as a 'residual' income in the Ricardian scheme – the 'leavings of wages' as one contemporary put it – and this is reflected in Ricardo's standard turn of phrase to the effect that 'profits depend on wages' rather than the reverse. Yet at the same time Ricardo recognised that the profit rate acts upon the rate of savings not only by way of the income effect ('the ability to accumulate') but also by way of the substitution effect ('the motive to accumulate'). Accordingly, labour demand and the wage rate and in turn the growth rate of population are effected by alterations in the rate of profit. Viewed from this perspective profits appear to be a residual in nothing more than a formal sense – in the sense that the sole contractual payment in the system is that made to labour, and not in the substantive sense of a 'rent' or 'surplus value.' That Ricardo utilized a labour-embodied accounting unit and did not provide a label for the relationship between savings decisions and the rate of interest (such as that of 'abstinence') should not be allowed to detract from his recognition of such a relationship.

It was Ricardo's position that assuming an unchanged cost of production of the monetary metal, wage-rate increases are non-inflationary (at most generating an alteration in relative prices) and must reduce the rate of return. (The issue, it will be recalled, was formulated initially by Ricardo as a direct challenge to received doctrine based upon Adam Smith's analysis whereby wage-

3 See in particular ibid., 473, 490, 558f, 569, 590f, 653.
4 Ibid., 592
5 An increase in labour's *per capita* share implies, of course, an increase of the total wage share in the aggregate output to be divided between labour and capital.

rate increases are passed on by capitalists in the form of higher prices and lower rents.) But his conclusion that wage-rate increases are non-inflationary is maintained quite generally – that is to say, it is applied to the 'real world' where the conditions required of the theoretical medium are not fulfilled.[6] (For example, it is applied to a world where a paper currency circulates in which a cost of production theory is inapplicable.) Ricardo's model (or engine of analysis) was designed to throw light on the underlying processes, which are not always apparent to the naked eye, whereby the rate of return is governed by the proportion of the work-day devoted to the production of wage goods.

It is this doctrine which represents the 'New Political Economy,' a term coined by contemporaries to describe Ricardo's particular contribution and his divergence from Smith. I exclude both Say's Law and the Comparative-Cost doctrine quite deliberately as secondary to Ricardo's primary concern, which was to demonstrate that nothing but an alteration in the real cost of producing wage goods can affect the rate of return.[7] (In any event both were acceptable to neo-classical writers so that they scarcely represent doctrines which are *peculiarly* Ricardian.) I will have something to say, subsequently, about the Ricardian theory of employment capacity, or his version of the wages-fund theory. But this analysis is not so much of a breakaway from the Smithian position; it is rather an important extension. This is also perhaps an opportune moment to remark that the 'four fundamental propositions on capital'[8] usually attributed to Mill are in fact part and parcel of the Ricardian analysis.

There exists considerable accord amongst Marxist and non-Marxist historians regarding the fate of 'Ricardianism,' despite apparent differences.[9] For it

6 Professor George Stigler, *Essays in the History of Economics* (Chicago 1965), 191, has made the point as follows: 'Ricardo argues, almost paranthetically, that under certain conditions the inverse relationship between wages and profits holds also when they are expressed in terms of ordinary money rather than in an ideal standard. If a country is on the gold standard, its price level cannot vary (much) because of changes in domestic factor prices; gold flows will soon restore its former level. If, further, the productivity of capital and labour do not change, a rise in money wages would lead to a fall of money profits – in no other way can international monetary equilibrium be restored.' In our view, this characteristic is not 'parenthetical' but quite crucial to Ricardo's position. And, as we shall show, it is a feature of the positions of McCulloch and J.S. Mill.

7 See the evidence presented by R.L. Meek, regarding the status of Say's Law as hallmark of Ricardian economics in *Economics and Ideology and Other Essays* (London 1967), 51ff. Compare also F.W. Fetter, 'The Rise and Decline of Ricardian Economics,' *History of Political Economy*, I, spring 1969, 68–9, 70–2

8 'Industry is limited by capital'; 'capital is the result of saving'; 'all capital is consumed'; 'demand for commodities is not the demand for labour': see *Principles of Political Economy, Collected Works*, II (Toronto 1965), 63ff.

9 See Karl Marx's Afterword to second German edition (1873), *Capital*, I (Moscow 1965), 14–15; Meek, *Economics and Ideology*, 62, 67, 68–73; Meek, 'Marginalism and Marxism,' *History of Political Economy*, IV, fall 1972, 500–1; P. Schwartz, *The New Political Economy of J.S. Mill* (London 1972), 16

is generally agreed that Ricardian economics in the narrow and specific sense of the term which I outlined above – the use of a special theory of value (involving an absolute standard) in the derivation of the inverse relation between proportionate wages and proportionate profits – came to a very early end, while Ricardian economics in a broad sense had a pervasive influence.[10] It is this consensus that I wish to challenge. I shall try to justify the contention, with particular reference to J.S. Mill,[11] that Ricardianism in the strict and narrow sense lived on to a ripe old age.

MILL ON VALUE AND DISTRIBUTION

Much of Schumpeter's case for the early demise of Ricardianism is based upon the appearance and supposed influence of Samuel Bailey's *Critical Dissertation on Value* (1825): 'Bailey,' we read, 'attacked the Ricardo-[James] Mill-McCulloch analysis on a broad front and with complete success. His *Dissertation*, which said, as far as fundamentals are concerned, practically all that can be said, must rank among the masterpieces of criticism in our field, and it should suffice to secure to its author a place in or near the front rank in the history of scientific economics.'[12] And it is precisely because J.S. Mill, in Schumpeter's view, rejected on Bailey's grounds the conception of a measure of absolute value that he must be excluded from Ricardo's school. The value that really mattered to him, runs the contention, was *relative price*, and since value was a ratio all values could not vary simultaneously. Similarly, there was no such thing as 'the total value of all the services of wealth (or of all wealth) taken as a whole,' in contrast to the position adopted by Ricardo – and Marx.[13] Indeed, 'the energy with which Mill insisted on the relative character of [exchange value] completely annihilated Ricardo's Real Value and reduced other Ricardianism to insipid innocuousness.'[14] Precisely the same view of Mill's position is adopted by Professor Blaug:

10 By Ricardian economics 'in a broad sense' I have in mind, for example, an emphasis upon economic progress and the laws of distribution in a progressive economy subject to diminishing agricultural returns; an approach to the problem of value from the cost side; and an acceptance of Say's Law. On this see Meek, ibid., 73; and Mark Blaug, *Ricardian Economics* (New Haven 1958), 226: 'The Ricardian emphasis on economic growth and the changes in the distributive shares so permeated economic thinking in the period that even those who revolted against Ricardo's authority in fact accepted its essential outlook.' The distinction is implied in Lord Robbins' well-known review of Schumpeter's *History*: see *The Evolution of Modern Economic Theory* (London 1970), 58–9.

11 Supporting evidence might also be drawn for our proposition from the works of J.R. McCulloch, Robert Torrens, and Samuel Bailey.

12 *History of Economic Analysis*, 486

13 Ibid., 589

14 Ibid., 603

Mill does not derive the theorem about profits and wages, as Ricardo has done, from the concept of an invariable measure of value. Even the standard Ricardian thesis that 'general wages, whether high or low, do not affect values' is entirely divorced from the notion that value is to be measured by an invariant standard ... There is no mention in Mill's discussion ... of the important role assigned to the invariable measure of value in Ricardo's system.[15]

The issue can best be evaluated by consideration of the evolution of Mill's position from the youthful review of Malthus's objections to the so-called 'New School' (1825) and the paper 'On Profits and Interest' (1829), to the *Principles*, and finally to the famous *Fortnightly Review* article of 1869.

If Mill's position as stated in his first major paper were his final word there would be little doubt of the justice of the view according to which Mill rejected the fundamental Ricardian position. For Mill neglected the analysis of deviations of price from labour value which served as a preliminary step in the derivation of the inverse profit-wage relationship.[16] However, in the essay 'On Profits and Interest' the perspective is entirely altered and Mill presents favourably the Ricardian position, accepting it with the 'slight modification' that the rate of profit is related not to the value of *per capita* wages – the direct and indirect labour embodied in the wage bill – but to the 'cost of wages' which includes the profit of the wage-goods producer.[17] But even this modification is withdrawn in Book II of the *Principles* where Mill adopts the proposition that the profit rate varies inversely with the fraction of a man's labour time devoted to the production of his wages.[18]

We may take the matter a step further. The analysis of profits as presented in his Book II was, Mill observed, correct but nevertheless provisional, for a complete treatment required a discussion of value: 'It will come out in greater fulness and force when, having taken into consideration the theory of Value and Price, we shall be enabled to exhibit the law of profits in the concrete – in the complex entanglement of circumstances in which it actually works.'[19] A preliminary word is in order regarding Mill's position on the conception of absolute value.

Throughout the *Principles*, indeed in his first major article of 1825 mentioned above, Mill insisted upon the *relativity* of exchange value, and like

15 *Ricardian Economics*, 172–3. Compare Stigler, *Essays in the History of Economics*, 190–1: 'Ricardo's basic theory on distribution – 'a rise of wages ... would invariably lower profits' – is thus strictly dependent on his measure of value.' (This view is slightly modified subsequently. See above, 69, n6.)
16 *Westminster Review*, III, 1825, in CW, IV, 30ff
17 CW, IV, 293ff
18 The 'cost of labour' is thus finally identified with labour embodied in *per capita* wages and with labour's share in *per capita* output. CW, II, 411ff
19 Ibid., 415

Bailey, rejected the notion of a general alteration in exchange values as logically incomprehensible. But he did of course allow for a general change in *prices* which he pointed out 'is merely tantamount to an alteration in the value of money.'[20] Mill, in the Ricardian manner, decided to use as *numeraire* a commodity money 'with the proviso that money itself do not vary in its general purchasing power, but that the prices of all things, other than that which we happen to be considering, remain unaltered.'[21] The constancy of purchasing power is the consequence of a presumed constant cost of producing the monetary metal.

In the light of this procedure we may perhaps better appreciate Mill's formal discussion in the chapter 'Of a Measure of Value' (iii,xv). Here he rejects on Bailey's grounds the notion of a measure of exchange value as a conceptual impossibility but *accepts* that of a measure of cost of production. The conditions for the measure are stated as follows:

[Economists] have imagined a commodity invariably produced by the same quantity of labour; to which supposition it is necessary to add, that the fixed capital employed in the production must bear always the same proportion to the wages of the immediate labour, and must be always of the same durability: in short, the same capital must be advanced for the same length of time, so that the element of value which consists of profits, as well as that which consists of wages, may be unchangeable.[22]

Now such a measure of cost, Mill insists, 'though perfectly conceivable, can no more exist in fact, than a measure of exchangeable value,' because of the likelihood of changes in production cost for any commodity chosen. Nevertheless, gold and silver 'are the least variable' and, if used, the results obtained must simply be 'corrected by the best allowance we can make for the intermediate changes in the cost of the production itself.' This is far from an out-of-hand rejection of the measure of absolute value, and in fact represents precisely the position adopted by Ricardo.

The full analysis of the effects of wage-rate changes is undertaken in the important chapter 'Distribution, as affected by Exchange' (iii,xxvi). Now much is made by commentators of Mill's treatment of production, distribution, and exchange in three consecutive books, as indicative of a failure, characteristic of classicism, to envisage any relation between value theory and distribution. This is clearly a misunderstanding. The early discussion of distribution was

20 cw, iii, 459; compare 479
21 Ibid., 458
22 Ibid., 579. All that is missing is the condition that the metal is produced by a process representing the mean proportions of those in the economy as a whole. But Mill may have been assuming identical proportions in all commodities, and for this reason neglected to be explicit about the matter.

provisional only; in the chapter at hand the order is reversed and the problem of distribution is analysed in light of the theory of exchange value.

When the distribution of national income occurs via the mechanism of exchange and money, Mill argues, the 'law of wages' remains unchanged insofar as the determination of commodity wages is concerned, for this depends upon 'the ratio of population and capital.'[23] As Mill has already explained, from the perspective of the employer it is not merely *commodity* wages that are relevant but the 'cost of labour'; the new point is that under certain circumstances this cost will be reflected accurately by the *money* wages paid. This situation will obtain when money represents 'an invariable standard':

Wages in the second sense, we may be permitted to call, for the present, money wages; assuming, as it is allowable to do, that money remains for the time an invariable standard, no alteration taking place in the conditions under which the circulating medium itself is produced or obtained. If money itself undergoes no variation in cost, the money price of labour is an exact measure of the Cost of Labour, and may be made use of as a convenient symbol to express it.[24]

Assuming money to be such an invariable measure, the rate of money wages will depend upon the commodity wage and the production costs and accordingly the money prices of wage goods, particularly agricultural produce, which in turn is dependent upon 'the productiveness of the least fertile land, or least productive agricultural capital.'[25] It is upon the 'cost of labour' that the rate of profit depends, as he had concluded earlier in Book II of the *Principles*, but the cost of labour is now identified with 'money' wages.[26]

In the present context Mill thus defines an inverse relation between the profit rate and the cost of labour, the latter identified with the *money wage rate*. He does not bother to equate the cost of labour, in contrast to his practice in Book II of the *Principles*, with the proportionate share of the labourer in *per*

23 Ibid., 695
24 Ibid., 696
25 Ibid., 697
26 An application of the principle appears in correspondence with Cairnes: 'Have you formed any opinion, or can you refer me to any good authority, respecting the ordinary rate of mercantile and manufacturing profit in the United States? I have hitherto been under the impression that it is much higher than in England, because the rate of interest is so. But I have lately been led to doubt the truth of this impression, because it seems inconsistent with known facts respecting wages in America. High profits are compatible with a high reward of the labourer through low prices of necessaries, but they are not compatible with a high cost of labour; and it seems to me that the very high *money* wages of labour in America, the precious metals not being of lower value there than in Europe, indicates a high *cost* as well as a high remuneration of labour.' (Letter to Cairnes, 1 Dec. 1864, CW, XV, 967. Compare ibid., XVI, 1002, 1009)

capita output. But there is no reason to believe that he no longer maintained this relation.[27] In effect, Mill has adopted the Ricardian 'proportions–measuring' money in terms of which a rise of wages implies an increased share of the labourer in the 'value' of his output and a reduced profit share and rate of return.[28]

The full analysis of the effects of 'money' wage increases upon profits – money presumed to be 'invariable' – involves a demonstration that such increases cannot be passed on in the form of higher commodity prices.[29] The entire argument is beautifully summarized by Mill in a passage which emphasizes that the wage increase which reduces profits is one involving a greater labour embodiment in wage goods, or a rise in labour's *proportionate* share: 'If the labourers really get more, that is, get the produce of more labour, a smaller percentage must remain for profit. From this Law of Distribution, resting as it

27 In fact Mill refers back in the present context (cw, iii, 698) to the earlier analysis of Book ii.

28 An index of the extent of Mill's Ricardianism is provided by his treatment of capital-saving technical change. Mill raises the question whether the relationship between profits and wages – whereby 'the rate of profit and the cost of labour vary inversely as one another, and are joint effects of the same agencies or causes' – must not be modified in light of the fact that a reduction in the *time* for which capital is invested in all commodities (including the monetary metal) appears to raise the rate of return. His answer is revealing for it indicates the strictest adherence to the Ricardo position. In the case at hand, 'since values and prices would not be affected, profits would probably be raised; but if we look more closely into the case we shall find, that it is because the cost of labour would be lowered. In this as in any other case of increase in the general productiveness of labour, if the labourer obtained only the same real wages, profits would be raised: but the same real wages would imply a smaller Cost of Labour; the cost of production of all things having been, by the supposition, diminished. If, on the other hand, the real wages of labour rose proportionally, and the Cost of Labour to the employer remained the same, the advances of the capitalist would bear the same ratio to his returns as before, and the rate of profit would be unaltered.' (Ibid., 700–1)

The essence of the matter clearly lies in the assumption that the technical change in question, because it affects all goods, also affects wage goods and for *this* reason the rate of profit rises. (For a similar emphasis upon technical change which affects wages-goods as distinct from those which do not, see ibid., 724, 742–5, 751.)

In this context Mill refers his readers to the analysis in the essay 'On Profits and Interest' in which he had discussed the question of a capital-saving technical change. It is by no means clear that Mill is justified to do so. For it will be recalled that in the essay Mill had introduced a 'slight modification' relating the rate of profit to the cost of wages including therein the profits of the capital goods' producers. In the *Principles*, however, Mill reverts to a view which envisages the cost of wages as consisting entirely of labour (direct and indirect). The problem is a serious one for it is only by dint of the latter view that Mill was able to relate the cost of wages to labour's proportionate share.

29 Ibid., 479–80, 692, 698–9

does on a law of arithmetic, there is no escape. The mechanism of Exchange and Price may hide it from us, but is quite powerless to alter it.'[30] In his chapter on 'Distribution, as affected by Exchange' Mill simply makes it clear that a measure of proportionate wages is provided by *money wages* but only if money satisfies the conditions required of a stable absolute measure.

MILL ON WAGES AND PRICES

The theme which we have isolated – the effect of a wage-rate change upon the rate of return – is obviously not one introduced by Mill as a casual aside. It reappears throughout the *Principles*, and clearly the analysis of the issue was of the first importance to him in light of the common opinion that wage-rate increases can be passed on to consumers. The sharp distinction between Ricardo's position and that of Smith is kept to the fore as, for example, in Mill's criticism of Smith's analysis of the 'tendency of profits to a minimum' in terms of the competition of capital.[31] Moreover, in dealing with the contention that an increase in wages generates higher commodity prices, Mill, for the edition of 1871, replaced the introductory phrase 'it used formerly to be said' by 'it is not infrequently said,' implying that the analysis remained of immediate relevance. But the clearest indication of the critical nature of the matter at hand appears in a letter to Cairnes some six months before Mill's death wherein he expressed the inverse relation between wages and profits in terms more forceful than ever before:

You must have been struck as I have been, by the thoroughly confused and erroneous ideas respecting the relation of wages to price, which have shewn themselves to be almost universal in the discussions about the recent strikes. The notion that a general rise of wages must produce a general rise of prices, is preached universally not only by the newspapers but by political economists, as a certain and admitted economical truth; and political economy has to bear the responsibility of a self-contradicting absurdity which it is one of the achievements of political economy to have exploded. It provokes one to see such ignorance of political economy in the whole body of its self-selected teachers. The Times joins in the chorus ... Certainly no one who knows, even imperfectly, what the Ricardo political economy is, whether he agrees with it or not,

30 Ibid., 479–80
31 Ibid., 733. Similarly, Mill made explicit the divergence between Ricardian and Smithian theory in the context of taxation of wages: 'On whom, in this case, will the tax fall? According to Adam Smith, on the community generally, in their character of consumers; since the rise of wages, he thought, would raise general prices. We have seen, however, that general prices depend on other causes, and are never raised by any circumstance which affects all kinds of productive employment in the same manner and degree. A rise of wages occasioned by a tax, must, like any other increase of the cost of labour, be defrayed from profits.' (Ibid., 830)

can suppose this to be it. I hope you will come down upon it with all the weight of your clear scientific intellect, your remarkable power of exposition, and the authority of your name as a political economist.[32]

The importance of the issue cannot be exaggerated, particularly in light of the contemporary buoyancy of trade-union activity.[33]

I shall now show that for Mill, as for Ricardo, the substantive prediction – that an increase of 'real' wages (that is of labour embodied in wages) is necessarily accompanied by an inverse movement in the rate of return – holds good quite generally, irrespective, that is to say, of the satisfaction by the medium of exchange of the necessary properties required to guarantee its theoretical suitability as invariable standard.

In the first place, Mill makes it clear that even were prices to rise following an increase of wages, producers would not benefit therefrom since all their expenses rise: 'It must be remembered too that general high prices, even supposing them to exist, can be of no use to a producer or dealer, considered as such; for if they increase his money returns, they increase in the same degree all his expenses.'[34] Ricardo's identical rendition will be recalled: 'If the prices of commodities were permanently raised by high wages, the proposition would not be less true, which asserts that high wages invariably affect the employers of labour, by depriving them of a portion of their real profits ... [The employer] would be in no better situation if his money profits had been really diminished in amount, and everything had remained at its former price.'[35]

Secondly, Mill relies on the gold-standard mechanism involving the quantity theory to assure the result that wage increases are non-inflationary. Ricardo's rendition may first be noted: 'All commodities cannot rise at the same time without an addition to the quantity of money. This addition could not be obtained at home ... nor could it be imported from abroad. To purchase any

32 Letter dated 4 Oct. 1872, CW, XVII, 1909–10. The issue was also taken up in correspondence of 13 Sept. 1865, ibid., XVI, 1102; 15 Dec. 1865, ibid., 1127; 22 Dec. 1867, ibid., 1335; and – in particular – 21 June 1870, ibid., XVII, 1734–5 (see text below, 78). See also a letter dated 30 May 1872, ibid., 1901, on the impossibility of a general tax on profits resulting in an increase in the price level.

33 It should be kept in mind that a Royal Commission on Trade Unions was appointed in 1867; the working-class vote was granted by the Reform Act of 1867, and the unequal Master and Servants Acts were amended in the same year; and complete legal recognition was accorded trade unions in 1871. It has been stated that 'in 1863 began the campaign for the amendment of the Master and Servant Acts which was the true starting point of that remarkable decade of successful pressure from 1866 to 1876 which produced more legislative gains for the working class than all the mass agitations of the preceding half century.' (Harold Perkins, *The Origins of Modern English Society: 1780–1880* [London 1969], 401)

34 CW, III, 479

35 *Principles of Political Economy*, in *Works and Correspondence of David Ricardo*, ed. P. Sraffa, I (Cambridge 1951), 126–7

additional quantity of gold from abroad, commodities at home must be cheap, not dear. The importation of gold, and a rise in the price of all home-made commodities with which gold is purchased or paid for, are effects absolutely incompatible.'[36]

I would like to demonstrate Mill's position regarding the latter mechanism by reference to his discussion of the inverse relation between wages and profits as it appears in his famous review article of W.T. Thornton's work, *On Labour.*[37] While Mill here refuted the wages-fund theory, for which of course the review is so well known, he in no way abandoned the basic Ricardian theorem on distribution. Consider then the following comment upon Thornton's analysis of the potential efficacy of trade-union activity, an analysis that Mill in general adopted:

[There] is a view of the question, not overlooked by the author, but hardly, perhaps, made sufficiently prominent by him. From the necessity of the case, the only fund out of which an increase of wages can possibly be obtained by the labouring classes considered as a whole, is profits. This is contrary to the common opinion, both of the general public and of the workmen themselves, who think that there is a second source from which it is possible for the augmentation to come, namely, prices. The employer, they think, can, if foreign or other competition will let him, indemnify himself for the additional wages demanded of him, by charging an increased price to the consumer. And this may certainly happen in single trades ... But though a rise of wages in a given trade may be compensated to the masters by a rise of the price of their commodity, a rise of general wages cannot be compensated to employers by a general rise of prices. This distinction is never understood by those who have not considered the subject, but there are few truths more obvious to all who have.[38]

The reasons given by Mill for the inability of employers to pass on wage increases include the necessity for an increase in the money supply,[39] which would not, under the circumstances supposed, be forthcoming:

36 Ibid., 105
37 'Thornton on Labour and its Claims,' *Fortnightly Review*, ns, v (1869), in CW, v, 631ff
38 Ibid. Dr Pedro Schwartz, *New Political Economy of J.S. Mill*, 98, asserts that Thornton 'continued to hold that a general rise of wages could be passed on to prices, despite Mill's arguments showing that, in the circumstances of the time, it could only take place at the expense of profits.' In point of fact, Thornton, 2nd ed. (London 1870), 299–301, is quite clear that a truly general wage increase will not be passed on to consumers. He may differ from Mill, however, in requiring that the wage increase be (literally) world-wide.
39 While Mill was critical of the Bank Charter Act of 1844, he at no time agreed with Fullarton and Tooke that notes do not affect prices but simply adjust to price movements, or that the money supply is a 'passive' response. Compare F.W. Fetter, *The*

There cannot be a general rise of prices unless there is more money expended. But the rise of wages does not cause more money to be expended. It takes from the incomes of the masters and adds to those of the workmen; the former have less to spend, the latter have more; but the general sum of the money incomes of the community remains what it was, and it is upon that sum that money prices depend. There cannot be more money expended on everything, when there is not more money to be expended altogether. In the second place, even if there did happen a rise of all prices, the only effect would be that money, having become of less value in the particular country, while it remained of its former value everywhere else, would be exported until prices were brought down to nearly or quite their former level. But thirdly: even on the impossible supposition that the rise of prices could be kept up, yet, being general, it would not compensate the employer; for though his money returns would be greater, his outgoings (except the fixed payments to those to whom he is in debt) would be increased in the same proportion. Finally, if when wages rose all prices rose in the same ratio, the labourers would be no better off with high wages than with low; their wages would not command more of any article of consumption; a real rise of wages, therefore, would be an impossibility.[40]

Precisely the same position was reiterated by Mill in correspondence after the appearance of the review. In June 1870 he wrote to George Adcroft:

... I differ from you when you say that a general rise of wages would be of no use to the working classes because it would produce a general rise of prices. A general rise of prices, of anything like a permanent character, can only take place through a general increase of the money incomes of the purchasing community. Now a general rise of wages would not increase the aggregate money incomes, nor consequently the aggregate purchasing power of the community; it would only transfer part of that purchasing power from the employers to the labourers. Consequently a general rise of wages would not raise prices but would be taken out of the profits of the employers; always supposing that those profits were sufficient to bear the reduction.

The case is different with a rise of wages confined to a single, or a small number of employments ... The supply of these particular articles would fall short, their prices would rise so as to indemnify the employers for the rise of wages. But this would not happen in case of a rise of all wages, for as all capitalists would be affected nearly alike they could not as a body relieve themselves by turning their capital into another employment.[41]

The evidence presented thus far suggests a firm conviction on Mill's part of the justness of strict Ricardianism – that is to say a body of doctrine including, first, the relation between the rate of return on capital and the wage rate, iden-

Development of British Orthodoxy: 1797–1875 (Cambridge, Mass. 1965), 190, 226–7

40 CW, V, 661   41 CW, XVII, 1734–5

tified with the often-called 'peculiar' principle of proportionate wages and profits; second, the formal derivation of the relation in terms of a money of invariable value, despite an emphasis upon the relativity of exchange value; and third, the view that the inverse relation holds good independently of the measure in that wage-rate increases can be shown to be non-inflationary.

It is this latter characteristic of Mill's work, in conjunction with a too hasty reading of the chapter formally devoted to the measure, which may be responsible for the view expressed by Blaug and Schumpeter, that, unlike Ricardo, Mill discusses the inverse relation without making use of an invariable measure. This view is misleading in two regards. First, the measure is in fact used as a conceptual device as we have seen; and second, Ricardo too maintained that the inverse relation holds in the real world independently of the measure. There is a complete identity of opinion between Mill and Ricardo on these fundamental issues. To refer to Mill's maintenance of an 'emasculated' version of Ricardo's system is surely unjustified.[42]

MILL'S CONSISTENCY: RICARDIANISM AND NEO-CLASSICISM

My argument thus far has been that Mill's economics retained the truly characteristic Ricardian elements. I also believe, although space limitations preclude any development of this contention, that the attack against Mill and orthodoxy in the 1860s and 1870s, including that implicit in Mill's recantation, was to a large extent misdirected and thus failed to reach the fundamental core of Ricardianism. There is a further matter, however, which remains for consideration here – that of Mill's consistency.[43]

The issue can fruitfully be envisaged from the perspective of the so-called

42 It is a fundamental weakness of the account by Dr Schwartz, *The New Political Economy of J.S. Mill*, that while reference is made to Mill's 'adoption of the Ricardian dictum that "profits depend on wages"' it is implied that Mill took this position only *after* he had rejected the wages-fund theory in 1869 (101). Compare ibid., 97: 'Mill was to reject the idea of a general rise in prices as impossible.' The essence of our argument is that these themes were quite central to Mill from at least 1830, reappearing continuously throughout the essay 'On Profits and Interests' and the *Principles*.

43 In his *New Political Economy of J.S. Mill*, 3–4 (compare 235) Dr Schwartz asserts that 'it would be unrewarding ... to ask whether it was inconsistent of Mill to attempt to build a new political economy on the basis of the Ricardian system,' and that 'questions as to the originality or coherence of Mill's economic thought are irrelevant and unimportant, distracting attention from the real problem. Of course he was both original and coherent, but the questions that go to the heart of the matter are others. What were Mill's relations to his teachers? What was Mill aiming at with his 'New Political Economy'? Was he successful? And whether he achieved his goal or no, how valuable is his doctrine from the point of view of today's economics and social philosophy?' These latter questions may indeed be the important ones, but I do not see how the matter of Mill's consistency can be thus dismissed in attempting to provide answers. And a mere assurance of Mill's coherence simply begs the question.

marginal revolution. Jevons, unlike Walras, failed to develop in the *Theory of Political Economy* (1871) an alternative structure to the one he was criticizing.[44] His work, he frankly informs us, without understatement, 'was never put forward as containing a systematic view of Economics.'[45] Nevertheless, he did suggest in the celebrated Preface to his second edition (1879) what the features of a 'true system of Economics' must be. Distribution must be envisaged as a matter of service pricing 'entirely subject to the principles of value and the laws of supply and demand' in which all prices are subject to the same rule; costs of production would reflect alternative opportunities foregone; and input prices would be 'the effect and not the cause of the value of the produce.'[46] Now what is quite fascinating in this account is the fact that Jevons found so much to admire in the work of the arch-villain himself. Thus

44 The point is fairly made by Léon Walras who contrasted Jevon's failure in this regard with his own achievement: 'Jevons a eu le tort de ne pas dire que le système de Ricardo et Mill est remplacé. Je remplace dans ma *Théorie mathématique de la Richesse Sociale* et dans mes *Eléments d'Economie politique pure* le système de Ricardo et Mill par un système très beau, très simple dans ses éléments et très vaste dans ses détails ...' *Correspondence of Léon Walras and Related Papers*, ed. W. Jaffé (Amsterdam 1965), I, 626. Walras recognized, however, Jevon's 'ten remarkable pages' (discussed below) which state 'that the formula of the English school, in any case the school of Ricardo and Mill, must be reversed, for the prices of productive services are determined by the prices of the products, and not the other way round.' *Elements of Pure Economics* (Preface to 4th ed.; def. ed. 1926, London 1954), 45

45 *Theory of Political Economy*, 4th ed. (London 1924), xliii–xliv

46 Ibid., xlvif. In his introduction to Jevons's *Theory of Political Economy* (Harmondsworth 1970), 17–20, Professor R.D.C. Black rejects the usual criticism of Jevons that he failed to develop a theory of factor pricing and therefore a full neo-classical perspective. His intention, Black suggests, was Benthamite; he was not concerned with a general pricing system.
   This interpretation merits careful consideration for it is by no means self-evident, since Jevon's Preface to the Second Edition does imply a preoccupation with the general pricing problem, both by the suggestions made regarding a 'desirable' approach and by the criticisms of orthodoxy. Jevons's reference to input prices as the *effect* rather than the *cause* of value, on the other hand, lends some support to Professor Black's argument whereby Jevons was not groping towards a general-equilibrium system of the Walras-Pareto type. At the same time, it will be recalled that Walras himself applauded this passage; frequently, however, Walras used the term 'cause' in a particular sense – that of 'universal concomitance and exact proportionality' – and it is not certain how much weight to place upon Walras's approbation. On Walras's use of the expression 'rareté is the cause of value' see W. Jaffé, 'Léon Walras's Role in the "Marginal Revolution" of the 1870's,' *History of Political Economy*, IV, 1972, 398. Professor Black in his most recent contribution ('W.S. Jevons and the Foundation of Modern Economics,' ibid., 373–4) suggests that Jevons's adherence to Benthamism may have held him back from developing a full-fledged theory of factor pricing. This interpretation would be fully consistent with Jevons's position in his Preface.

he referred to J.S. Mill's own recognition of alternative cost in the case of land: 'When land capable of yielding rent in agriculture is applied to some other purpose, the rent which it would have yielded is an element in the cost of production of the commodity which it is employed to produce.'[47] He pointed to the 'remarkable section' in which Mill 'explains that all inequalities, artificial or natural, give rise to extra gains of the nature of Rent.'[48] He was equally impressed by Mill's analysis of pricing in the case of joint-production wherein, as he put it, Mill reverted 'to a law of value anterior to cost of production, and more fundamental, namely, the law of supply and demand.'[49] Jevons might have gone further, as Professor Stigler's study of scientific originality makes clear.[50] I myself would add to the list Mill's recognition, in correspondence with Cairnes, of the substitution effects generated by relative price changes in consumption,[51] and the recognition both in the *Principles* and the *Fortnightly Review* of a version of the derived-demand principle.[52]

In this context, Mill's objections to Smith's analysis of the wage structure deserves mention. Both financial and social obstacles, Mill insisted, prevented the attainment of skills by sufficiently large numbers to assure the eradication of monopoly returns in skilled trades, even in the absence of institutional constraints. The recognition that *within* the working class there were non-competing groups is the essence of the change.[53] But Mill's objections went further. According to Smith it was to be expected that the least pleasant occupations would, *ceteris paribus*, be the highest paid. It was pointed out by Mill that, quite apart from impediments to mobility, the result envisaged presumed the (aggregate) labour market to be in equilibrium. Should unemployment exist in the labour market as a whole, it is likely that the least agreeable (and unskilled) trades would be the worst paid since the excess supplies therein would be relatively great: 'Partly from this cause, and partly from the natural and artificial monopolies ... the inequalities of wages are generally in an opposite direction to the equitable principle of compensation erroneously represented by Adam Smith as the general law of the remuneration of labour.'[54]

The problem then which I wish to raise relates to the relative status in Mill's work of the Ricardian and non-Ricardian elements. For it seems clear

47 *Theory of Political Economy*, xlviii, regarding Mill's *Principles of Political Economy*, III, vi
48 Ibid., li, regarding Mill's *Principles*, III, v
49 Ibid., 197, regarding Mill's *Principles*, III, xvi
50 *Essays in the History of Economics*, 6–11
51 See S. Hollander, 'The Role of Fixed Technical Coefficients in the Evolution of the Wages-Fund Controversy,' *Oxford Economic Papers*, xx, 1968, 334.
52 CW, III, 747; V, 644
53 CW, II, 386–7
54 Ibid., 383

enough that some, at least, of the propositions I have referred to are incompatible with pure Ricardianism.[55] For example, the wage-structure analysis casts into doubt the entire conception of a *general* movement in wage rates. (It will be recalled that Ricardo commenced his value analysis with the assumption that 'the estimation in which different qualities of labour are held, comes soon to be adjusted in the market with sufficient precision for all practical purposes, and depends much on the comparative skills of the labourer, and intensity of the labour performed. *The scale when once formed, is liable to little variation.*'[56]) The introduction of derived demand has no place in the Ricardian scheme of things. The recognition of substitution-in-consumption, and of rent as a cost of production when land has alternative uses, are further instances. Jevons himself pointed out that Mill's generalization of the rent conception 'when properly followed, will overthrow many of the principal doctrines of the Ricardo-Mill economics.' Jevons, however, was quite satisfied to leave the matter there with the remark that 'those who have studied Mill's philosophic character as long and minutely as I have done, will not for a moment suppose that the occurrence of this section of Mill's book tends to establish its consistency with other positions of the same treatise.'[57]

Now it is not uncommon to suggest in Mill's defence that 'a textbook,' such as the *Principles*, 'was not the place to rehearse technical anomalies.'[58] There doubtless is something to this,[59] but I do not think it provides the whole solution. In the first place it is not clear to what extent Mill was in fact aware that certain of his propositions were problematic. And second, even if we assume that he was fully aware, it is not apparent how the inconsistencies could have been dealt with even for a technical audience. Whatever the reason it is clear enough that Mill was much concerned to avoid even the impression

55 Professor Stigler does not raise this question, although he envisages Mill as attempting 'to add improvements here and there to the Ricardian system' (*Essays in the History of Economics*, 11), a position also adopted by Dr Schwartz (*The New Political Economy of J.S. Mill*, 3, 236).

56 See *Works and Correspondence of David Ricardo*, I, 20. On the significance of this assumption see T.W. Hutchison, 'The "Marginal Revolution" and the Decline and Fall of English Classical Political Economy,' *History of Political Economy*, IV, 1972, 457.

57 *Theory of Political Economy*, li. Mill's emphasis upon interest as a reward for abstinence does not create a problem from the point of view of his consistency. The conception of profit as a residual arising from the productive power of labour (see CW, II, 411) is the basis for investment demand, while abstinence relates to the supply side and explains the constraints on the growth of capital. (See Mark Blaug, *Economic Theory in Retrospect*, 2nd ed. [Homewood 1968], 193; Bela A. Balassa, 'Karl Marx and John Stuart Mill,' *Weltwirtschaftliches Archiv*, LXXXIII, 1959, 149.)

58 Donald Winch, Introduction to Mill's *Principles of Political Economy* (Harmondsworth 1970), 29

59 See CW, III, 701, where Mill refers the reader to his *Essays on Some Unsettled Questions* on a question which 'is too intricate in comparison with its importance, to be further entered into in a work like the present.'

that he was at any significant point diverging from Ricardo's authority.[60] His allowance that variations in the wage or profit structure will affect relative prices provides an interesting example: 'It thus appears,' he wrote, 'that the maxim laid down by some of the best political economists, that wages do not enter into value, is expressed with greater latitude than the truth warrants, or than accords with their own meaning.'[61] Now in light of Mill's great emphasis elsewhere upon the phenomenon of non-competing groups we might have expected that the weaknesses inherent in the concept of a general change in the level of wages would have been considered ruinous to any view that emphasizes relative labour embodied as the main variable acting upon values.[62] Yet in fact Mill concludes that while 'in strictness ... wages of labour have as much to do with value as quantity of labour' – a fact, he insists, that 'neither Ricardo nor any one else' had ever denied – 'in considering, however, the causes of *variations* in value, quantity of labour is the thing of chief importance; for when that varies, it is generally in one or a few commodities at a time, but the variations of wages (except passing fluctuations) are usually general, and have no considerable effect on value.'[63] Mill refused to allow his own innovation to damage the main structure.

It is frequently suggested that Mill's fidelity to Ricardo may lie in his conception of scientific development, whereby 'once humanity was purged of its prejudices, science could grow steadily through accumulation, each scientist adding a storey to the edifice initiated by his predecessors ... The idea that the theories of gifted economists like Ricardo could need a fundamental revision was alien to his idea of the cumulative growth of science.'[64] The problem, however, is that Mill's 'innovations' were scarcely *consistent* with Ricardianism, and the suggestion fails to account for this significant characteristic of the *Principles*.

The failure to face squarely the problems created for the Ricardian scheme by various incompatible elements must remain something of a problem. Nonetheless, we know enough now of the innovatory process to realise that the presence of 'anomalies,' even when they are recognized as such, may be quite inconsequential and fail to generate an alternative to the established structure – irrespective of any peculiarly powerful ingredient labelled 'filial respect.' It is

60 Jevons was quite correct to emphasise that the non-Ricardian features which he enumerated were presented in Mill's *Principles* as exceptions to the rule, or special cases. See *Theory of Political Economy*, xlviii.
61 cw, III, 480
62 And indeed Mill points out (ibid.) that 'wages in different employments do not rise or fall simultaneously, but are, for short and sometimes even for long periods, nearly independent of one another.'
63 Ibid., 481
64 Schwartz, *The New Political Economy of J.S. Mill*, 236–7; compare Thomas Sowell, *Say's Law* (Princeton 1972), 164; and Schumpeter, *History of Economic Analysis*, 530

worth while staying a moment with this issue, for it was consideration of the non-Ricardian features which led Schumpeter to his position that Mill's system was 'free from the objections which could be directed against that of Ricardo' and 'offered all the elements of the complete model that Marshall was to build.'[65] It is Schumpeter's reference to *Mill's system* which may be misleading. The choice as ultimate standard of reference of the micro-economic general-equilibrium model led Schumpeter, of course, to make the celebrated charge that the entire Ricardian episode was a mere 'detour' in the development of economic theory involving the construction of a 'faulty engine of analysis.'[66] It also led him to read far more into those writings which appeared to recognize the 'true' economic problem and deal with it appropriately. Thus it is that the scattered presence in Mill's work of properties which Schumpeter considered desirable reassured him that Mill's heart was in the right place. If it appeared otherwise it was an illusion created by Mill's 'filial respect.'[67] Faulty methodology, so it seems to me, led to an unjustified discounting of Mill's Ricardianism and to an undue premium upon the rest.[68] In the last resort, it is essential to remember, on the one hand, that the *only* full-fledged system in Mill's *Principles* is that of Ricardo, in light of which fact we should avoid referring to Mill's Ricardianism as a 'relic'; and on the other, that the recognition of theoretical elements which fit better into a neo-classical model must not be identified, even by inference, with the actual construction of such a model. Schumpeter, and in this regard Knight too,[69] were prone to minimize the horrendous conceptual difficulties which stood in the way. The significance of neo-classical elements in the *Principles* must not be overstated.

It is in fact legitimate, I think, to regard the central Ricardian model as a genuine paradigm basically concerned with the treatment of macro-economic issues. To envisage a transfer from this to the neo-classical system with its emphasis upon allocation by a process of shedding the weak elements and

65 *History of Economic Analysis*, 569–70: 'J.S. Mill's system ... absorbed enough of the Say conception – and in addition was sufficiently helped by Senior's notion of abstinence – to be free from any such objection [as Ricardo's inability to deal with simultaneous equations], and it offered all the elements of the complete model that Marshall was to build. But he retained so many Ricardian relics that there is some excuse for Jevons's and the Austrians' not seeing that they were developing his analysis and for believing instead that they had to destroy it.'

66 Ibid., 474, 568

67 Ibid., 529

68 Dr Schwartz, *The New Political Economy of J.S. Mill*, 243, refers to the 'merit' of 'writing the history of economic doctrines from the point of view of pure analysis.' It would seem, however, that serious misinterpretations may result from a failure to justify with sufficient care the standard of reference chosen in such an historical approach.

69 F.H. Knight, 'The Ricardian Theory of Production and Distribution' (1935), in *On the History and Method of Economics* (Chicago 1956), 37ff

replacing them by superior ones – a view for which Marshall himself is partly responsible[70] – may be misleading, for there is an important sense in which the two schemes are incommensurable.[71] It is for this reason that I would avoid the designation 'Half-way House' sometimes attached to Mill's *Principles*.[72]

The force of the contemporary challenge to orthodoxy must also not be exaggerated. Much is frequently made of the so-called French tradition of regarding commodities and factor services as subject to the same rules.[73] But Ricardo himself was fully aware of Say's criticisms of his approach along these lines, yet deliberately stayed with his chosen path.[74] In other words, the challenge in this key respect was not a *new* one. Accordingly, much of the case against Ricardianism should be temporally discounted, as it were, when considering Mill's position; he was aware of the case for the prosecution from the very outset. In this regard I would like to refer to a recent demonstration by Professor de Marchi that on methodological grounds Mill saw little cause for rejoicing in Jevons' attempt to render consumption theory in mathematical terms.[75] There is a difference of 'principle' involved and not merely a question of wearing Ricardian blinkers, or of 'filial respect.'

Finally, we must keep in mind the crucial fact that Mill found the basic Ricardian approach genuinely useful. 'Filial respect' may have played some part in the Mill concoction, but it should not be given pride of place. For you will recall that Mill referred to the problem which the Ricardian model was designed to treat as one of topical and immediate concern, and not one of mere antiquarian interest. Its attempt to distinguish conceptually in the analysis of the rate of return on capital between nominal and real wage-rate changes (reflecting an altered share of wages in *per capita* income), it may be added, had by no means been undermined by direct challenge.

70 '... [My] acquaintance with economics commenced with reading Mill ... and translating his doctrines into differential equations as far as they would go; and, as a rule, rejecting those which would not go.' *Memorials of Alfred Marshall*, ed. A.C. Pigou (London 1925), 412

71 Even G.F. Shove, who commenced his famous study of Marshall's *Principles* with the proposition that the latter 'is nothing more or less than a completion and generalisation, by means of a mathematical apparatus, of Ricardo's theory of value and distribution as expounded by J.S. Mill,' conceded that 'if the Ricardian analysis was our starting-point, by the end of the journey we have entered a new world.' Cf 'The Place of Marshall's *Principles* in the Development of Economic Theory,' *Economic Journal*, LII, 1942

72 Mark Blaug, *Ricardian Economics*, 165

73 See the references in N.B. de Marchi, 'Mill and Cairnes and the Emergence of Marginalism in England,' *History of Political Economy*, IV, 1972, 345n.

74 See *Works and Correspondence of David Ricardo*, VIII, 379–80; IX, 35, 171–2.

75 N.B. de Marchi, 'Mill and Cairnes and the Emergence of Marginalism in England,' 349. Compare Schwartz, *The New Political Economy of J.S. Mill*, 238

John Stuart Mill as a Sociologist: The Unwritten Ethology

L.S. FEUER

In 1843, at the height of his intellectual powers, and with his *System of Logic* published and recognized at once as an intellectual landmark, John Stuart Mill prepared for his next book. Virtually announced at the end of his *Logic*, his aim now was to be to establish the foundations of sociology. Ethology, the science of 'the laws of human character,' was to have been the core; then he would set forth the laws both of social statics and dynamics. For a 'considerable time' Mill tried to write this book. But, as Alexander Bain, his friend, tells us, he 'despaired, for the present time at least' of bringing such a work to fruition. Thereupon Mill turned in the autumn of 1845 to composing instead a volume on *Political Economy*.[1]

Among the great social thinkers of the nineteenth century, Mill was the only one who failed to write a system encompassing the evolution of humanity. Hegel, Comte, Marx, and Spencer felt they could enunciate and derive the law of social progress. Mill too would have wished greatly to prove that an empirical law of progress followed from the basic laws of mind. But Mill, author of 'On the Logic of the Moral Sciences,' the most enduring essay on the method of the social sciences which has ever been written, was aware that their simple 'derivations' collapsed under scientific scrutiny.

Comte, Marx, and Spencer could enunciate laws of historical development because their perception was pre-selected by their categorical schemes; they saw a reality, censored through ideological prisms, which arbitrarily excluded

---

1 Alexander Bain, *John Stuart Mill: A Criticism With Personal Recollections* (London 1882), 78–9, 84

a whole set of possible developmental sequences consistent with observable facts. Comte ruled out the likelihood that religious revivals might occur, a possibility which Tocqueville had documented, and he altogether vetoed the notion that anti-civilizational waves might reinstate astrology and fetishism in people's minds. Marx excluded the possible advent of technocratic, totalitarian societies, characterized by managerial rule rather than by the workers' self-administration. Spencer set aside the possibility that the militant motive in men might manifest itself with a renewed intensity to engulf industrial societies; nor did his law of the differentiated progress of societies allow for the possibility of their decline. Mill alone tried to do justice to all the competing drives and motives of human nature; he would never banish from his consciousness the knowledge of the many-sidedness and many-levelledness of social reality. With his immense learning, practical experience, and logical acumen, Mill was more qualified to write the masterpiece of sociology than any other man in the nineteenth century. To understand why he failed in this design will perhaps bring to light truths of social existence that only great failures make explicit. What intellectual problems arose to make it impossible for Mill to compose his sociological treatise?

Mill in his *Logic* had explicated the character of the social sciences in a manner which has basically withstood all criticism. The inverse deductive method, as he called it, distinguished between the three levels of social analysis. Underlying all social truths there were first the elementary, fundamental laws of mind, the laws of psychology, known to us through introspection and empathetic understanding. These provided the basic premises for sociology considered as a deductive science. The sociologist as a deductive theorist knew his major premises and indeed his empirical conclusions; he then sought the intervening minor premises which were still unknowns. The conclusions to be derived were the empirical laws of sociology, confirmed in statistical studies and surveys – such empirical laws, for instance, as those concerning the frequencies and variations of suicide which Quetelet was investigating in Mill's time.[2] Between the major premises of psychology and the empirical laws of sociology was the domain of the middle principles – the *axiomata media,* the laws of ethology. These were to constitute the science of the formation of national character, or social character as it would be called today. To every system or structure of social institutions, Mill affirmed, there was a corresponding formation of social character. The social institutions were the social initial conditions under which the universal laws of human psychology operated. And they gave rise to the laws of ethology, or social psychology – those forms of

2 Quetelet, it should be observed, created the science of social statistics during the early 1830s when he and the young Belgian intellectuals were, like young Mill in England, under the influence of Saint-Simonian ideas. See Lambert A.J. Quetelet, *A Treatise on Man and the Development of his Faculties,* facsimile of 1842 translation, introduction by Solomon Diamond (Gainesville 1969), vi, vii.

human feeling, thought, and behaviour which social circumstances educed from the universal psychological nature of man. The observed empirical laws would then in turn be derivable from the laws of mind and the ethological premises.

Mill's conception of sociology is today part of its common sense. For instance, it provides the framework for the study of suicide, an example in which Mill was interested. Persons of Calvinist background usually show higher rates of suicide than Roman Catholics; again, for many years, the suicide rates among Negro men were about one-third those of white men in corresponding age groups. To explain these empirical uniformities of suicide, we would avail ourselves in Millite fashion of such psychological laws as we may possess. We might use the psychological law that where frustrations persist or increase, the aggressive energies accumulate; and that where the latter cannot be directed toward causative external objects, they are redirected inward against one's self. As sociologists, we should seek the ethological middle laws which would take us to the empirical uniformities. We might use the ethological law that the Calvinist upbringing made for a more rigorous, severe, unbending conscience, that its reproaches, moreover, were alleviated by no social servomechanism, and that the resultant guilt feelings were more intense. We might note that because the Negro family had for many years a matriarchal pattern, with the fathers of the children unknown or transient, the character-structure of the sons, therefore, was such in which the father's commands had a weaker part. And from these ethological laws we could derive the empirical uniformities of suicide.

As a model of what a science of ethology could do, Mill had before him his father's *History of British India*, a book which he had read in manuscript and which, as he said, guided his thoughts by its analysis of Hindu society and civilization; the son regarded it as perhaps the most instructive history ever written.[3] James Mill had traced the causes of the Hindu national character to their political institutions. His character-sketch of them was scarcely flattering: 'No other race of men are perhaps so little friendly and beneficient to one another as the Hindus.' Their 'listless apathy' was not the outcome of their climate; other nations such as the Chinese had lived under as warm a sun but were 'neither indolent, nor weak.' If the Hindus disliked work, it was for one basic reason – their subjection to a wretched government, under which the fruits of their labour were never secure. Other Britons might find profundities in Hindu religious philosophy, but to James Mill their conception of nature was 'the most grovelling and base' and their writings replete with 'a more gross and disgusting picture of the universe' than any other people could adduce.[4]

3 *Autobiography*, ed. J. Stillinger (Boston 1969), 16–17
4 *The History of British India*, 5th ed. (1858; reprinted New York 1968), I, 466, 469, 480, 481, 371, 385, 347

There is a simplicity and comprehensiveness in John Stuart Mill's conception of sociology. It is utterly free of the exaggerations of later methodological
schools which, fastening on one of Mill's three levels of analysis, have declared
it to be the all-exclusive sociological one. Thus, Durkheim's school maintained
that no psychological components should enter into a sociological explanation,
though its own practice contravened its theory; on the other side, empirical
surveyors have wished to pursue their inquiries without regard to underlying
causal laws; while phenomenologists have argued that only the inner psychological processes, bracketed from the external world, were the social reality. Mill
stood above such academic ideologies.

It was the very comprehensiveness of Mill's inverse deductive method,
however, that made it impossible for him to bind together the contrary empirical laws he wished to affirm. To begin with, there was the flat contradiction
in Mill between the manifest nineteenth-century optimist and the underlying
pessimist. As an optimist, he accepted Auguste Comte's law of the three stages
– the evolution from the religious to the metaphysical to the positive stage – as
a valid empirical generalization; Comte's 'main conclusions,' he wrote, were
sound, and the chain of causation Comte outlined as 'in all essentials irrefrag-
able'; this intellectual movement, Mill said further, was 'at the root of all the
great changes in human affairs.'[5] But then there was the pessimist Mill who
discerned that the law of the future would be the dominance of mediocrity:
'the general tendency of things throughout the world is to render mediocrity
the ascendant power among mankind.' '[I]n the world at large,' wrote Mill,
there was 'an increasing inclination to stretch unduly the powers of society
over the individual ...' It was the sociological analogue to the great generalization which William Thomson, later Lord Kelvin, had enunciated at almost
the same time on the universal tendency to the dissipation of energy. In not
dissimilar words, Mill affirmed: 'the tendency of all the changes taking place
in the world is to strengthen society, and diminish the power of the individual ...' The creative energies of men would become increasingly unavailable.

Most unfortunately, according to Mill, no social class or stratum was exempt
from the tendency toward mediocrity. The middle classes, the masses, and
the reforming intellectuals were all alike mediocrats and intolerant. In England, said Mill, it was 'chiefly the middle class' which imposed the stamp of
its 'collective mediocrity' on social existence;[6] in democratic America, it was
the 'whole white population' expressing itself through the force of public opinion;[7] and as for the intellectuals, 'almost all the projects of social reformers of
these days are really *liberticide*.'[8] From Saint-Simon to Auguste Comte, their

5 *Auguste Comte and Positivism, Collected Works*, x (Toronto 1969), 317, 319, 322–3
6 *On Liberty*, 4th ed. (London 1869), 119
7 Ibid., 118–19
8 Letter to Harriet Mill, 15 Jan. 1855, CW, XIV, 294

aim had been 'dictatorship,' and with Comte it seemed indeed that the crypto-despot in every revolutionizing intellectual emerged explicit: in his scheme for 'the absolute and undivided control of a single Pontiff for the whole human race – one is appalled at the picture of entire subjugation and slavery ...'[9]

Here then were two empirical laws which stood as contraries to each other – progress and mediocritization. The contraries in his ethological laws also tore apart the psychological basis which Mill provided for his sociology. In his *Logic*, following in his father's footsteps, Mill asserted that the laws of association were a sufficient foundation for the explanation and derivation of sociological laws. Yet, it became clear to Mill, a far broader conception of human drives was required. He noted in his essay 'Nature' (begun in 1854) that there was 'an instinct for domination' in men, 'a delight in exercising despotism, in holding other beings in subjection to our will'; it was linked to an 'instinct for destructiveness,' 'an instinct to destroy for destruction's sake'; men were 'naturally cruel.'[10] Comte too had observed that there were two 'very powerful instincts,' 'a downright taste for destruction' and a repugnance toward labour, which impelled men toward military rather than industrial societies.[11] If so, however, civilization rested on a precarious 'victory over instinct' through self-discipline. There were 'bad instincts' in men which, said Mill, 'it should be the aim of education not simply to regulate, but to extirpate ...'[12] But if so, on what psychological ground could an empirical law of progress safely repose? The laws of mind, as Mill set them forth, were consistent not only with mediocritization, but indeed with a decline of civilization. What combination of psychological axioms with middle principles would underwrite the empirical law of progress?

Now Karl Marx, confronted by essentially the same problem, could avail himself of the salvaging motor force of the dialectic. According to Marx and Engels, greed and the lust for power could themselves be enlisted to transform a system beset with 'contradictions' into a higher one. But this conception was explicitly repudiated by Mill, most clearly so in his essay on Guizot's theory of history. Guizot, Marx's forerunner as a historian of class struggles, had affirmed that feudal society, 'by its own nature and tendencies,' evolved toward its dissolution. Mill, however, saw no such dialectic transmutation of evil to a higher good. 'That is an easy solution,' he wrote, 'which accounts for the destruction of institutions from their own defects; but experience proves that forms of government and social arrangements do not fall merely because they deserve to fall. The more backward and the more degraded any form of

9 *Considerations on Representative Government*, 3rd ed. (London 1865), 38–40; *Auguste Comte and Positivism*, cw, x, 351

10 'Nature,' cw, x, 398

11 Auguste Comte, *System of Positive Polity*, tr. E.S. Beesly et al. (London 1875–7), III, 47

12 cw, x, 393, 398

society is, the stronger is the tendency to remain stagnating in that state, simply because it is an existing state.'[13] Existing societies, far from being 'rational' or 'functional,' were, from Mill's standpoint, as likely or likelier to be irrational and otiose. Then, how then did the feudal society evolve into a free commercial and industrial one? Progress, according to Mill, took place not because of any dialectical breakdown, but rather the spirit of liberty, the aspiration toward improvement, had found within the feudal order a sufficient support. Given the 'imputed causes of the fall of feudalism, the question recurs,' wrote Mill, 'what caused the causes themselves? ... There can be but one answer; the feudal system with all its deficiencies, was sufficiently a government, contained within itself a sufficient mixture of authority and liberty ... to enable the natural causes of social improvement to resume their course.' The feudal age, in Mill's view, had been wrongly 'vilified,' for 'at no period of history was human intellect more active, or society more unmistakably in a state of rapid advance' than during a great part of it.

Only once did Mill in an ethical fervour allow himself to endorse the notion that an evil institution must perish of economic necessity. That was during the American Civil War when Mill argued in 1862 that the confinement of slavery to the Southern states would mean its 'death-warrant,' its 'nearly inevitable and probably rapid' extinction.[14]

Underlying all progressive change, in Mill's view, was simply a persisting moral aspiration in men which could never be stifled but rather endured through all the 'compressions' of human character to avail itself of the rare social circumstances which enabled humanity to resume its linear advance. 'All political revolutions, not effected by foreign conquest, originate in moral revolutions,' wrote Mill.[15] Revolutions of progress were in his view the consequence of an uprising of the spirit of liberty and improvement against the 'yoke of authority.' Mill thus attributed the rise of capitalist society, or in his terms, the rise of 'the principle of accumulation,' to conditions which allowed 'the growth of mental activity, making the people alive to new objects of desire.' Under such conditions of a better government and more complete security, foreign arts were welcomed; 'by instilling new ideas and breaking the chains of habit, if not by improving the actual condition of the population, [it] tends to create in them new wants, increased ambition, and greater thought for the future.'[16] If Mill was ranged against any Marxist dialectical conception, he would also have rejected the involuted dialectic of Max Weber where-

13 'Guizot's Essays and Lectures on History,' *Dissertations and Discussions: Political, Philosophical, and Historical*, II (London 1859), 268–70

14 J.S. Mill, 'The Contest in America,' *Dissertations and Discussions*, III (London 1867), 191

15 J.S. Mill, 'A Few Observations on the French Revolution,' *Dissertations and Discussions*, I (London 1859), 56

16 *Principles of Political Economy*, CW, II, 186–7

in Calvinist asceticism somehow gave rise to its precise opposite, the development of new industries and new wants. According to Mill, Calvinism constituted a 'narrow theory of life' making for a 'pinched and hidebound type of human character,' for people 'cramped and dwarfed,' crushing the individual and his will through self-denial, and refusing to conceive of God as a Being who takes delight in every increase of human 'capabilities of comprehension, of action, or of enjoyment.'[17] As such, it would be inimical to the free development of the sciences and technology essential to the rise of capitalism. Calvinist doctrine too easily afforded a justification for what Mill called 'an equal chance to everybody of tyrannizing,' a desire, he said, as 'fully natural to mankind' as the desire not to be tyrannized over.[18]

Nonetheless, a sociological mystery still persisted as to the circumstances in which the spirit of liberty and advancement would prevail over the drives toward enslavement and retrogression.

Mill at one point tried to found the empirical law of progress on two universal human motives – the pursuit of truth and 'the desire of increased material comforts.' The latter, the hedonistic ingredient, was, he wrote, 'the impelling force' to most improvements. But, he went on to observe, the 'progress of industry must follow, and depend on, the progress of knowledge.'[19] Every advance in material civilization has been preceded, wrote Mill, by an advance of knowledge; changes in the mode of thought, in the Comtist pattern, have set the stage for these advances, but these changes in the mode of thought have themselves not arisen from the requirements of practical life but solely from the inner tendency of the previous system of beliefs to evolve. Once again, however, Mill's sociological theory was in straits. For what immanent law prescribed that a system of beliefs had to evolve? If it was dominated by myths, why could not a society stagnate in the mythological mode even as it did in its economy? What gave power to the pursuit of truth so that it could triumph over the contrary will to illusion?

At this juncture Mill tended to shift the causal primacy in social evolution to the character of a people's political institutions. He asserted in his *Logic* as a basic principle 'the necessary correlation between the forms of government existing in any society and the contemporaneous state of civilization ...'[20] The greatness of the Athenian achievement, he thus affirmed, was derived from their free social institutions.[21] By contrast, the impoverished backwardness of many fertile tracts of Asia received its 'acknowledged explanation' in the tyrannical insecurity of rapacious governments, whose agents could deprive one arbitrarily of the fruits of one's labour. Why did the Roman empire decline? Mill felt that Finlay had explained this phenomenon better than had

17 *On Liberty*, 112
19 *Logic*, cw, viii, 926 (vi, x, 7)
21 *Dissertations and Discussions*, ii, 286

18 *Principles*, cw, iii, 944
20 cw, viii, 919 (vi, x 5)

Gibbon,[22] for Finlay traced the decrease in the Italian population to evils inherent in the political system of the Roman government, its public distribution of grain, its arbitrary mode of taxation.[23] But the relation between social institutions and a people's mode of thought and feelings was also asserted by Mill to be circular, interdependent, and interactive, with neither variable ontologically independent: 'The creed and laws of a people act powerfully upon their economic conditions; and this again by its influence on their mental development and social relations reacts upon their creed and laws.'[24]

Mill, however, could scarcely be satisfied with a theory of the multiple causal interdependence of social institutions and modes of thought. It was adequate for what he (following Comte) called static rather than dynamic situations. Thus an equilibrium was defined by the uniformities between a society's different elements of coexistence; the society's institutions would all be values to interdependent mathematical functions, and the static state of affairs would be the counterpart of mathematical conditions of equilibrium. Yet these static mutual correlations themselves arose out of dynamic processes; they were the terminal points of equilibrium of processes in which one variable might well indeed be the primary independent. The aspiration for liberty, truth, and improvement seemed never to be confined to particular static forms consistent with their coexistent society; the dynamic variables always had a degree of freedom which resisted their simply being assigned the values appropriate to the existing institutions.

Mill at this point verges on a complete declaration for sociological voluntarism as against sociological determinism. For years he had struggled with the problem of determinism. It weighed on him not only logically, but psychologically, part of that 'nightmare' which (in Thomas Henry Huxley's expression) haunted British thinkers of that era. During the 'mental crisis' of his early manhood, it took the form, as Mill described it, of his being 'seriously tormented by the thought of the exhaustibility of musical combination.' He compared 'this source of anxiety' to 'that of the philosophers of Laputa, who feared lest the sun should be burnt out.' Then in 'later returns of my dejection,' as Mill wrote, 'the doctrine of what is called Philosophical Necessity weighed on my existence like an incubus. I felt as if I was scientifically proved to be the helpless slave of antecedent circumstances ...'[25] He struggled to remove this incubus all his life. He drew the distinction in later years between

22 John Morley, *Recollections* (London 1917), I, 66
23 'The social organization of nations affects their vitality as much as their political constitution affects their power and fortunes.' George Finlay, *A History of Greece, from its conquest by the Romans to the present time, B.C. 146 to A.D. 1864*, new ed. (Oxford 1877), I, 89–90
24 *Principles*, CW, II, 3
25 *Autobiography*, 87, 101

two kinds of fatalism, the Asiatic and the modified, which he contrasted with his own doctrine. 'Real Fatalism is of two kinds. Pure, or Asiatic fatalism – the fatalism of the Oedipus – holds that our actions do not depend upon our desires.' In the case of modified fatalism, 'our actions are determined by our will,' wrote Mill, 'our will by our desires,' and the last are determined by our motives and character; our character, however, is supposed to have 'been made for us and not by us, we are not responsible for it ...' The true doctrine of causation, on the contrary, said Mill, affirmed that our character is 'in part amenable to our will ...' Yet it scarcely seemed that Mill had escaped the fatalism of the Oedipus. All the varieties of fatalism and his own causation as well reduced to an Oedipal determinism. For our decisions and efforts to improve our characters were all in principle predictable; the behaviour of Mill and the modified fatalist were as predictable as that of the Oedipal subject in whose case a superior power intervened as an added variable. This common predictability pervaded all of Mill's thought with something akin to an Oedipal determinism.[26] His sociological theory tried to make real the power of mankind to choose and be unbound by universal laws. But he could never define a sense of freedom which would liberate him from Philosophical Necessitarianism. Perhaps his choice of the Oedipal metaphor to convey the sense of the extreme of fatalism reveals something of the emotional source of the hold of determinism upon Mill.

It was in his *Political Economy* above all that Mill explicated what he thought was the scientific basis for social choice; he drew the distinction between the laws of production with their necessitarian character and the laws of distribution which were voluntarist. Mankind, rescued from sociological fatalism, was acknowledged to be able to choose the kind of society it wanted:

The laws and conditions of the production of wealth, partake of the character of physical truths. There is nothing optional or arbitrary in them ...

It is not so with the Distribution of Wealth. That is a matter of human institution solely. The things once there, mankind, individually or collectively, can do with

26 Freud in 1880 translated a volume of Mill which included his essays on the labour question, Harriet Taylor Mill's 'The Enfranchisement of Women.' Grote's *Plato*, and the posthumous writings on socialism. He did so at the request of Mill's Viennese friend and editor, Theodore Gomperz. Did Freud read the other translated volumes, and imbibe Mill's usage of the 'fatalism of the Oedipus'? In any case, Freud regarded Mill 'as perhaps the man of the century who best managed to free himself from the domination of customary prejudices.' (Ernest Jones, *The Life and Work of Sigmund Freud* [New York 1953], I, 55, 176) Apart from the essays on socialism, the contents of the volume Freud translated were drawn from Volume II of *Dissertations and Discussions*. Mill's views on the hatred-vector in revolutionary socialism clearly became the basis for Freud's analysis of communism. Compare Adelaide Weinberg, *Theodor Gomperz and John Stuart Mill* (Geneva 1963), 60

them as they like ... The rules by which it is determined, are what the opinions and feelings of the ruling portion of the community make them, and are very different in different ages and countries; and might be still more different, if mankind so chose.[27]

Thus, the law of diminishing returns was, according to Mill, essentially a law of chemistry and physics stated with reference to agricultural technology; the laws of distribution, on the other hand, bore the stamp of men's varying choices. Mill drew on his own experience and knowledge of Indian affairs to illustrate how human choices could be made among diverse possible social systems. The British authorities had introduced different social systems in India; sometimes they displaced an oligarchy of usurpers and collected the taxes directly; in other cases they decided to create landed aristocracies; and in still others they co-operated with the representatives of village communities to arrest social change. Thus, human choice had been efficacious in deciding among the alternatives to the existent system of land ownership.[28]

If choices were genuine, mankind might then choose to progress rather than retrogress or stagnate. The incubus of sociological necessitarianism would be lifted. Yet, choice remained a kind of surd in Mill's sociological theory. For a sociology of choices always was at hand in his own terms to subsume them under causal laws. Mill strongly rejected the doctrine, akin to the Marxian, that 'the forces ... on which the greater political phenomena depend, are not amenable to the direction of politicians or philosophers.' According to this doctrine of sociological necessitarianism, 'the government of a country, it is affirmed, is in all substantial respects, fixed and determined beforehand by the state of a country in regard to the distribution of the elements of social power.'[29] Choice, according to such a doctrine, was the experience of a social epiphenomenon; the deliberations of philosophers never liberated the so-called choices from their determinants of social power. 'Whatever is the strongest power in society will obtain the governing authority ... A nation, therefore, cannot choose its form of government.' And James Mill had long previously analyzed the situation of a country divided into a ruling class and a subject class as one in which the members of the former had sympathies almost exclusively for themselves.

To this doctrine of economic determinism, Mill replied that purely ethical convictions, contravening the material interests of economic and social power, did intervene at critical junctures to transcend the latter: 'It was not by any

27 *Principles*, CW, II, 199–200
28 'Mr. Maine on Village Communities,' *Fortnightly Review*, ns IX, 1871, 554–5
29 *Representative Government*, 12. The action of the British people in abolishing the slave trade and in emancipating the slaves was, Mill wrote, ' a cause in which we not only had no interest, but which was contrary to our pecuniary interest ...' (*Dissertations and Discussions*, III, 180)

changes in the distribution of material interest, but by the spread of moral convictions that negro slavery has been put an end to in the British Empire and elsewhere.' The emancipation of the Russian serfs was, he felt, another decision which transcended material interests. Then wrote Mill: 'It is what men think, that determines how they act ...'[30] Even on his own showing, however, it was very rare that men's thoughts contravened their economic interests. For as he affirmed in *On Liberty*: 'Wherever there is an ascendant class, a large portion of the morality of the country emanates from its class interests ...'[31]

And, indeed, was that segment of men's ideas which transcended material interests free from causal determination? Were acts which transcended selfishness likewise choices in the sense of transcending causal laws? There were moments in the world's history, as in the February Revolution of 1848 in France, when it seemed to Mill that there appeared 'that almost unheard-of-phenomenon – unselfish politicians'; decisions then seemed to become choices rather than the resultants of polygons of social forces.[32] One might argue that the causal processes of individual psychology would account for these materially transcending actions. But there was no causal account at hand to explain how these idealistic motives, so powerless ordinarily, could have persisted in human history to shape its outlines and demarcate its future development. The instinct of domination was so much more forceful; hatred, selfishness, and brutality were so omnipresent that one asked: How had this puny vector of aspiration to truth and fellow-feeling survived in this welter of barbarian forces? That civilization had risen as far as it had against the evil inscribed in man's animal nature seemed a cosmo-historical fact of such improbable proportions that its actual occurrence defied the categories of sociological understanding. Thus it was that Mill was driven toward a sociological theology.

Mill's last essay, on theism, 'dismayed his disciples,' wrote John Morley. It was a natural conclusion, however, to his lifetime of sociological reflections. Mill had survived troughs of despair, such times as when he found human beings so abhorrent that he speculated with a certain pleasure upon the conditions under which there might take place a 'universal & simultaneous suicide of the whole human race.'[33] He had reflected on how beautiful the English environment would be but for its people: 'The nuisance of England is the English.'[34] Nonetheless, this human race seemed somehow to have surmounted

30 J.S. Mill, *Representative Government*, 15. James Mill, *Analysis of the Phenomena of the Human Mind*, 2nd ed. (London 1869), II, 275n
31 *On Liberty*, 16
32 'Vindication of the French Revolution of February 1848,' *Dissertations and Discussions*, II, 337
33 Letter to Harriet Mill, 30 Dec. 1854, CW, XIV, 272
34 Letter to Harriet Mill, 2 Jan. 1855, CW, XIV, 277

partially and periodically the trammels of its heredity and circumstances. Man had fashioned for himself, wrote Mill, 'a second nature, far better and more unselfish than he was created with.'[35] The virtues – courage, cleanliness, truthtelling – were all conquests of instinct; man evolved not through conforming to nature, but from his resolve to amend it, to challenge the maleficient powers. Whence, however, did he derive the resolve to challenge his own given character and status in animal existence? There was the feeling, Mill wrote, that in such an effort 'we may be co-operating with the unseen Being to whom we owe all that is enjoyable in life.' This God was a Limited God, not omnipotent. To his closest disciples Mill seemed suddenly and inexplicably to have subscribed to a Manichaean theology. Yet Mill found himself drawn to such postulates by processes of thought not dissimilar to those which have moved such scientists as Einstein, Bohr, Heisenberg, Russell. Einstein discerned the counterpart of Spinoza's Substance in the all-embracing simple laws of nature; Niels Bohr was moved in his conception of physical quanta by a vision of Kierkegaardian stages; Heisenberg and Max Born sought to realize conceptions of free will; while Russell hoped that a Kropotkinite anarchism prevailed at least among the world of logical atoms. In a similar sense, Mill found himself affirming a meta-sociological postulate: 'a battle is constantly going on, in which the humblest human creature is not incapable of taking some part, between the powers of good and those of evil, and in which every even the smallest help to the right side has its value in promoting the very slow and often almost insensible progress by which good is gradually gaining ground from evil ...' This postulate in Mill's view was 'the most animating and invigorating thought which can inspire a human creature,' and he allowed that it might be grounded in a hope which reached toward the supernatural.[36]

Thus Mill at the close of the utilitarian cycle moved toward views which his father James Mill had set aside seventy-five years earlier. John Stuart Mill regarded himself as 'one of the very few examples, in this country, of one who has not thrown off religious belief, but never had it ...'[37] The father had 'after many struggles' painfully shed his Presbyterian creed, and affirmed that 'concerning the origin of things nothing whatever can be known.' He had, however, kept open for consideration 'the Manichaean theory of a Good and an Evil Principle, struggling against each other for the government of the universe ...'[38] And the son now felt that such an inarticulate premise was adumbrated in his experience; the sociologist's inverse deductive method, the laws

35 'Theism,' cw, x, 459
36 Ibid., 488–9
37 *Autobiography*, 27–8. Bain, however, writes that 'John as a little boy, went to church; his maiden aunt remembered taking him, and hearing him say in his enthusiastic way "that the two greatest books were Homer and the Bible." ' (*James Mill*, 90)
38 *Autobiography*, 25–6

of mind, and the empirical sociological laws, required the intervening meta-sociological principle of a Limited God.

Mill's sociological Manichaeanism, moreover, was not a sudden aberration of old age. He had used its vocabulary and metaphors spontaneously at the outset of the American Civil War when he had pleaded that England should not for the sake of cotton render aid to the Confederacy and make 'Satan victorious'; the Southern secessionists, he wrote, were undertaking 'to do the devil's work.'[39] And, indeed, a Manichaean world-view has been a largely unspoken axiom of sociologists; only Mill had the courage to articulate it. Physicists such as Einstein might find in the conception of God a regulative principle leading to the discovery of simple, mathematical laws. Is this the way God would have done it? was the question Einstein always asked. Not so, however, with social reality. The sociologist asks as well: How would social reality have been contrived if Satan had had his share in designing it? If God provides a methodological regulative criterion in physical science, Satan provides a partial one in social science. Malthus seeing disaster latent in every happiness of man, Marx and Engels writing of history as a goddess demanding human sacrifices, Weber describing a rationalization of life which made people ever more disenchanted, Pareto seeing idealists pursuing illusions in an endless circulation of élites, all shared a common standpoint with Mill who brooded in 1848 that 'it is questionable if all the mechanical inventions yet made have lightened the days' toil of any human being.'[40]

Indeed, Mill's Manichaeanism led him to enunciate what was perhaps his most original sociological theorem – his theory of the stationary state. The evolution of society, according to Mill, has an upper limit: 'It must always have been seen, more or less distinctly, by political economists, that the increase of wealth is not boundless: that at the end of what they term the progressive state lies the stationary state, that all progress in wealth is but a postponement of this, and that each step in advance is an approach to it. We have now been led to recognise that this ultimate goal is at all times near enough to be fully in view ...' Gone was Condorcet's vision of the indefinite progress of man. His was a law of sociological impotence (to use the term of the physicist Edmund Whittakers): 'This impossibility of ultimately avoiding the stationary state – this irresistible necessity that the stream of human industry should finally spread itself out into an apparently stagnant sea ...'[41] In essence, Mill derived this theorem from the simple consideration that the practice and development of the industrial arts always involved the depletion of energy-resources. The stationary state was a corollary of the second law of thermodynamics applied to the closed system of the planet Earth. But where

39 'The Contest in America,' *Dissertations and Discussions*, III, 181
40 *Principles*, CW, III, 756
41 Ibid., 752

other economists and sociologists such as Marx paid homage to the everlasting development of the forces of production and industrial civilization, and would have regarded the stationary state as too remote to enter the sociological purview, Mill avowed himself frankly as not charmed by 'the trampling, crushing, elbowing, and treading on each other's heels, which form the existing type of social life.'[42] He wanted solitude and the preservation of natural beauty. To Marx who wrote of 'the idiocy of rural life' he counterposed the imbecility of urban life, and he spent his most joyous days in botanizing, in long tramps, which led to 'frequent notes and short papers' in the *Phytologist*, an obscure journal for botanical collectors.[43] The Limited God of Mill had his counterpart in the finitude of energy resources. If the human species must finally vanish, its one hope was at least to postpone that not distant event by the wise cultivation of a stationary state, stationary in capital, population, and the productive arts.[44]

Is Mill's theory of the stationary state a viable one? Mill felt that in the stationary state 'there would be as much scope as ever for all kinds of mental culture'; the art of living, the arts and sciences would indeed, he argued, improve even more 'when minds ceased to be engrossed by the art of getting on.'[45] What Mill failed to pursue, however, were the social consequences of a stationary state. For such a society would probably evoke the most intense generational conflicts; bereft of the sense of open frontiers and opportunities, the young would expend their energies of aggression and hatred even more unidirectionally upon the old. In pre-historic stationary societies, the middle-aged men evidently died by violence.[46] The Chinese stationary society, which Mill studied, was characterized by a severe discipline imposed on the young; the sciences and arts of living were virtually transfixed. A stationary society would be one without the experience of renaissances. The condition for healthy social existence is that it be revivified for the young with the breath of fresh new industries and material obstacles; otherwise aggressive energies might turn inward, toward self-destruction.

42 Ibid., 754
43 Henry Trimen, 'His Botanical Studies,' H. Fox Bourne, ed., *John Stuart Mill – His Life and Works* (Boston 1873), 44. Mill's botanizing was throughout his life the avocation in which he found the most complete pleasure. He first became a plant-collector during his sojourn in Southern France, 1820–1, 'the happiest six months of my youth.' He would pursue it intensely day after day in arduous climbs and hikes whenever he could. When the 'battle of the Barricades' was raging in 1832 during the crisis of the Reform bill, Mill was off botanizing quietly at Highgate. He told Herbert Spencer his 'murderous propensities' were 'confined to the vegetable world.' (Anna Jean Mill, ed., *John Mill's Boyhood Visit to France* [Toronto 1960], 65)
44 *Principles*, cw, iii, 752–7
45 Ibid., 756
46 See Carlo M. Cipolla, *The Economic History of World Population*, rev. ed. (Middlesex 1964), 74

Moreover, every wave of human improvement has been founded on a contemporaneous expansion of capital. It is sociologically doubtful that the arts
of life could progress without such a corresponding material progress. And
with the depletion of energy resources, a society would be unable to maintain
its stationary position without progress in the use of its industrial capital and
available resources.

The author of *On Liberty* feared slackening and stagnation; the theorist
of the stationary state, however, regarded it as the best compromise with
Manichaean reality that the human race might hope to achieve. Here was
still another reason why Mill was unable to write his sociology. Not the contradictions of Victorian England were laid bare in his thought but rather the
eternal unresolvable oppositions within all human life.

Some might say that Mill's theory of the stationary state was a reflection of
the death-instinct which periodically waxed strongly in him.[47] To which Mill
could reply that he alone in the nineteenth century had not flinched from
drawing the ultimate consequences of Thomas Malthus's mode of thought.[48]
And perhaps the Limited God, if not himself possessed of a death-instinct,
was finally incapable of sustaining the human race against the harsh odds of
the material universe.

Withal, it is probably true that Mill's sociological pessimism, his pervasive
sense of pending exhaustion, had its highly personal sources as well. His upbringing by his father had so constrained him that he wrote poignantly: 'Let
any man call to mind what he himself felt on emerging from boyhood ... Was
it not like the physical effect of taking off a heavy weight ..? Did he not feel
twice as much alive ..?'[49] Above all, the strains of the two decades of his sexual
repression with respect to Harriet Taylor had exacted their toll. To mitigate
these strains, Mill cultivated a mocking attitude not unlike Harriet's toward
those who made much of the strength of the sexual drive. He railed at those
who said it was difficult to control the sexual appetite.[50] He declared that the
possibility of progress itself depended on the reduction of sexuality, that no
great improvement in human life could be looked for 'so long as the animal
instinct of sex occupies the absurdly disproportionate place it does therein';
and he anticipated confidently that this passion would become 'with men, as
it is already with a large number of women, completely under the control of

47 Leslie Stephen felt that Mill's theory of the stationary state was rather a temporary
protest than a settled conviction. (*The English Utilitarians* [London 1900], III, 200)
48 When young Oliver Wendell Holmes, Jr, visited Mill in 1866, Mill took him to a
meeting of the Political Economy Club where the subject for discussion was 'whether
the financial policy of England should be governed by the prospective exhaustion of
coal in H years as predicted by Jevons ...' (Mark De Wolfe Howe, *Justice Oliver
Wendell Holmes: The Shaping Years* [Cambridge, Mass. 1957], 226–7)
49 *The Subjection of Women* (London 1869), 180–1
50 Bain, *John Stuart Mill*, 149

reason – that is, as disciplined as he was in emulation of Harriet.[51] He persuaded the historian George Grote to delete from the Preface to his *History* the words 'feminine' and 'masculine' in the discussion of the aspects of the ancient Greek character. He showed an unusual sympathy toward the mediaeval institution of a celibate clergy.[52] Mill's *Autobiography* impressed Freud as 'so prudish or so ethereal that one could never gather from it that human beings consist of men and women, and that this distinction is the most significant one that exists.'[53]

Yet, periodically, resentment against the régime of sexual attenuation would break forth. He had ridiculed as a young man the search of the Saint-Simonians for 'la femme libre,' which had indeed sent them to a quest among the harems of Constantinople. But in his old age, his final tribute to the Saint-Simonians was to 'the boldness and freedom from prejudice with which they treated the subject of the family, the most important of any, and needing more fundamental alterations than remain to be made in any other great social institution, but on which scarcely any reformer has the courage to touch.'[54] He responded with dislike to the statue of the Venus de Medici, saying 'the expression of the face is complete old maidism.'[55] Above all, in his unconscious he argued, thought not very successfully, with Harriet's high discipline. He wrote her an account of a memorable dream: 'I was seated at a table like a table d'hôte, with a woman at my left hand & a young man opposite – the young man said, quoting somebody for the saying, "there are two excellent & rare things to find in a woman, a sincere friend and a sincere Magdalen." I answered "the best would be to find both in one" – on which the woman said "no, that would be *too* vain" – whereupon I broke out "do you suppose when one speaks of what is good in itself, one must be thinking of one's own paltry self-interest? no, I spoke of what is abstractedly good and admirable." '[56] Mill finally recognized explicitly that his father James together with his fellow Associationists obliterated sexuality and the biological basis of emotions from psychology. James Mill had dismissed the whole subject delicately with one sentence: 'The affection of the husband and wife is, in its origin, that of two persons of different sex, and need not be further analysed.'[57] By contrast, John wrote: 'there is evidently in all our emotions an animal part ... which

51 Letter to Lord Amberley, 2 Feb. 1870, CW, XVII, 1693; Diary entry, 26 March, in Hugh Elliot, *Letters of John Stuart Mill* (London 1910), II, 382
52 Bain, *John Stuart Mill*, 78, 86. J.S. Mill, 'Michelet's History of France,' *Dissertations and Discussions*, II, 159
53 Ernest Jones, *The Life and Work of Sigmund Freud* (New York 1953), I, 176
54 Letter to Carlyle, 11 & 12 April 1833, CW, XII, 150; *Autobiography*, 101
55 Letter to Harriet Mill, 8 June 1855, CW, XIV, 480
56 Letter to Harriet Mill, 17 Feb. 1857, CW, XV, 523–4; *John Stuart Mill and Harriet Taylor*, 254
57 James Mill, *Analysis*, II, 218–19

these philosophers have passed without any attempt at explanation.'[58] The phenomenon of 'intense bodily suffering,' the 'screams, groans, contortions, etc.,' the experience and manifestations of Fear, were systematically omitted by the Associationist.

Mill's own experience, borne too stoically, had left him imprinted with a permanent dislike for human society. One wonders finally whether Mill at the last would have interceded with any enthusiasm with his Limited God to spare the human race. He could scarcely engage in the kind of panoramic mythologizing and ideologizing to which Karl Marx could surrender himself; he lacked Marx's capacity to disregard doubts, and to rely on dialectical paste-paper to bridge the transitions between the stages of society as well as collapsing arguments.

There are signs that the father James Mill felt at times a restiveness with his own life and was rebellious with the austere Calvinist asceticism which still underlay his Benthamite associations of pleasure. He was strangely drawn to the personality of the South American revolutionary general, Francisco de Miranda. As the French Saint-Simonians later fed the exotic longings of his son, so General Miranda delighted the Calvinist calculating utilitarian with his effervescence and spontaneity. The general was famed for exploits which had likened him to Casanova; the lover of the admired Delphine de Custine, who had escaped the guillotine which annihilated her family, he had been characterized by the Emperor Napoleon as 'a Don Quixote except that he is quite sane.' Under Miranda's influence, James Mill felt himself fortified to reject his traditional religion. James worked together with the general on an article 'Emancipation of Spanish America,' published in 1809 in the *Edinburgh Review*. He rendered tribute to the general as one in whose 'breast the scheme of emancipation, if not first conceived, seems at least to have been first matured.'[59] Betrayed in the revolutionary war, Miranda died in 1816 in a Spanish dungeon. Meanwhile, James Mill had found in vicarious revolutionary participation an alleviation of the strains of a grey doctrine, a harsh Presbyterian upbringing, and an unhappy marriage. The son John repeated the pattern. The misfortune of James Mill's life was that he too had known a Harriet Taylor, but in his case their separation was inevitable. She was the daughter of the Scottish baron, Sir John Stuart, after whom James had named his son. James wrote about her as his son did of Harriet: 'besides being a beautiful woman, [she] was in point of intellect and disposition one of the most perfect human beings I have ever known.' They grew up and studied

---

58 'Bain's Psychology,' *Dissertations and Discussions*, III, 132–3
59 Bain, *James Mill*, 89. William Spence Robertson, *The Life of Miranda* (Chapel Hill 1929), II, 48–50; I, 57. Joseph F. Thorning, *Miranda: World Citizen* (Gainesville 1952), 126. George F. Kennan, *The Marquis de Custine and his Russia in 1839* (Princeton 1971), 3–4

together from childhood on, 'and were about the best friends that either of us ever had.' When she was dying, she spoke of James 'with almost her last breath.'[60] James Mill could never forget that his wife was not the one he loved. His utilitarianism was as much the outcome of a personal quarrel with society as his son's *On Liberty*.

Mill did try periodically to alleviate the pessimistic tendencies in his character and his sociological theory by partaking in the enthusiasm and fellowship of socialist movements. Nevertheless, in the final consideration, he always refrained from any overt commitment to socialism, and at the time of his death was writing what even in its fragmentary form was the most powerful critique of socialism written in the nineteenth century. As a young man, Mill had long, eager discussions with the young French Saint-Simonian Jew, Gustave d'Eichthal, whom he admired almost as much as his father had venerated the Dutch-English Jew David Ricardo. He shared the revolutionary zeal of the Saint-Simonians, and almost became one of them; tactical considerations alone, he said, kept him from enlistment in their ranks. Meanwhile, he awaited the revolutionary hurricane:

And if the hour were yet come for England ... I know not that I should not renounce everything and become, not one of you, but as you.

But our 10 août, our 20 juin, and perhaps our 18 Brumaire, are yet to come. And which of us will be left standing when the hurricane has blown over, Heaven only knows.[61]

This period of high revolutionary zeal was also that of his growing involvement with Mrs Harriet Taylor, the period of his own most intense rebellion against the authority of his father James Mill. He wrote in 1831 to his close friend Sterling with the swathes of the revolutionary intellectual: 'until the whole of the existing institutions of society are levelled with the ground, there will be nothing for a wise man to do ...' And he looked forward with pleasure to what later would be called the 'physical liquidation' of the English middle class and its intellectual advocates. It will be recalled that the father James was an unashamed admirer of the middle class.[62] The son, however, wrote that if only 'a few dozens of persons' were salvaged to be 'missionaries of the great truths' for posterity, he would not care though a revolution were to ex-

60 Graham Wallas, *The Life of Francis Place: 1771–1854* (4th ed., London 1925), 70–1
61 Letter to Gustave d'Eichthal, 30 Nov. 1831, cw, xii, 89
62 Letter to John Sterling, 20–22 Oct. 1831, cw, xii, 78. The 'class which is universally described as both the most wise and the most virtuous part of the community, the middle rank ... which gives to science, to art, and to legislation itself their most distinguished ornaments ...' (James Mill, *An Essay on Government* [reprinted, Cambridge 1937], 71–2)

terminate every person in Great Britain and Ireland who has £500 a year. Many very amiable persons would perish, but what is the world the better for such amiable persons?'[63] Mill's ideological, Messianic mood coincided with his peaks of aggressive resentment. But with his awesome strength of character, he always regained his rationality and independence of judgment. He finally estimated the Saint-Simonians as having a 'narrow & bigoted understanding, & a sordid & contracted disposition,' and being so fixated on the notion that history was governed by a unidirectional progressive law that they forgot it could go backwards.[64] He welcomed the advent of the International Working-men's Association in 1864 when Karl Marx, to please the British labour leaders, allowed himself to write like a Millite rather than a Marxist. But when the secretary of its Nottingham branch sent Mill its literature, he responded that, though he 'warmly approved' of its principles: 'What advantage is there in designating the doctrines of the Association by such a title as "the principles of the political and social Revolution?" '[65] Mill in his *Autobiography* classed himself and Harriet 'under the general designation of Socialists.' During the intervening years, however, he kept himself well-informed through reading the journals of the Association.[66] His misgivings concerning socialism deepened. He had always been troubled by what he saw as 'the social problem of the future' – how to preserve 'the greatest individual liberty' within the framework of a socialist society.[67] He now however observed those whom he called 'the revolutionary socialists,' and concluded that the motives which impelled them were malevolent. Those 'who play this game,' he wrote, 'unconfirmed as yet by any experimental verification ... and [who] would brave the frightful bloodshed ... must have a serene confidence in their own wisdom on the one hand and a recklessness of other people's sufferings on the other, which Robespierre and St. Just, hitherto the typical instances— ... scarcely came up to.' For Mill stated clearly what he took to be the tenets of 'the revolutionary socialists'; they were exactly those of Marx. They proposed on the economic side, wrote Mill, 'the management of the whole productive resources of the country by one central authority,' while on the political side 'their purpose' was 'that the working classes, or somebody in their behalf, should take possession of all the property of the country, and administer it for the general benefit.' Thus, the three elements of the revolutionary socialist programme were

63 Letter to Sterling, 20–2 Oct. 1831, cw, xii, 84
64 Letter to Gustave d'Eichthal, 8 Oct. 1829, cw, xii, 37
65 Edward S. Mason, *The Paris Commune: An Episode in the History of the Socialist Movement* (New York 1930), 50
66 Letter to Georg Brandes, 4 March 1872, cw, xvii, 1874–5. A subscription on Mill's behalf to the journal *Progress* was made by Cowell Stepney, an eccentric blind millionaire who was a member of the International's General Council. (See James Guillaume, *L'Internationale: Documents et Souvenirs* [Paris 1905], i, 139.)
67 *Autobiography*, 138

total central planning, the alleged ownership of the national property by the working class, and its achievement by a revolutionary act. Their avowed aim was 'to substitute the new rule for the old at a single stroke, and to exchange the amount of good realized under the present system, and its large possibilities of improvement, for a plunge without any preparation into the most extreme form.' The programme had 'great elements of popularity,' Mill noted, not shared by 'the more cautious and reasonable form of Socialism.' For it made its appeal above all to the emotions of hatred. This, then, was the ethological middle principle of revolutionary socialism: 'for if appearances can be trusted, the animating principle of too many of the revolutionary Socialists is hate.' One might undertake to excuse their absorption in hatred by invoking their dialectical belief, in Mill's words, 'that out of chaos would arise a better Kosmos.' But this entirely overlooked, wrote Mill, 'that chaos is the very most unfavourable position for setting out in the construction of a Kosmos, and that many ages of conflict, violence, and tyrannical oppression of the weak by the strong must intervene ...' In the character of the dialectical revolutionists Mill perceived a readiness to destroy the world if it could not be changed: 'its apostles could have only the consolation that the order of society as it exists now would have perished first, and all who benefit by it would be involved in the common ruin ...'[68]

The leaders of the English workingmen alone, Mill observed with some pride, refused to be drawn into the destructivism of the European revolutionary socialists. 'The leaders of the English working-men – whose delegates at the congresses of Geneva and Bâle contributed much the greatest part of such practical common sense as was shown there – are not likely to begin deliberately by anarchy ...'[69] The congresses of the International Workingmen's As-

---

68 *Chapters on Socialism*, cw, v, 737, 749
69 Ibid., 709. George Odger, the secretary of the London Trades Council, supported Mill increasingly while he denounced the intransigence of the General Council of the International, 'the most unfit persons I have ever come in contact with to represent the working classes.' George Howell, who in 1871 became secretary to the Parliamentary committee of the Trades Union Congress, advised workers to 'get Mill on Liberty and Political Economy. There are many other works, but go to the fountain head at once.' Marx fought Mill's influence in the labour movement by supporting the Land and Labour League against Mill's Land Tenure Reform Association. Mill in turn deplored 'the furious and declamatory virtue' of the former's resolutions. (Compare Royden Harrison, *Before the Socialists: Studies in Labour and Politics, 1861–1881* [London 1965], 234, 143, 223)

Mill always exerted his logical powers to dissuade the English labour leaders from being captivated by revolutionary rhetoric and violent postures. In March 1867 he wrote to William Randal Cremer in sharp disapproval of the calls for force which the Reform League was making to secure enactment of the bill for enfranchisement. Ultimate success in Britain, Mill said, could only be obtained 'by a succession of steps.' No justification for 'revolutionary expedients' existed in the British case (cw,

sociation in September 1866 and 1869 had been the scene of a struggle between Marx's faction and the followers of Proudhon. Marx's initial programme for the International, adopted at Geneva, was rather moderate,
placing the empasis on achieving the eight-hour day and a system of public
education; it stressed, however, the importance of trade unions as agencies for
'complete emancipation' whereas the Proudhonists advocated co-operative
associations and denigrated the recourse to strikes. At Basel, however, the
legendary figure of Mikhail Bakunin emerged to lead the most formidable
challenge to Marx's 'centralized Communism' on behalf of anarchy; Bakunin
indeed won majorities against Marx in the actual voting on resolutions. The
English trade-union leaders supported Marx's proposals as against Bakuninist
anarchy, yet they too were unhappy with the underlying note of Marx's
'centralized Communism.' Mill stood with such trade unionists as Odger,
Cremer, and Applegarth, against both Marx and Bakunin; the English trade
unionists soon dissociated themselves from the International. Marx at the last
Congress of the International in 1872 insulted all the English labour leaders
by saying publicly that 'almost every recognised leader of English working
men was sold to Gladstone, Morley, Dilke and others.'[70] The English labour-

XVI, 1247–8). He argued in September 1865 with George Howell, who placed an
inordinate faith in the strike weapon; where strikes were successful in the generality
of trades, said Mill, there would be a general rise in prices, which would be of 'no
benefit to the labouring classes' (CW, XVI, 1102). But he subscribed in 1869 to the
Labour Representation League on whose executive Howell was active (CW, XVII,
1673). He vigorously supported Odger in his efforts to win election to Parliament:
'No one has taken a warmer interest than I have in the candidatures of working men
in general & Mr Odger in particular, & I believe Mr O. is well aware of this,' Mill
wrote in 1870 (ibid., 1688). And when Odger lost again in February 1870 Mill
still wrote him a letter of congratulation (ibid., 1697). He wrote in terms of admiration of the English labour leaders, and in December 1867 advised Thomas Hare,
the exponent of proportional representation: 'if you could make a convert of even
one such man as Odger, or Cremer, or Howell – the gain would be immense' (CW,
XVI, 1342). He introduced to Odger his 'very old friend,' the former Saint-Simonian,
Gustave d'Eichthal, when the latter was visiting Britain in May 1871 (CW, XVII,
1816). It was Odger who rose to commend Mill at the celebrated meeting when
Mill, a candidate for Parliament, acknowledged that he had written that the English
working class were 'generally liars.' When the 'vehement applause' subsided, Ogder
said that the working class 'wanted friends, not flatterers,' and were grateful to one
who spoke sincerely of their faults (Mill, Autobiography, 168). To John Hales, the
secretary of the General Council of the International, Mill wrote on 28 May 1871
saying that if any demonstration 'could arrest or mitigate the horrors now being per-
petrated at Paris' there was hardly anything he would not do; but he saw no such
hope (CW, XVII, 1821–2). He gave his support to preventing the dismissal from
University College of Professor E.S. Beesly, the courageous Comtist professor of
classics who in 1867 had spoken in defence of the trade unions (CW, XVI, 1297).
70 Henry Collins and Chimen Abramsky, Karl Marx and the British Labour Movement:
Years of the First International. Socialists and trade unionists generally admired the

ites never forgave him for that slur. The enfranchisement of 1867 had opened up to the British working class the prospect of using Parliament to achieve social reforms; thus seeds which were being planted for the Labour party were far more Millite than Marxist. Mill's last chapters on socialism must be regarded as essentially an evaluation founded on the added experience of the English trade unionists with the International. He knew that they had been at odds with all the ideologists, with Marx, Bakunin, and Proudhon. The too generous hopes of Mill in 1848 for the principle of association were now basically amended in the light of this new phenomenon of the revolutionary ideologists – this permeation of socialism with a ferocity and hatred which Mill had not previously foreseen.

No doubt Karl Marx was informed through their various common associates, the labour leaders and the positivist intellectuals, of Mill's opinion of 'revolutionary socialists.' Nothing else would explain Marx's outburst against John Stuart Mill in the closing days of the International, on 16 April 1872, months after Mill had protested the sanguinary suppression of the Paris Communards.[71] Mill still continued to place some hope in a moderate, experi-

record of John Stuart Mill as a member of Parliament. William Morris said Mill had been 'a real success in Parliament.' (See James Mavor, *My Windows on the Street of the World* [London, 1922], i, 209.) J. George Eccarius, Marx's collaborator on the General Council, wrote: 'As a member of Parliament Mill conducted himself in exemplary fashion, and showed he had the courage to come forward in the interest of the working class to oppose both the aristocracy as well as the gelfackelbourgeoisie. His political behaviour is in contradiction with his economic philosophy.' (*Eines Arbeiters Widerlegung der National-okonomischen Lehren John Stuart Mill's* [Berlin 1869], iv) On the reaction of the British labour leaders to Marx's insult, compare Boris Nicolaievsky and Otto Maenchen-Helfen, *Karl Marx: Man and Fighter*, tr. Gwenda David and Eric Mosbacher (Philadelphia 1936), 360. John Hales moved a vote of censure against Marx in the British Federal Council; it was adopted. An amendment charging Marx with political deception got an equally divided vote. (See Franz Mehring, *Karl Marx: The Story of His Life*, tr. Edward Fitzgerald [New York 1935], 518.)

71 Marx ridiculed what he called 'John Stuart Mill's compendium of political economy,' and the proposal, for instance, that the state should lend capital to co-operative societies, a proposal made by Ferdinand Lassalle and in keeping with Mill's idea. (*The General Council of the First International, 1871–1872: Minutes* [Moscow nd], 160) Marx's ire was especially directed against Henry Fawcett, professor of Political Economy at Cambridge, and Mill's disciple. Fawcett, after studying the documents of the International and after 'frequent conversations with many of its members,' gave a series of lectures in 1872 against its principles. Though himself, like Mill, an advocate of co-operation on the Rochdale model, Fawcett argued that the effort to realize the programme of the International would make for a 'weakening and lessening of individual responsibility' and a decline of the 'industrial virtues.' (Henry Fawcett, 'The Nationalisation of the Land,' *Fortnightly Review*, ns LXXII, [1872], 627, 637, 638. Leslie Stephen, *Life of Henry Fawcett*, 5th ed. [London 1886], 158–66, 470)

mental, piecemeal socialism which could 'be brought into operation pro-
gressively, and ... prove its capabilities by trial.' With sympathy toward com-
munitarians (exemplified in later years by Martin Buler and William Morris),
Mill looked to modest efforts 'on the scale of a village community.' Aware, no
doubt, that experiment had often shown that such associations deteriorated
into village tyrannies, Mill as a pluralist noted the aim for 'the multiplication
of such self-acting units.'[72] Perhaps individual liberty might be safeguarded
in a society of competing communal associations. Yet, in 1849 Mill had affirmed his belief that co-operative associations would not prove themselves as
efficient as competitive societies.[73]

The notion of central planning itself, 'the very idea of conducting the whole
industry of a country by direction from a single centre,' was in Mill's view
'obviously chimerical.'[74] 'Communistic management' would be 'less favourable than private management to that striking out of new paths'; it would
lack the venturesomeness 'generally indispensable to great improvements in the
economic condition of mankind ...'[75] It would of necessity decide 'in a more
or less arbitrary manner' those questions which 'on the present system' for all
its imperfections decide themselves spontaneously – that is, in predominant
accord with rational criteria.[76] Thus in a few sentences Mill raised those
problems concerning the irrationality of socialist economy which have haunted
the halls of socialist proponents of later generations, and whose phantom still
attends the sessions of the Soviet Planning Council. Curiously, the corollary
latent in Mill's analysis was that for a communist society taken in isolation the
optimal equilibrium would be that of a stationary state. Mill indeed had written Harriet Taylor in 1849 that the objection to communism that it would
make life 'a kind of dead level' could never be taken away.[77] Nevertheless, he
always clung to elements of a socialistic ethic even though his analysis dis-

72 *Chapters on Socialism*, cw, v, 737
73 'The French Revolution of 1848 and its Assailants,' *Dissertations and Discussions*,
    II, 394
74 *Chapters on Socialism*, cw, v, 748
75 Ibid., 742
76 Ibid., 743
77 Letter to Harriet Taylor, 21 Feb. 1849, cw, xiv, 11. Mill's concern for Harriet
    Taylor's approbation led him to mute his criticism of communism. In revising his
    Political Economy in 1849 he had stated the objections to communism that he
    thought were valid, but he wrote in conciliatory fashion: 'if you do not think so, I
    certainly will not print it.' (Ibid.) Mill argued with her that she 'greatly' overrated
    'the ease of making people unselfish,' and that even if they had absolute power, 'all
    our plans would fail from the impossibility of finding fit instruments.' (21 March
    1849, ibid., 19). This passage in my opinion is not given sufficient weight by H.O.
    Pappé in his *John Stuart Mill and the Harriet Taylor Myth* (Melbourne 1960), 40.
    Not until Harriet was long dead was Mill able to bring all his critical acumen to
    bear on the socialist proposals.

sociated socialist society from any law of progress with which it had been joined so facilely by socialists.

Meanwhile, however, Mill finally rejected the notion that the misery of the working classes was increasing under capitalism. This was one of the 'Socialist exaggerations,' he wrote. 'The present system is not, as many Socialists believe, hurrying us into a state of general indigence and slavery from which only Socialism can save us. The evils and injustices suffered under the present system are great, but they are not increasing; on the contrary, the general tendency is towards their slow diminution.'[78] He still looked for guidance to the moral principles of socialism, but doubted whether in the trials of experiment the power of the 'higher' motives would be sufficient even in a large minority to sustain such a society.[79] It had become clear to Mill that for the revolutionary socialists the experience of the revolutionary leap and the opportunities it afforded for the release of aggression was the primary purpose; they disliked an experimental approach toward socialist ventures precisely because it deprived them of the chance for revolutionary experience. In 1849 Mill had charged that the fear of socialism drove the bourgeoisie into an 'insane terror.'[80] At the end of his life he might have amended this statement to make central instead the fear not so much of socialism as of socialists, such as Blanqui, whose aim was the savouring of revolutionary dictatorship far more than the improvement of the human lot. What the sources of this compulsion for revolutionary experience might be was a problem that was left unsolved for a more developed science of ethology.

Mill was, it must be remembered, part of that corps of British sociologists whose ideas were largely shaped by their experience in the administration of India. Though Mill's work was confined to the London headquarters of the East India Company, he was dealing with the same problems that Sir Henry Maine and James Fitzjames Stephen met in India directly.[81] The administrative experience provided Mill's judgment with a ballast which Marx and Comte never had. He knew the inefficiencies and arbitrariness in the bureaucratic administration in a way the bookmen-revolutionists never did. With respect to problems where he lacked that ballast, Mill too tended to veer toward radical proposals otherwise foreign to him. He, for instance, like his friend John Cairnes, demanded in Abolitionist fashion that all Negro ex-slaves be given the right to vote at the end of the American Civil War. He

---

78 *Chapters on Socialism*, cw, v, 736

79 Ibid., 736, 741–2

80 *Dissertations and Discussions*, ii, 394

81 For twenty-three years Mill wrote almost every 'political' despatch of the East India Company; two huge volumes, five or six inches thick, were each year written by Mill alone. (See W.T. Thornton, 'His Career in the India House,' *John Stuart Mill*, ed. Fox Bourne [Boston 1873], 32.)

would have repudiated such a demand for the people of India whom he regarded as still in their 'nonage.' In the former case, he was moved by pure ethics; in the latter, he weighted ethics with sociological experience. Ethical zeal, at times, could obliterate Mill's social judgment. For instance, he finally opposed the secret ballot because he felt that all men should be fearless in character, and not afraid to say openly what they thought. But the Cooperative leader, George Jacob Holyoake, thought that Mill had forgotten that a secret ballot gave the average man his only chance to be independent – that Mill expected the average citizen to have the character of a John Stuart Mill.[82]

What then is Mill's place in the development of sociological science? His enduring greatness is as the conscience of science. Virtually alone he sought steadfastly to keep his sociology free from ideology. He articulated the problems which others repressed by a variety of devices. Where Marx and Engels projected a dialectical leap which would take human society from the kingdom of necessity to that of freedom, Mill, too honest to succumb to the allure of sociological metaphor, enquired into the threats which socialism would pose for individual liberty. While Weber built a whole theory of the origins of capitalism on a presumed psychological law that guilt-ridden people will embark more frequently upon technological innovation, Mill, with his analysis of the Calvinist character, would scarcely acquiesce to such an assumed law of mind. Where Durkheim as a Radical Republican exalted society and claimed that religion was society's worship of itself, Mill would observe that religious ideals provided a basis for the critique of every existing society; if religion was society's self-worship, then the tension between religion and society was unintelligible. Mill could never write a complete system of sociology because he alone would not confuse the subjective completeness of a narrowed mind with the objective completeness of sociological explanation.

That is why when we look for intellectual guidance today with respect to the problems of freedom in communist societies, the exhaustion of the environment, and the pressure of population, Mill is the only sociologist of the nineteenth century whose pages are not discoloured with the acid of bias. Others claiming to prefigure the law of history, were obsessed by the demon of making history; Mill held to the more modest ethic of acting as circumstances allowed on behalf of human happiness. In so doing, the 'saint of rationalism' held to the conception of scientific truth with an integrity which the prophet-ideologists never approached.

82 George Jacob Holyoake, *Bygones Worth Remembering* (London 1905), I, 276

Mill and Tocqueville on Liberty

JOSEPH HAMBURGER

John Stuart Mill, influential in many ways in his own time and since, might be said to be exerting his greatest influence just now. This judgment is particularly true of his essay *On Liberty*. Ever since publication it has had continuing appeal and authority among those seeking toleration and responsibly free expression, but it seems that only in our time have the full implications of Mill's argument been considered. Today when 'emancipation' and 'liberation' are words used to justify proposals for new social policies and novel life styles, we are bound to consider their possible connections with Mill's famous arguments. The question seems especially relevant because the quest for liberty is no longer confined to the political or economic realms, but, as Mill wished, is extended to considerations of the development of personality and all social institutions. In this sense it can be said that only in our time have Mill's practical teachings in *On Liberty* been taken seriously.

That Mill's rationale for liberty could come to be more persuasive and meaningful today than in previous generations would have been in accord with his plans, for during the last half of his life this was the kind of influence he hoped to achieve. This ambition to be influential on the thoughts and beliefs of future generations came only after 1840 – after he lost hope of having an immediate influence on his own generation. Until 1840, it will be recalled, he was engaged in politics, seeking an immediate impact. His greatest wish at that time was to be a member of Parliament – a wish that was incompatible with his appointment at India House. Since he could not be in the House of Commons, Mill sought to direct the ambitions and policies of the Radicals in Parliament by his journalism. His purpose was to provoke nothing less than a realignment of political parties in order to establish an independent Radical party led by his close associates. Realigned parties would reflect, respectively, the popular and the aristocratic interests in society, and ultimately their antagonism would lead to the democratization of the constitution. This scheme occupied Mill during the 1830s, however much he mixed its pursuit with purposes inspired by the writings of the Saint-Simonians and Coleridge.

His tactics and his dedication bore the marks of the doctrinaire politician. He was insistent that reform be fundamental, thorough, total, and he was entirely opposed to half-measures. The Radical party and no other was the agent by which reform was to be achieved. Consequently he was contemptuous of the moderate Left and its efforts, and was anxious to distinguish, indeed to separate, Radicals even from liberal Whigs. There was a willingness to be alone in virtuous isolation rather than compromise. Mill, like the other Philosophic Radicals, was convinced that an independent Radical party could be established and realignment could be effected. Believing that there was an underlying reality of class conflict and a latent radicalism in the populace that could be brought to the surface, he thought there was no great difficulty in transforming institutions and redefining party boundaries. The expectation that great changes could be quickly accomplished seemed reasonable because he thought his tactics were grounded in reality. Thus Mill could believe in what he called 'the practicability of Utopianism.'[1]

He was to be disappointed in this vision. Realignment did not take place; the Radical party foundered and dissolved. Contemporary observers thought his plans highly unrealistic. The Radicals were called 'irreconcilables.' It was not a propitious time for Radicalism, for the country was beginning an epoch during which it was to celebrate its predominantly centrist politics. The spirit of whiggism was infused into all parties, making them conciliatory, flexible, and compromising. There was instinctive opposition to doctrinairism, whether found on Right or Left, which became, as Professor Butterfield has pointed out, a national attitude.[2] In face of it, doctrinaire politicians were bound to have difficulty.

Mill now directed his ambition to other goals. About 1840, having given up his hope to establish a strong and independent Radical party, he shifted his energies, for he undertook to develop the ideas and beliefs that would shape the politics of a future generation. He decided that 'the progress of liberal opinions will again ... depend upon what is *said* & *written*, & no longer upon what is *done* ...'[3] Mill became the architect of a new world, as he sought to

1 'Rationale of Representation,' *London Review*, I, 1835, 367
2 *The Englishman and his History* (Cambridge 1944), 83, 87, 97–8, 137–8
3 Mill to Macvey Napier, 30 July 1841, *Collected Works*, XIII (Toronto 1963), 483. This turning away from active politics had been briefly anticipated in his outlook in about 1830–1.

visualize the kinds of institutions that would be suitable for mankind once it entered a new historical era in which the prevailing, established authorities and traditions would be without force. He now thought of himself as one whose task was 'to make new trains of thought intelligible.'[4] The 'mental regeneration' of Europe that he wanted to bring about was a stepping stone to this future.[5] And when he came to write *On Liberty* he was still reaching for this goal.

Mill's impact has been immense. Not that his designs for institutions have been implemented. But his attitudes to authority and his sense of the possibility and reasons for change, to say nothing of his particular arguments on these matters, have come to prevail among the liberal intelligentsia. Indeed, it is remarkable that the recurring themes found in the cultural milieu of these intellectuals can be identified in *On Liberty*. There we find Mill deeply critical of society. It was intolerant and bigoted; there was a pervasive Puritanism; it was dominated by a desire for upward mobility; it was indifferent to intellectual values; it gave sensitive persons a sense of being oppressed; men in the mass were characterless and mediocre, subject as they were to custom and standardization in the way they lived and in the formation of their desires.

Responding to these views, the intellectuals found in Mill the message that they should be opposed to this kind of society. They were to be unconventional, eccentric, and to engage in 'experiments of living.'[6] The intellectuals were 'to commence new practices, and set the example of more enlightened conduct' (115) as they were 'in advance of society in thought and feeling' (17). They were the *avant garde*. In all this Mill can be seen as a prophet of Bohemianism and of the intellectual as outsider. In addition to providing for the intellectuals' emancipation from bourgeois society, Mill also anticipated their wish to have a niche for themselves. He visualized a society in which intellectual values would be honoured and where those who possessed them would have influence and perhaps power.[7]

These attitudes have since become part of the predominant tradition of the intelligentsia, though they did not yet have this status in Mill's time, at least not in his country. Mill was genuinely original in this attitude, as in many other ways, for he was, in the British context, the prototype intellectual. There had been journalists, publicists, men of letters, all of whom had places in the established social system. Mill, however, deserves consideration as the first intellec-

---

4 Mill to Edwin Chadwick, April 1842, ibid., 516
5 Mill to Robert Barclay Fox, 19 Dec. 1842, ibid., 563
6 Mill, *On Liberty*, 4th ed. (London 1869), 101. Subsequent references to *On Liberty* will be to this edition; page numbers will appear in parentheses following the passage cited.
7 This is not to say that the benefits of liberty were to be denied all individuals: see below, 118.

tual. In this role he was bound to be influential among the ever-expanding intelligentsia.

The adversary posture towards society, the anti-authoritarian outlook, and the romantic concern with self-cultivation, all found in Mill's *On Liberty*, have become widely-shared attitudes now that the culture of the intelligentsia has come to enjoy an enlarged influence. We find the tenets of Mill's most famous book clearly reflected in the ubiquitous rhetoric of liberation. It is evident in such varied fields as the arts, the family, psychotherapy, as well as in politics, and even more notably in general discussion of life styles and personality. And this being the case, we might ask what has been accepted, in addition to the attractive plea for toleration and open-mindedness. For the book also contains a theoretical foundation and unstated assumptions that accompany its rhetoric and its formal argument, and it includes an image of the society in which Mill's version of liberty was to be enjoyed. It is this aspect of the book that I shall consider – or, perhaps one should say, reconsider, for this is not the first time that attention has been drawn to Mill's presuppositions about society.[8]

What would Mill's society be like? For one thing, it would be without religion. Because nothing was to be undiscussable, nothing should be held sacred, as there should be 'fair and thorough discussion of heretical opinions' (61). Such discussion was to determine whether the alleged heresy was true, and Mill could not have believed that any religion of the kind that had historically existed would survive such discussion. Nor would he protect religious belief on the ground that it was at least useful. In the case of Christianity no problem arose for him, for he thought its utility quite limited. It was too negative; it encouraged private rather than public spirit; and, because it discouraged self-willing, it was oppressive. However, usefulness *per se* was not a defence. As he said, 'In the opinion, not of bad men, but of the best men, no belief which is contrary to truth can be really useful ...' (43). It should be noted that not only Machiavelli but also Tocqueville believed the opposite.

There have been some who have held that religious belief, even if false, performs morally and politically useful functions; that it helps sustain the moral capital on which the world may live before the deluge begins. Mill makes clear that he has no fears of a deluge. Indeed, he sees no need for conventional institutionalized religion, indicating that we are well rid of it, as it gave 'direction of men's consciences' and was 'the most powerful of the elements which have

---

8 In confining myself to *On Liberty* of course I neglect other writings in which contrasting views can be found – for example, *Logic*, 'Coleridge,' and the articles 'The Spirit of the Age.' My procedure is based on the fact that *On Liberty* is much more widely read and quoted than any of his other writings. It is not only the book most readily associated with him, it has also achieved an authoritative – it is tempting to say sacred – status in the liberal tradition.

entered into the formation of moral feeling'; thus it was one of 'the engines of moral repression' (28). It is no wonder he thought the contemporary 'revival of religion' was 'always, in narrow and uncultivated minds, at least as much the revival of bigotry' (57) which, Mill said, 'makes this country not a place of mental freedom' (58). Whatever he foresaw or hoped for, it would be religion only in name. His free society would be quite secular.[9]

Mill would not stop with the emancipation of men from the influence of false religion. Among all the social influences, in Mill's view, custom had the greatest and most harmful effect. Along with tradition and experience, custom was the enemy of the individuality and the spontaneity that Mill sought to establish. It encouraged acceptance and thoughtlessness. Custom embodied other people's experience, and each individual should have his own (104). These thoughts led him to make the famous statement: 'Customs are made for customary circumstances, and customary characters' (105). Even if customs were good they ought not to be followed, for to do so was to avoid choice, and consequently not to be fully free. 'The despotism of custom,' Mill said, 'is ... in unceasing antagonism to ... the spirit of liberty' (126).[10]

Mill would also free men from those influences that operated through social classes. He complained that all persons, regardless of social position, asked themselves what was suitable to their station in life (or, if they were upwardly mobile, what was suitable to the station to which they aspired), and they conformed to the role as it was defined by society. This was the 'hostile and dreaded censorship' under which his contemporaries lived. It was not the censorship of a church or a government but a self-censorship, for man's inclinations were themselves shaped only to want what society prescribed. In this way, he said, 'the mind itself is bowed to the yoke' (110). As he visualized his free society, social stratification was not to affect behaviour. However, we should note in passing that there have been libertarians – for example, Tocqueville – for whom stratification was not incompatible with the enjoyment of liberty; indeed, in his view it was an obstacle to despotism.

9 Also see 92ff. While he held out this view for the future, in the meanwhile he would not eliminate religion. 'I am not anxious to bring over any but really superior intellects and characters to the whole of my own opinions – in the case of all others I would much rather, as things now are, try to improve their religion than to destroy it.' (Mill to Alexander Bain, 6 Aug. 1859, in CW, xv, 631)

10 There are passages, it is true, where Mill assumes the existence of custom; for example, 'it is important to give the freest scope possible to uncustomary things, in order that it may in time appear which of these are fit to be converted into customs' (121). Yet after an interval of only one sentence he also states, 'There is no reason that all human existence should be constructed on some one or some small number of patterns. If a person possesses any tolerable amount of common sense and experience, his own mode of laying out his existence is the best, not because it is the best in itself, but because it is his own mode.' This position is hardly compatible with the existence of custom in any usual meaning of the word.

Since Mill's theme is emancipation from society and all its despotic influences, he seeks to minimize and perhaps eliminate all the means by which society prevents the emergence of the free and spontaneous individual. Because he minimized the influence of class, custom, and religion, it should not be surprising that he was not sensitive to the usefulness of informal social organization, which consists of those associations larger than the family and yet less comprehensive than the state.

His description of social structure in a libertarian régime is meagre, but we can infer what it would be from his discussion of obligation. There were three kinds of obligation. First, there was obligation to share the labours and sacrifices required for defence of society, entailing responsibility for such things as policing, soldiering, and tax-paying (134–5, 145–7). They related one to the state. But the obligations were minimal, and the relation was distant, formal, and impersonal. Second, there were obligations arising from contracts. But these obligations were not necessarily based on enduring or socially significant relations, for there was to be liberty of retraction from most of them, even from the marriage contract, although if children were involved this step was not to be taken mindlessly or without hesitation (185–6).[11] So far, the obligations that Mill recognizes do not reflect close and intimate relations of the individual to society, the state, or its social institutions.

The third kind of obligation was to those who 'through their sympathies and their interests ... [were] nearly connected.' These were the 'distinct and assignable obligations' that take conduct out of the self-regarding class (145). Such obligations were only to those persons sufficiently close and dependent to be vulnerable to injury. The language – with its reference to near connections and sympathies and 'assignable individuals' (147) – suggests that he had the family in mind, as does one of the infrequent examples, in which the father is held to be obliged to provide education for his children. However, since he did not exclude the possibility of easy retraction from the marriage contract, the family was not in itself the occasion for an obligation.

Obligation was limited to a very small circumference. Apart from duties involving defence of society and contracts, it existed in a context of social relations that were close enough for there to be shared interests and sympathies and vulnerability to injury among particular and identifiable and therefore

11 The expectations of the other contracting party and the interests of children were to make one hesitate before breaking the contract. 'It does not follow, nor can I admit, that these obligations extend to requiring the fulfilment of the contract at all cost to the happiness of the reluctant party; but they are a necessary element in the question; and even if as von Humboldt maintains, they ought to make no difference in the *legal* freedom of the parties to release themselves from the engagement (and I also hold that they ought not to make *much* difference), they necessarily make a great difference in the *moral* freedom' (186–7). Of course if a contract related to money there was no liberty of retraction (185).

comparatively few other individuals. All else was self-regarding and presumably involved relations that were distant, tenuous, and impersonal. Not that beyond the family there were to be no groups or organizations; indeed, the provision for liberty of combination suggests the contrary. But individuals were not expected to have the kind of binding and mutually-sympathetic relations that created obligation. 'No person is an entirely isolated being,' Mill said (143). He was involved with others, and his conduct affected the interests and happiness of others. The more directly and forcefully it did so, the more it came under the jurisdiction of society. On the other hand, moving in the other direction, the more *isolated* an individual became, the fewer were his obligations, the more self-regarding his conduct, the more free he would be. Is it possible that for Mill liberty depended on very loose and distant relations of individuals to social groups and institutions – or, to use Mill's word, on isolation?[12]

When he looked forward to a society of fully free men, Mill visualized a multitude of self-determining individuals who, because they did not have many strong bonds or close ties, were a multitude of isolated, socially unconnected men. Mill's fully free man does not achieve his condition by virtue of membership in any group but, on the contrary, by separation and independence from groups and organizations. His ideally free individual is self-governing, which has nothing to do with his being a citizen in a democracy, but refers, as Mill said, to 'the government of each by himself' (12). He is to follow his own nature (110) and to form his own character. Such a person is exemplified by men of genius who are not capable of 'fitting themselves, without hurtful compression, into any of the small number of moulds which society provides in order to save its members the trouble of forming their own character' (116). Free men will 'break their fetters' and be more like the Niagara River than a Dutch canal(117). Having resisted the 'tyranny of opinion'(120) and the 'yoke of authority' (63), they could be independent of public opinion, custom, most obligations, and authority. Such men would be not only spontaneous but also self-made.

This is an ideal condition for Mill. As a choice-making person the free man is more fully human, for he uses the faculties of perception, judgment, and discrimination. Of course, he is also useful; since he is more sceptical and more inventive he contributes to the discovery of truth and so to improvement and national greatness. Thus the best historical periods were those in which 'the mind of a people [was] stirred up from its foundations' – for example, during the years immediately following the Reformation, when 'an old mental despotism had been thrown off, and no new one had yet taken its place.' From such periods all improvements came, and at such times there was an 'impulse

12 There is a biographical parallel, for Mill experienced a sense of isolation and had a preference for it: see the Editor's Introduction to *Later Letters*, cw, xiv, xxviii, xxxiii–iv, xxxvii; also 97, and xv, 589.

given which raised even persons of the most ordinary intellect to something of the dignity of thinking beings' (63). Thus freedom was a matter of inherent worth. Since liberty is inherently good, it is to be enjoyed by all. Men of genius would be the first to benefit from it (116–17), but it was not to be the privilege of an intellectual élite. Freedom, he said, 'is as much and even more indispensable, to enable average human beings to attain the mental stature which they are capable of' (62).[13]

The viability of Mill's free society is a matter of some importance, especially as there is another libertarian, with as good a claim to the label as Mill, who visualized the society of free men in a radically different way. I refer to Tocqueville, and a comparison is illuminating.

We are often reminded of their similarities. They both accepted democracy and appreciated its advantages; and they both discerned difficulties with it. Both were concerned about centralization and bureaucracy and they shared a sense of the importance of the educational effect of participation in politics. And of course Tocqueville's telling phrase 'tyranny of the majority' became useful and particularly meaningful to Mill when *On Liberty* was written. In addition, there were Mill's two reviews of *Democracy in America* and the author's gratification in reading them. Above all, there was their shared belief in liberty as the greatest good for modern men. All this especially makes the differences between them worthy of notice.

The first difference to be considered concerns religion. For Tocqueville religion was necessary if there was to be liberty in a democratic regime. In a democracy there was no political obstacle to what might be done. Therefore the check on men's actions and the source of guidance was to be found in moral ideas, which for most men were to have been derived from religion. Religion was the most important boundary that divides good and evil. 'Despotism may govern without faith,' he said, 'but liberty cannot. Religion ... is more needed ... in democratic republics than in any others.' He also said, 'while the law permits the Americans to do what they please, religion prevents them from conceiving, and forbids them to commit, what is rash or unjust.' Religion as a source of virtue gives men a rule to live by, thus making political rule less necessary and liberty possible. Consequently Tocqueville wanted, if possible, to reawaken religious belief.[14]

Could the contrast with Mill be greater? For him religion was the subject

---

13 'We *must* be satisfied with keeping alive the sacred fire in a few minds when we are unable to do more – but the notion of an intellectual aristocracy of *lumières* while the rest of the world remains in darkness fulfils none of my aspirations – & the effect I aim at by the book is, on the contrary, to make the many more accessible to all truth by making them more open minded' (Mill to Alexander Bain, 6 Aug. 1859, CW, XV, 631).

14 *Democracy in America*, ed. Phillips Bradley (New York 1946), I, 7, 305, 307, 327. Of course these views are not inconsistent with his personal religious views, which

of false feeling, of hypocrisy; it had authority and so encouraged mindlessness; and it was the source of persecution and bigotry. What Tocqueville wanted to encourage, Mill wanted to eliminate.

So also with conscience, which might be seen as an ally to religion. To Mill it was puritanical and therefore an obstacle to self-willing. He saw the moral feelings that entered into conscience as having come from religion. Thus conscience was literally a matter of internalized norms – that is, it was, in effect, external guidance. For Tocquevile, on the other hand, freedom meant not absence of regulation but self-regulation. This meant compliance with some rule or norm, and it would come from conscience or religion. In contrast, Mill's self-determining individual was to be subject to nothing external.[15]

There is another important difference between the two. Mill's free man – the immediate beneficiary of liberty and the agent of social improvement – tends to become the isolated individual that for Tocqueville is the bane of libertarian society. For Tocqueville the very worst thing that can happen in a democracy is that all men are equal but isolated from one another, so that there is a multitude of individuals, each 'living apart,' as he said, and 'a stranger to the fate of all the rest; his children and his private friends constitute to him the whole of mankind. As for the rest of his fellow citizens, he is close to them, but he does not see them ... he exists only in himself and for himself alone; and if his kindred still remain to him, he may be said at any rate to have lost his country.' Tocqueville called this condition of society 'individualism,' and he considered it a diseased condition, for it made men self-concerned, indifferent to others, and impotent. It was the condition that would give rise to despotism – indeed, to that new kind of despotism that would be worse than any yet experienced by mankind.[16]

Yet this condition also appears to be alarmingly similar to the social conditions Mill would create in order that men might enjoy his kind of liberty. To achieve this goal he would make the individual free from societal influences – from religion, from custom, from any need to conform to the role requirements of class or station. He would also make man free by minimizing his enforceable obligations to most persons other than his 'near connections' – that is, his family. The result would be, as suggested above, only tenuous relations to the world beyond. Mill's free man, as a consequence of his being self-determining and free of most obligations, would be one of a multitude of isolated and unconnected individuals.

It might be asked, what about Mill's and Tocqueville's common concern

varied and included disbelief in Christian doctrines. On Tocqueville's religious beliefs see Richard Herr, *Tocqueville and the Old Regime* (Princeton 1962), 48–9 and esp. n10.

15 Mill acknowledged the usefulness of conscience (25, 107); yet he also complained about the way conscience operated to prevent liberty (28–9, 61–2).

16 *Democracy in America*, II, 318; also Second Part, Bk II, Chaps. ii–iv

about the tyranny of the majority? But even here there is a difference that is concealed by their sharing of the phrase. Mill included as an example of the tyrannical majority the influence of social groups which for Tocqueville were the essential bulwarks against the potential tyranny of that majority. Whereas Tocqueville welcomed the existence of associations in which group cohesion and authority were sustained by custom and tradition, for Mill such groups were oppressive, for they were obstacles to liberty and individuality.

If we take note of the sociological dimension that Mill did *not* take into account in his theory of liberty, we can say that what for Mill was an ideally free society was Tocqueville's nightmare. To put this conversely, Tocqueville's best possible régime (libertarian democracy) was, from Mill's point of view, one in which there was despotism of custom, the authority of religion, individuals suffering under tyrannical majorities in all their many social activities, and an absence of improvement. Perhaps the difference arose from Mill's wish to see a libertarian utopia established, whereas Tocqueville more modestly hoped to avoid disaster – that is, despotism.[17]

In this context it is not surprising that Mill's two reviews of *Democracy in America* were so insensitive to Tocqueville's argument. His statement in his letter to Tocqueville (in 1840) – 'You have changed the face of political philosophy' – is misleading if it suggests endorsement of all Tocqueville's argument.[18] Although Mill appreciated much in Tocqueville's book, he especially appreciated what was congenial to his own views at the time. That is, Mill in 1835 was a spokesman for what he called the true idea of a representative democracy, a notion he had most recently propounded in his review of Samuel Bailey's *Rationale of Political Representation*. By the true idea of democracy Mill meant a government that combined popular control of a legislature with deference to enlightened leadership. After all, 'the best government, (need it be said?) must be the government of the wisest, and these must always be a few,' or, as he also described it, 'the omnipotence of the

17 In view of their differences on the meaning of liberty and on the preferred relation between the individual and society, the controversial question as to whether Tocqueville had a significant influence on Mill in this respect appears to be anything but urgent. By asking the question one assumes a similarity of outlook. For scepticism about Tocqueville's influence see H.O. Pappé, 'Mill and Tocqueville,' *Journal of the History of Ideas*, xxv, 1964, 220, 225–6, 228, 230–1.

18 Mill to Tocqueville, 11 May 1840, cw, xiii, 434. Tocqueville's appreciative statements to Mill about the reviews also cannot be taken as evidence of close similarity in their views; see Tocqueville to Mill, 3 Oct. 1835 and 18 Oct. 1840: Alexis de Tocqueville, *Oeuvres Completes*, vi, *Correspondence anglaise*, eds. J.P. Mayer and G. Rudler (Paris 1954), 302–3, 329–30. Mill sent Tocqueville a copy of *On Liberty*. Tocqueville acknowledged it without having read it, but he said he expected that liberty was a subject on which they would agree. Tocqueville died a couple of months later and may not have read the book. (Tocqueville to Mill, 9 Feb. 1859, ibid., 351–2)

majority would be exercised through the agency and at the discretion of an enlightened minority, accountable to the majority in the last resort.'[19] This ideal was the criterion by which he evaluated Tocqueville's analysis of democracy as it appeared in the part of his book that was published in 1835.

Consequently Mill welcomed Tocqueville's argument that democracy was inevitable, and he was critical of Tocqueville's generous assessments of aristocracy.[20] More importantly, Mill seized upon Tocqueville's observations that in American democracy the people did not select as their rulers the ablest and that this led to hasty and unskilful legislation. Anxious to believe that the true idea of democracy could exist, yet sharing some of Tocqueville's concern, Mill responded accordingly. On the one hand, uneasy lest Tocqueville's observation tell against democracy itself, Mill said 'we do not share all the apprehensions of M. de Tocqueville from the unwillingness of the people to be guided by superior wisdom'; indeed, 'this source of evil tells for very little with us in the comparison between democracy and aristocracy.' On the other hand, having defended democracy against what might have appeared a criticism of it, Mill then turned to the defence of the true idea of democracy and agreed that, although excessive, Tocqueville's fears were not misplaced. 'If democracy should disappoint any of the expectations of its more enlightened partisans, it will be from the substitution of delegation for representation; of the crude and necessarily superficial judgment of the people themselves, for the judgment of those whom the people, having confidence in their honesty, have selected as the wisest guardians whose services they could command. All the chances unfavourable to democracy lie here.'[21] Indeed, he also said that 'the substitution of delegation for representation is therefore the one and only danger of democracy.'[22]

Such was not Tocqueville's view. As we know, for him the greatest danger in a democracy was the threat to liberty. But Mill in 1835 was not especially interested in this most important theme of Tocqueville's book. The yoke of public opinion was seen by Mill as a threat to the discretion of representatives and other members of the élite; he was not yet prepared to call it a threat to the individuality of all men. Whereas Tocqueville was deeply, almost single-mindedly, worried about the fate of liberty, Mill played down the threat, as

19 'De Tocqueville on Democracy in America,' *London Review*, II, Oct. 1835, 110–11. By using this essay and the review of Tocqueville published in 1840 I am making an exception to the restriction described in note 8, an exception that, I trust, is justified by the immediate relevance of these two reviews to the comparison with Tocqueville.
20 *Ibid.*, 91, 116
21 *Ibid.*, 109, 112, 117–18. Tocqueville took note of Mill's distinction between delegation and representation and acknowledged its importance; and Mill explained that he had been using it since 1830 (Tocqueville to Mill, 5 Dec. 1835, *Correspondance anglais*, 303; Mill to Tocqueville, 11 Dec. 1835, CW, XII, 288)
22 'Tocqueville,' *London Review*, II, Oct. 1835, 112

is indicated even by his choice of words. Tocqueville's overriding concern with the omnipotence of the majority is described by Mill as merely that which Tocqueville 'regards as the most serious of the inconveniences of democracy.'[23] In addition, Mill does not always describe the potentially serious consequences of democracy in the language of one with a concern for liberty. Whereas Tocqueville was worried about the status of liberty in the inevitable democracy, Mill was content to describe the alternatives as 'between a well and ill-regulated democracy.'[24] Furthermore, I have not found Tocqueville's memorable and crucial phrase 'tyranny of the majority' in Mill's entire essay.

There is still more evidence in this essay of Mill's insensitivity to Tocqueville's concern with liberty. Mill denies the suggestion that minorities are vulnerable. Most minorities are fluctuating – that is, their composition varies – so that all men have an interest in preventing oppression of them. There are the rich, but they are not oppressed by the poorer majority. Mill concludes that 'it is not easy to see what sort of minority it can be, over which the majority can have any interest in tyrannizing.' He grants that antipathies of religion or race might provide exceptions, but he does not pause to consider this possibility apart from noting that such oppression is not peculiar to democracy and that it can be avoided only through moral and intellectual improvement.[25]

In turning to Tocqueville's fear of majoritarian suppression of individual opinion Mill had yet another opportunity of demonstrating his concern for liberty, for he recognized that 'it is a tyranny exercised over opinions, more than over persons, which [Tocqueville] is apprehensive of. He dreads lest all individuality of character, and independence of thought and sentiment, should be prostrated under the despotic yoke of public opinion.' But Mill refused to accept Tocqueville's analysis and depreciated his fear. Mill implied that Tocqueville's picture was 'overcharged'; in any case, it was not a problem peculiar to democracy; and (begging the question) he said that where there was an educated, leisured class there was no great danger. Thus in Europe 'there is a security, far greater than has ever existed in America, against the tyranny of public opinion over the individual mind.'[26] Since Tocqueville had France in mind, this is the very opposite of his view. Yet Mill went on to say that, while a debt of gratitude was owed to Tocqueville for pointing to the possible evils of democracy, he was confident that there was no danger, provided superior spirits engaged in the instruction of democracy. Thus he could say, 'we see nothing in any of these tendencies, from which any serious evil need be apprehended.'[27]

Even in the review of Tocqueville's completed book in 1840 Mill neglected some of the more important aspects of Tocqueville's argument. It is true that

23 Ibid., 118
25 Ibid., 118–19
27 Ibid., 125

24 Ibid., 93
26 Ibid., 119, 122, 124

he wrote more forthrightly about the despotism of the majority, and although he still thought oppression of minorities not a formidable evil,[28] he did recognize the seriousness of the problem arising from 'the tendency of democracy towards bearing down individuality, and circumscribing the exercise of the human faculties within narrow limits.'[29] Unlike his review in 1835, that of 1840 does not depreciate the importance of this phenomenon. It should also be noted that Mill clearly alluded to what Tocqueville described as individualism: 'M. de Tocqueville is of opinion, that one of the tendencies of a democratic state of society is to make every one, in a manner, retire within himself, and concentrate his interests, wishes, and pursuits within his own business and household.' And for this condition Mill used a brilliant simile: 'The members of a democratic community are like the sands of the sea-shore, each very minute, and no one adhering to any other.' Thus there are no permanent classes, and no *esprit de corps*; there are few local attachments, and scarcely any ties to connect men together, except patriotism (of which there is very little in a large democracy).[30]

But this is as far as Mill's sympathetic understanding of Tocqueville's argument went. For Tocqueville individualism was important because it made men vulnerable to despotism. It made them prefer comfort and equality to liberty. Mill did discuss one of Tocqueville's remedies for individualism – participation in politics – no doubt because it was congenial to Mill's belief in democratization.[31] But religion, which was equally important to Tocqueville as an obstacle to despotism, was not mentioned by Mill. And even more notable was Mill's neglect of Tocqueville's discussion of despotism as the most serious consequence of individualism.[32] Mill appears to have been insensitive to Tocqueville's really great sense of urgency, not unmixed with despair,

28 'Democracy in America,' *Edinburgh Review*, LXXII, 1840, 24. However he now had, as he had not had in 1835, examples of oppression of minorities based on antipathies of religion, politics, and race (see 23).
29 Ibid., 36; also 24, 35
30 Ibid., 28–29. However, he did not use Tocqueville's word, individualism.
31 Ibid., 29
32 It would have been appropriate to discuss it in the seven pages (29–35) following his allusion to individualism, but such discussion does not occur. Mill does point to 'Chinese stationariness' as an obstacle to change; this was a consequence of equality of condition. Mill connects this tendency with the growth of central government and the sense of insignificance among citizens; and with a 'danger of losing the moral courage and pride of independence which make [men] deviate from the beaten path either in speculation or in conduct' (35). Although there is a libertarian ingredient in this argument, Mill's position is more that of the Radical worried about obstacles to political change. This judgment is confirmed in a contemporary letter to Tocqueville (11 May 1840) in which he says 'the real danger in democracy, the real evil to be struggled against ... is not anarchy or love of change, but Chinese stagnation & immobility.' (CW, XIII, 434)

about the threat of despotism arising from modern social conditions. (It hardly matters whether these conditions are described as middle-class and commercial, as Mill preferred, or as egalitarian, in Tocqueville's usage.) Tocqueville foresaw a new form of oppression, unlike anything that had ever existed. The old words despotism and tyranny were inappropriate. As it was new, although he could not name it, he would grope to define it. This effort occupied much of Book IV, which Mill quoted but once in his review, and then not to this point.

It is true that Mill in 1859, when *On Liberty* was published, was different from Mill in 1835 and 1840. But there is no evidence that in 1859 his appreciation of Tocqueville's nightmare had increased.

Why did Mill fail (or choose not) to assimilate Tocqueville's concern and his argument? One answer is to say that they understood liberty differently, that for Tocqueville it was the condition of participating in a régime that was not despotic, whereas for Mill, so far as the narrowly political realm was concerned, this result had been achieved and in any case was insufficient, as full individuality was the goal to be reached.[33] This can be put differently by saying that Mill was visualizing a libertarian utopia, and in doing so he ignored – he had to ignore – what did not suit this purpose. In this he was a visionary; not the wild kind – his moderate tone, his sobriety, his willingness to consider opposing arguments prevent our seeing him in this way. And we need only recall his criticism of the later Comte to realize how much Mill saw himself as one whose feet were on the ground. Yet he was visionary in the sense that he made assumptions about the functioning of his ideal society that other observers thought questionable. He assumed that his libertarian society would 'work' – that without religion there would be morality; that without authority there would be allegiance and compliance with law; that with full individuality there would be a sense of social responsibility and cohesion; and that with the individualization that he thought necessary there would be no despotism.

These are empirical questions – not the kind, alas, that social scientists usually deal with. At the very least we can say that they are still undecided. But they were not problems for Mill. It was his theory of history, a legacy of his earlier Saint-Simonian beliefs, that allowed him to assume that his ideal society would function satisfactorily. He was confident that old creeds and institutions decayed; that transitional periods made for drastic changes; and that regeneration would take place, with new institutions and new beliefs that would make men incredulous that the old ones could have existed. With this understanding of historical change it was necessary to have great confidence

---

33 Although in somewhat different terms, the differences in their understandings of liberty are discussed in Jack Lively, *The Social and Political Thought of Alexis de Tocqueville* (Oxford 1965), 13–15.

in the flexibility of human nature and in the variability of social arrangements. Mill had such confidence, and it allowed him to assume that society in the future could be fundamentally different from what is was during the transitional period to which he was confined as an observer of men and society.

With his assumption that the future could be fundamentally different, in *On Liberty* he proceeded to describe full and complete individuality without very much consideration of the kind of society that would be compatible with it. This procedure was unobjectionable, for, as he said (in a letter to Bain), 'One must never suppose what is good in itself to be visionary because it may be far off.'[34] And this was in accord with 'utility in the largest sense,' for the famous phrase has a futuristic meaning. The 'permanent interests of man as a progressive being' (14) surely were the interests of man as he would be when the libertarian society was finally established. Of course over the decades Mill had changed in many ways; but there is a continuity with the early Mill when he was a Radical politician: he still believed in the 'practicability of Utopianism.'

It is evident that we ought not make an easy assumption of great affinity between Mill and Tocqueville; and that we ought to recognize that the liberal tradition, which of course involves many things, should provide quite separate places for them. And the evidence that supports such conclusions suggests an additional question. If we accept Tocqueville's analysis as valid and the reasonableness of his warnings about the tyranny of the majority and the risk of despotism, can we, with consistency, also endorse the entirety of Mill's argument about liberty?

34 Mill to Bain, 17 March 1859, cw, xv, 606

The Principles of Permanence and Progression in the Thought of J. S. Mill

EDWARD ALEXANDER

According to the historical theory of the young J.S. Mill, the outbreak of the French Revolution was the first spectacular manifestation of Europe's entry into an age of transition.[1] Mill was helped to see the revolution as the symbol of a new age characterized by disregard of the authority of ancestors by the fact that his own early attachment to its principles constituted a flouting of the authority of ancestors named James Mill and Jeremy Bentham, neither of whom could be stirred by declarations of rights attaching to the human being *per se*. James Mill had sent his son to France not for high thinking but for cheap living, so that it was not until two years after his return that young Mill read a history of the French Revolution. From it he 'learnt with astonishment, that the principles of democracy, then apparently in so insignificant and hopeless a minority everywhere in Europe, had borne all before them in France thirty years earlier, and had been the creed of the nation ... From this time ... the subject took an immense hold of [his] feelings.'[2]

For about a decade Mill immersed himself intellectually and emotionally in the revolution in the manner of those Frenchmen and Englishmen who devoutly believed that the revolution had substituted for the old Trinity of the church that other trinity – 'Liberty! Equality! Fraternity!' Sometimes he would identify himself with the early revolutionists and dream of becoming 'a Girondist in an English Convention'; at other times, 'the French *philosophes* of the eighteenth century' were the example he and his friends 'sought to imitate, and,' he says, 'we hoped to accomplish no less results.'[3] By 1832 the larg-

1 J.S. Mill, *The Spirit of the Age*, ed. F.A. von Hayek (Chicago 1942), 67
2 J.S. Mill, *Autobiography*, ed. Jack Stillinger (Boston 1969), 40
3 Ibid., 40, 66

est segment of his private library consisted of materials on the revolution. His claim to have read 'innumerable books'[4] on the subject is confirmed both in his own writings of this period and in reports by those who met him in the late twenties or early thirties that the revolution was his favourite topic of conversation.[5] After meeting him in 1832, Henry Crabb Robinson wrote in his diary that Mill 'Is deeply read in French politics, and bating his ... unmeaning praise of Robespierre ... and ... the respect he avowed for the virtues of Mirabeau, he spoke judiciously enough about French matters ...'[6]

In 1828 Mill made the French Revolution the subject of the final and the most ambitious article he wrote for the original *Westminster*, a detailed review and rebuttal of that segment of Walter Scott's *Life of Napoleon* which is a history of the French Revolution. This elaborate defence of the early revolutionists against Scott's Tory calumnies was for Mill both 'a labour of love'[7] and the natural reaction of one who intended writing the history of the French Revolution against the premature effort of a biased and ignorant interloper. Mill was at this time convinced that he alone of all living Englishmen could do justice to the subject, a rather considerable claim in view of the fact that early in the article on Scott he lays it down that no one short of a universal genius can deal with so unprecedented and unimaginable an event. Not only are the facts of the revolution 'incapable of being elicited but by one who possesses all the endowments of the most sagacious and practised judge,' but the interpretation of the facts would require 'along with the most minute knowledge of the circumstances of France and of the French people for centuries back, a mind profoundly conversant with human nature ... and the deepest insight into the springs of human society.'[8] Since Scott is neither God nor J.S. Mill he proves inadequate to the task.

We might suppose that in April 1828 the Mill who had recently recovered from his mental crisis by an exercise of the imagination that enabled him to conceive of and be moved by an experience of bereavement, which was not his own but Marmontel's, would seek in imaginative literature the instrument for making that which is strange, absent, and past into that which is familiar, present, and immediate. He does stress the fact that the French Revolution was an historically unique event, unimaginable not only to those who did not witness it but perhaps even to those who, having acted or witnessed, tried to record their experiences 'when the genuine impression of the present events' had faded and they had returned to the realm of normal experience. Yet Mill

---

4 Letter to Carlyle, 2 Feb. 1833, *Collected Works*, xii (Toronto 1964), 139. Cf letter to Carlyle, 22 Oct. 1832, cw, xii, 129
5 *John Stuart Mill and Harriet Taylor*, ed. F.A. von Hayek (Chicago 1951), 35
6 *The Diary of Henry Crabb Robinson: An Abridgement*, ed. Derek Hudson (London 1967), 114
7 *Autobiography*, 79
8 cw, xii, 25; 'Scott's *Life of Napoleon*,' *Westminster Review*, ix, 1828, 256

insists that Scott's novelistic gifts, far from enabling him to imagine the unimaginable, are among his prime disqualifications for writing the history of the revolution. The gift of narrative, for example, is held dangerous to 'real history,' and Mill accepts the disjunction between objective chronology of naked facts and a novelistic presentation of them. The novelist's talent is derided as 'nothing less than the art of so dressing up a fact, as to make it appear to mean more than it does; of so relating and arranging the events to be related, as to make them tell a different story from what would be implied in the mere chronological recital of them.' This method, though not always blameable, becomes mischievous when an author's theory of an event is so entirely disproved by the evidence as is Scott's Tory misrepresentation of the revolution. The writer of novelistic romances, Mill alleges in a self-interested argument, escapes the drudgery of the conscientious historian by the simple expedient of allowing his biases to determine his presentation: 'It is for Sir Walter Scott to assert: *our* part must be to *prove*. Assertion is short, and proof is long: assertion is entertaining, and proof is dull: assertion may be read, as glibly and as cursorily as it is written; proof supposes thought in the writer, and demands it of the reader.'[9]

Another luxury of the novelistic approach to the events of the French Revolution, according to the Mill of 1828, is that of moral judgment. Scott's history presents the revolutionists as free moral agents, and so holds them wholly responsible for their misdeeds. Ignoring the contingent nature of human actions, Scott 'blames men who did the best they could, for not doing better; treats men who had only a choice of inconveniences, as if they were the masters of events, and could regulate them as they pleased ...' The dramatic exigencies of literature oblige Scott to ascribe to persons what were the effects of circumstances, and to give each of his historical characters a conscious, premeditated part.[10]

Mill does not, by deploring Scott's propensity for moral judgment, seek to exonerate the Terrorists. He refers, at various times in the long essay, to 'the opprobrium which is justly due to the terrorists alone,' to the absolute separation between 'all the more ardent and enthusiastic partisans of the Revolution' and 'the party called the Terrorists ...' and to 'the extinct, and now universally detested, sect of Jacobins.' Yet it is also true that he tries to keep the Terror and the moral ambiguities linked with it decently out of view, that he hazards an explanation of the cruelties of the peasantry by the oppression they had endured, and that he wants to see the whole revolution as, what at one point, in language redolent of apologies for a later revolution, he calls it, 'that great experiment.'[11]

9 'Scott's *Life of Napoleon*,' 275, 296
10 Ibid., 258, 276
11 Ibid., 275, 296, 312n, 262–3

Mill does seek to exculpate the Girondists and through them the central purposes of the revolution itself, and this with an urgency, with a passion, that might be supposed as deeply antipathetic to pure disinterestedness as a gift for novelistic characterization and the displacement of chronology by narrative. For amassing mountains of evidence to confute Scott's Tory misrepresentations of well-intentioned constitutional monarchists, Mill offers no excuse to the reader: 'we do not *solicit* attention to this mass of evidence, we *demand* it. We demand it in the name and in behalf of the whole human race, whom it deeply imports that justice should be done ... to the few statesmen who have cared for their happiness. Does the man exist who, having read the accusation brought against such men, will consider it too much trouble to listen to the defence? Let such amuse themselves with romance; it belongs to other men to read history.'[12]

Why, then, having invested tremendous amounts of time and energy in studying the revolution, having convinced himself that the cause of human improvement itself hinged upon vindication of the great revolutionary experiment and that England too would feel the revolutionary 'hurricane,' did Mill eventually abandon the project of writing the history of the French Revolution and consign it, along with many of his books on the subject, to Carlyle? The answer may lie in the fact that just a few months after publishing his attack on Scott, which represents the high water mark of his enthusiasm for the revolution, Mill read Wordsworth for the first time. Wordsworth, who had once celebrated the revolution as a new dawn but now saw it as the introduction to a lengthy nightmare, taught Mill two things that may have lessened his devotion to the revolution. One was that there existed perennial sources of happiness, available to all human beings, which had nothing whatever to do with struggle and conflict. The other was that 'happiness may coexist with being stationary and does not require us to keep moving.'[13] Wordsworth seemed, that is, to have called into question the fundamental principle of the transitional age which the revolution announced: that the world was in perpetual motion and that everything was to be valued not as it was in itself but as a stage of some further development.

In the early thirties Mill was still telling friends that he planned to put his knowledge of the revolution into the shape of a history; but meanwhile he was composing his first literary essays and facing up to the distinction between a literary and an historical view of human actions. In 1828 he had decried Scott's reliance on imagination and insisted on the unique authenticity of eyewitness accounts of historical events, but by 1831 he was celebrating the actor's power of imagination as the ability 'to conceive correctly, and paint vividly

12 Ibid., 306
13 CW, XII, 89; *Autobiography*, 89; 'Wordsworth and Byron,' in *John Stuart Mill: Literary Essays*, ed. E. Alexander (Indianapolis 1967), 353

within himself, states of external circumstances, and of the human mind, into which it has not happened to himself to be thrown ...' In the next year he argued that the knowledge of general truth is just as likely to emerge from 'that kind of self-observation which is called *imagination*' as from 'simple *observation*'; and in 1833 he was assuring Carlyle that there is more truth about private and social life during the revolution in novels than in histories.[14]

Mill blamed his failure to become the historian of the French Revolution upon the impossibility of declaring to English readers that Christianity, though it was the greatest thing that ever befell the human species, was historically, perhaps even biologically, obsolete and unsuited to the species in its present state of development. 'One could not, *now*, say this openly in England, and be read at least by the many ... *A propos* I have been reading the New Testament; properly I can never be said to have *read* it before.' That Mill should simultaneously own up to the secret vice of gospel-reading and complain of Christian prejudice against truth-telling suggests that it was his own rather than the public's doubts about the adequacy of a purely historical judgment of historical events that kept him from his intended project. If Christianity had indeed been, in Mill's words of 1833, 'the greatest and best thing which has existed on this globe,'[15] was not one obliged to call into question the belief that the French Revolution was a great milestone in an infinitely progressing historical sequence? Or was progress perhaps something wholly distinct from improvement?

Both his correspondence and his angry review of Alison's *History of Europe* suggest that such questions were very much present to his mind in 1833. History, he now argued, had both a scientific and a moral aspect. As a scientific enterprise, it 'exhibits the general laws of the moral universe ... and enables us to trace the connexion between great effects and their causes'; as a moral enterprise, it displays 'the characters and lives of human beings, and calls upon us, according to their deservings or to their fortunes, for our sympathy, our admiration, or our censure.' But Mill's review shows that it is not, at least when dealing with the revolution, easy to reconcile the scientific and the moral functions of the historian. Since the revolution was not distinctively French but 'one turbulent passage in a progressive revolution embracing the whole human race,' Mill has no patience with an English historian exclusively obsessed with 'the degree of praise or blame due to the few individuals who ... happened to be personally implicated in that strife of the elements.' The figure of speech implies that the revolution was as irresistible as – what he had already called it in 1831 – a 'hurricane,' and as little liable to moral judgment. Granting that the revolution paid a tremendous price in 'Immediate Evil' for

14 'French Theatre,' *Examiner*, 22 May 1831, 325–6; 'On Genius,' in *J.S. Mill: Literary Essays*, 36; cw, xii, 139
15 cw, xii, 182

the good it wrought, he nevertheless seeks refuge in the idea that it served the cause of improvement towards which history seems to be aiming. Might not any course 'which could have averted the Revolution ... have done so by arresting all improvement, and barbarizing down the people of France into the condition of Russian boors'? All that the revolutionists did was aimed only 'to *save* the Revolution.' As for the moral questions raised by the Terror, Mill pleads that 'We have not now time or space to discuss the quantum of the guilt which attaches ... to the ... revolutionary governments, for the crimes of the revolution.' Yet he feels constrained to confess that 'Much was done which could not have been done except by bad men.'[16] A few months earlier he had so far forgotten his devotion to the scientific aspect of history as to complain of Thiers and other French historians of the revolution that 'By dint of shifting their point of view to make it accord with that of whomsoever they are affecting to judge, coupled with their historical fatalism, they have arrived at the annihilation of all moral distinctions except *success* and *not success*.'[17]

The strife between the scientific and the moral principles in Mill's speculations on revolution is more a conflict between Mill the historiographer and Mill the literary critic than between Mill the radical and Mill the conservative. That a totally un-moral progressivism could coexist with Mill's newly-discovered reverence for conservatives and their pieties is indicated by a letter of 1831 to Sterling which expresses sentiments so appalling that we can only impute them to the influence of the woman who had hypnotized Mill in the previous year:

If there were but a few dozens of persons safe (whom you & I could select) to be missionaries of the great truths in which alone there is any well-being for mankind individually or collectively, I should not care though a revolution were to exterminate every person in Great Britain & Ireland who has £500 a year. Many very amiable persons would perish, but what is the world the better for such amiable persons. But among the missionaries whom I would reserve, a large proportion would consist of speculative Tories ...[18]

While Mill was trying to resolve the conflict between the scientific and the moral interpretation of the French Revolution, and to grasp the role of the literary imagination in the composition of history, there entered into his life a man whose ruling principle was that intellectual quandaries could be resolved only through action. Thomas Carlyle eagerly consumed his new friend's knowledge of the revolution and put it to immediate practical use in *The*

16 'Alison's History of the French Revolution,' *Monthly Repository*, VII, 1833, 513, 515–16
17 cw, XII, 139
18 Ibid., XII, 84

French Revolution, published in three volumes in 1837. In his laudatory review of what may have appeared to him partly a creation of his own brain, Mill praised Carlyle for completing history with literature and for validating imagination by fact. Carlyle, more in the tradition of Shakespeare than of the rationalistic historians, those men of 'mere science and analysis,' had revealed that the actors of history were individual human beings who could not be made merely coextensive with their social function or symbolic value. Carlyle had inherited the best gifts of historical dramatists and romancers, that of conveying the actuality of historical persons, but he had also anchored his poetical imagination in actuality, in fact. Whereas a decade earlier Mill had viewed the poetic and novelistic imagination as incompatible with historical accuracy, he now maintained that only the 'creative imagination' of the poet is equal to the full and accurate representation of historical reality: 'Not falsification of the reality is wanted, not the representation of it as being any thing which it is not; only a deeper understanding of what it is; the power to conceive, and to represent, not the mere outside surface and costume of the thing, nor yet the mere logical definition, and *caput mortuum* of it – but an image of the thing itself in the concrete ...'[19]

But there was one disturbing consequence of Carlyle's espousal of the artist's rather than the scientist's method for judging men and events. Although Carlyle had revealed how the scientific mind's allegiance to general principles and abstractions could blind it to concrete actualities, he had forgotten that 'without general principles no one ever observed a particular case to any purpose.' Even though he was at this time consistently elevating the poetic intelligence above the logical, Mill felt obliged at last to defend scientific generalization against exclusive reliance on artistic particularity and immediacy. From Carlyle's stress upon the moral actuality of individual men of the past Mill had learned that there could be a self-coercive force in logic which blinded one to actuality and was the opposite of genuine thinking, especially when the logic was modelled on the alleged logic of history. After reading Carlyle's work, Mill could no longer write of the French Revolution as if it were an inevitable event in the logical unfolding of the historical process. But he was determined to salvage what he believed to be the essentials of philosophical thought and scientific history. As Murray Baumgarten has pointed out, Mill now joined with Carlyle in emphasizing the moral values and lessons of the past, yet insisted on treating these scientifically and theoretically.[20]

The years immediately following his abandonment of the French Revolution project were for Mill years of intense speculation on the nature of the

19 'The French Revolution,' *London and Westminster Review*, xxviii, July 1837, 20–2
20 Murray Baumgarten, 'The Ideas of History of Thomas Carlyle and John Stuart Mill' (dissertation, University of California, 1966), 357. Baumgarten's is the best available study of Mill's historical thought.

historical enterprise, but rarely of comment on the revolution itself. In the late thirties and the forties the influence of Carlyle's poetic and moralized history converged with that of Coleridgean conservatism to move Mill to substitute perpetual antagonism for perpetual movement as the metaphor for history. Coleridge, Mill discovered, stood almost alone 'in having seen that the foundation of the philosophy of [politics] is a perception what are those great interests (comprehending all others) each of which must have somebody bound & induced to stand up for it in particular, & between which a balance must be maintained – & I think with him that those great interests are two, *permanence & progression*.'[21] The well-being of society and politics demanded a balanced antagonism between radical and conservative sympathies, with each party to this fruitful conflict tempering its opposite.

The decline of Mill's enthusiasm for the French Revolution was a function of his growing insistence upon institutionalized supports for the principle of permanence. The Enlightenment philosophers who prepared the revolution had destroyed the unifying spirit of the French nation because, lacking the historical sense, they failed to see that 'institutions and creeds, now effete, had rendered essential services to civilization, and still filled a place in the human mind, and in the arrangements of society, which could not without great peril be left vacant.' The Coleridgean conservatives, by contrast, recognized that an absolute condition of civil society was the establishment in the constitution of the State of '*something* which is settled, something permanent, and not to be called in question; something which ... has a right to be where it is, and to be secure against disturbance, whatever else may change.'[22]

What could this something be in 1840? To what object of absolute and eternal devotion does Mill wish the lovers of permanence to attach their unquestioning loyalty? The only icon he is willing to proffer them is 'the principles of individual freedom and political and social equality, as realized in institutions which as yet exist nowhere ...'[23] In other words, Mill's own deepest loyalties, despite all his misgivings about 'Civilization' as expressed in the essay of that name, are still to the seeming imperatives of the incomplete historical process, which in the view of such connoisseurs as Tocqueville was moving inevitably towards equality of condition. Permanence had come to be valued by Mill, but less for its own sake than for the sake of progression itself; for he now believed that without contraries there is no progression, and that organized antagonism between the party of progress and the party of stability

---

21 CW, XII, 408–9
22 CW, X, 138, 133–4
23 *System of Logic*, CW, VIII, 922 (VI, X, 5). It should be noted that this passage is quoted from Mill's own quotation from 'Coleridge' in *A System of Logic*. The original (1840) version of 'Coleridge' locates centres of permanence almost exclusively in the past.

was the only guarantee of progression. The certain guarantee of stationariness, he begins to argue in the late thirties, is the absolute preponderance of any one class or quality or party, including – or perhaps especially – the party of progress. The Enlightenment philosophers' intolerance of the principle of permanence found its natural expression in the enormities of Robespierre and Saint-Just, who had persuaded themselves that they murdered not as criminals but as executors of death-sentences passed by history itself upon unprogressive classes and ideas. What other conviction, asks Mill in 1838, 'could lead any man to believe that his individual judgment respecting the public good is a warrant to him for exterminating all who are suspected of forming any other judgment, and for setting up a machine to cut off heads, sixty or seventy every day, till some unknown futurity be accomplished, some Utopia realized.'[24]

Mill's numerous historical essays of this period are unified by the desire to analyze the whole of history and human nature to determine laws of historical evolution. They are as fully enlisted in the service of the idea of progress as anything Mill ever wrote, and study of them supports Gertrude Himmelfarb's assertion that Mill's conservatism was highly unorthodox. They offer the first full expression of his relentless Sinophobia, his image of China as the object lesson of what will happen to Europe should she come to believe that progress can be achieved in a homogeneous community. Repeatedly he maintains that there is no law of improvement in human nature, that Europe has continued, however slowly, to improve because she has never been ruled by one exclusive tendency. The great error to be avoided is the belief that to give complete preponderance to all those social forces which have made for improvement since the middle ages would make for yet greater and faster improvement; on the contrary, the complete ascendancy of the progressive spirit of European society 'would commence an era either of stationariness or of decline.'[25] Whatever else may have changed from the Mill of the early forties to the Mill of *On Liberty*, the insistence on collision of adversaries as the prerequisite of progress and improvement did not.

The incessant warnings against the Chinese stagnation which endangers democratic societies would seem to suggest that Mill had given up historicist notions of inevitable forces which override human will and render moral judgment pointless. In 1840 he maintains that ideas are not the 'mere signs and effects of social circumstances' but are 'themselves a power in history'; in 1844 he sympathetically sets forth Michelet's assertion of the primacy of mind and will over the 'fatalities' of race and geography, and praises Guizot for recognizing individual human agency as well as social and political causes in the formation of human affairs. Yet alongside the exhortations to the will

24 'Poems and Romances of Alfred de Vigny,' *London and Westminster Review*, xxix, 1838, 39
25 'Democracy in America,' *Edinburgh Review*, lxxii, 1840, 44

which flow from his belief that in this world we make our own good, or our own evil, we still find Mill invoking the principle of historical law and inevitability. He endorses Tocqueville's ascription of divine inevitability to history in general and to equality in particular. He chides the English for lagging behind the French in capacity 'to link together the events of history in a connected chain ...' He continues to equate historical with natural causes, though he is now more likely to speak of raging rivers, which man can harness to his use, than of hurricanes, which he cannot.[26]

Mill's ambivalence arose from his uncertainty about the proper role of literature in historiography. From the time he discovered Wordsworth, Mill tended to associate literary experience with the joy and wisdom that derive from stationariness, from bringing up the rear, from love of the past. If there is a political bias in his literary essays, which applaud Coleridge and Carlyle and Vigny, it is towards what Carlyle called the doctrine of standing still. In his essays of the thirties on the nature of poetry he had declared mere story-telling, whether in narrative verse or historical painting, alien to the nature of art, which at its best obliterates time and penetrates to that which is universal and permanent. Now, in 1843, he contends that in the minds of people of 'strong organic sensibility' the mental habit called Imagination will dislocate facts from the sequence in which they occurred and synchronize them in pictures of rich concreteness, whereas 'persons of more moderate susceptibility to pleasure and pain will have a tendency to associate facts chiefly in the order of their succession, and such persons ... will addict themselves to history or science rather than to creative art.' Nevertheless, that man of strong imaginative sensibility, Carlyle, had by Mill's own testimony given the world 'the history of the French Revolution, and the poetry of it, both in one ...'[27] Consequently, Mill had to incorporate in his theory of scientific history, which sought to define an elaborate network of cause and effect, literature's stress upon the life and death of individual actors.

This he tried to do in his long review in the following year (1844) of Michelet's *History of France*. Here he describes, in ascending order, the three stages of historical inquiry. Practitioners in the first stage show no respect for the integrity of past civilizations but judge all ages and forms of life by their own. In the second stage, the historian temporarily suspends his own rhythms of existence to see the past as contemporaries saw it and 'realize a true and living picture of the past time.' His gift is primarily a poetic one, for he is able to reconstruct the whole spirit of an age from mere fragments of the past. The writer who excelled in this form of history was Carlyle. But the third and highest stage of historical inquiry, which must incorporate the preceding stage, and which Carlyle could hardly conceive, requires as its starting point a scientific conception of history 'as a progressive chain of causes and effects ...'

26 Ibid., 44–5
27 *Logic*, cw, vii, 481 (iii, xiii, 6) ; 'The French Revolution,' 17

This scientific brand of history seeks to discover the law of progression by which one generation succeeds another. That such a law does exist, that everything which has befallen the human race is capable of rational explanation, Mill takes for granted; but he admits that the fundamental problem of the science of history is 'how to read that law.'[28]

The difficulties of reading that law of progression were manifold, but may be summed up in two questions: one is whether the law of progress is synonymous with a law of improvement or only one of change; the other is whether circumstances form human beings, or human beings form circumstances. In that chapter of the *Logic* devoted to 'The Historical Method,' Mill says that between human will and circumstances there exists a reciprocal relation in which every fact is at once effect and cause. This reciprocal relation is progressive rather than cyclical; but progress, Mill states unequivocally, is not to be understood as synonymous with improvement. Five years earlier, in 'Civilization,' he had admitted that moral improvement might not proceed hand in hand with progress in civilization. Now he admits it is conceivable 'that the laws of human nature might determine, and even necessitate, a certain series of changes in man and society, which might not in every case, or which might not on the whole, be improvements.'[29]

This is a salutary distinction, but a glance at the historical essays of the forties suggests that it is one which Mill reserved for emergencies. In 1840 he remarks that the barbarian dismemberment of the Roman Empire looked to witnesses like the destruction of civilization, but is now 'admitted to have been the necessary condition of its renovation.' He endorses Michelet's defence of the mediaeval church and papacy in order to vindicate 'the progressive movement of middle-age history,' and actually justifies the First Crusade because it gave a 'general start' to the Christian-European mind and eventually lessened the hatred of Christians for Moslems – which must have been a considerable consolation, one is tempted to add, to the Moslems, to say nothing of the Jews who had been murdered in the Rhineland. As for the system which succeeded the feudal one, it is admitted by Mill to have had a 'revolting exterior,' yet is held by him to have been, from the historical view, 'the mask of a great and necessary transformation.' In 1845 he argues that feudalism collapsed not because of its faults but because its good qualities and the 'progress in civilization' which took place under its ægis had prepared, in the natural order of things, the society which succeeded it as the overseer of the progressive movement of European civilization.[30]

Walter Houghton has remarked that Mill's theory of history as a natural

28 'Michelet's History of France,' *Edinburgh Review*, LXXIX, 1844, 4–8
29 CW, VIII, 911–15 (VI, x, 2–3)
30 'Democracy in America,' 37; 'Michelet's History of France,' 28–9, 36; 'Guizot's Essays and Lectures on History,' *Edinburgh Review*, 1845, 414

organic development in which each age is the child of the previous one is a prime example of Victorian optimism.[31] But it was optimism of a special kind. Mill's historicism never led him to assert that 'Whatever is, is right,' but in the forties it brought him very close to maintaining that nothing that ever was, was wrong, and that things could never at any point in history – European history at least – have been, in fact, better than they were. The essays have about them something of the odour of the Marxist interpretation of history as always a record of the right, never possibly an account of wrong triumphant, and for this reason they are deeply troubling. For who should understand more clearly than a reformer of society that things which have happened seem afterwards to have been inevitable, but were not inevitable until they happened?

Mill wanted to believe that the general tendency of European history was not merely progressive rather than cyclical in a neutral sense but 'one of improvement; a tendency towards a better and happier state.' He was therefore prepared to go a long way with the school of French scientific historians who were trying to discover and elucidate, by analysis of the general facts of history, a 'law of progress' as reliable for purposes of prediction as the axioms of geometry. Theirs was the nearest approach yet made to the third stage of historical inquiry, and yet it too fell short of perfection because it had not fully assimilated the prior stage dominated by poetic imagination. Mill charged that the French historians had made the error of assuming the all-sufficiency of history for determining a law of progress, when in fact the order of succession which the historian may be able to trace from one society to another can never amount to a law of nature but only an empirical law. 'The succession of states of the human mind and of human society cannot,' he argues, 'have an independent law of its own; it must depend on the psychological and ethological laws which govern the action of circumstances on men and of men on circumstances.' In other words, whatever empirical law of progress may be inductively derived from the study of history must be confirmed, before it can become truly scientific, by reference to 'the laws of human nature.'[32]

Long before 1843 Mill had learned from experience of the need to verify historical generalizations by their conformity to the constitution of the human mind. He had been trained to believe that in selfless dedication to the improvement of mankind lay the surest source of happiness: 'Of the truth of this I was convinced, but to know that a feeling would make me happy if I had it, did not give me the feeling.' Utilitarian laws of progress were proved faulty by the simple expedient of comparing them with such laws of human emotion as were inscribed in the mind of John Stuart Mill. That it was legitimate to deduce the laws of human nature from the mind of an individual was proved by the

31 *The Victorian Frame of Mind: 1830–1870* (New Haven 1957), 29
32 *Logic*, CW, VIII, 913–15 (VI, X, 3)

generalizing power of poetic imagination. Great poets, Mill had written, were often ignorant of life: 'What they know has come by observations of themselves; they have found within them one highly delicate and sensitive specimen of human nature, on which the laws of emotion are written in large characters ...' From the poets and novelists one learned little or nothing of the law of progress, but from a Wordsworth or a Carlyle one might gain moral and psychological knowledge of what Mill in the *Autobiography* calls 'the perennial sources of happiness.'[33]

A truly scientific history, then, requires the aid of literature in two ways. It must incorporate the power of imagination needed to recreate the spirit of an age, that which 'cannot be extracted literally from ancient records ...'[34] But it also has to recognize its obligation to compare historical laws of progress with the laws of human nature, which are universal and permanent, and as much, or as little, available to Homer as to the most knowing and recent of writers.

If the laws of historical evolution require validation by correspondence with the laws of human nature to become scientific, the key question would seem to become whether human nature matches the progressive character of European history. It is not a simple question to answer, and Mill does not answer it simply or perhaps even clearly. In his 1840 essay on Tocqueville, where the problem of reconciling historical inevitability with human will is central, Mill says that the 'law of progress' cannot be a universal attribute of human nature since it has hitherto manifested itself only in Europe, which has stayed progressive as a result of the happy circumstance that it was never ruled by one exclusive tendency. But three years later, in the *Logic*, he flatly states that there has been 'a progressive change both in the character of the human race, and in their outward circumstances so far as moulded by themselves ...' The prime agent of social progress is held to be 'the order of progression in the intellectual convictions of mankind ...' and yet Mill must concede that intellectual activity and the pursuit of truth are not among 'the more powerful propensities of human nature ...'[35]

Mill does not, in my view, ever resolve the contradiction between a progressive theory both of history and of the human intellect and a deep-seated conviction in the stationary character of human nature. But I think that his exploration of the implications of this contradiction, both in the world and his own mind, makes, far more than the influence of Harriet did, for what Mill called the greater breadth and depth of his work in the 'third period' of his 'mental progress,' in which, as he said, 'I understood more

33 *Autobiography*, 83–4, 89; 'What is Poetry?' in *J.S. Mill: Literary Essays*, 53
34 'Michelet's History of France,' 15
35 'Democracy in America,' 44; *Logic*, cw, viii, 914, 926–7 (vi, x, 3; vi, x, 7)

things, and those which I had understood before, I now understood more thoroughly.'[36] One thing which Mill understood more thoroughly in the fifties than he had in the forties was that there were serious and even dangerous flaws in the organic and necessitarian view of history, and that what kept laws of history from becoming laws of nature was not a flaw in contemporary historiography but in human nature itself. In 1853 he praises the Greeks because they 'decided for an indefinite period the question, whether the human race was to be stationary or progressive,' but 'that the former condition is far more congenial to ordinary human nature ... experience unfortunately places beyond doubt ...' *On Liberty* takes it for granted that truth does not always triumph over persecution, and that history makes appalling mistakes and is often the record of wrong triumphant. In 1855 Mill visited Syracuse and wept with regret over the defeat of the Athenians instead of consoling himself with the infallible rightness of the forward march of history. To his diary he confided in 1854: 'It seems to me that there is no progress, and no reason to expect progress, in talents or strength of mind; of which there is as much, often more, in an ignorant than in a cultivated age. But there is great progress, and great reason to expect progress, in feelings and opinions. If it is asked whether there is progress in intellect' – and we must recall that in the *Logic* Mill had made progress in intellect the basis of the historical method of the social sciences – 'the answer will be found in the two preceding statements taken together.'[37] Mill cannot resolve these antinomies, but he now shows a graceful willingness to rest in them.

Mill's retreat from the organic and necessitarian view of history was a partial, yet substantial, one. Expressions of belief in the organic progression of historical epochs still appear in the work of the fifties, but they are accompanied, almost obsessively, by expressions of scepticism about human nature and the moral pattern of history. *On Liberty* clings to the sanguine view that 'there is on the whole a preponderance among mankind of rational opinions and rational conduct,' but the only argument its author can muster in support is that there must exist such a preponderance 'unless human affairs are, and have always been, in an almost desperate state.' *On Liberty* also sets forth the organicist view of human nature as 'a tree, which requires to grow and develop itself on all sides, according to the tendency of the inward forces which make it a living thing.' But in the contemporaneous essay 'Nature' Mill maintains that some instincts require not merely to be controlled or perfumed

36 *Autobiography*, 137
37 'Grote's History of Greece,' *Edinburgh Review*, xcviii, 1853, 428; *On Liberty* (4th ed., London 1869), 52; *John Stuart Mill and Harriet Taylor*, 229; Diary entry for 15 Jan. 1854, in *Letters of John Stuart Mill*, 2 vols., ed. H.S.R. Elliot (London 1910), ii, 359

but to be rooted out, and that the 'artificially created or at least artificially perfected nature of the best and noblest human beings, is the only nature which it is ever commendable to follow.'[38]

John Robson has pointed out that Mill was never in danger of 'ascribing ethical qualities' to objective natural processes.[39] But he had been in danger of ascribing such qualities to history, of investing it with the powers and dignities formerly ascribed to providence, and of urging political philosophers to concentrate their view on 'agencies lying deeper than forms of government, which, working through forms of government produce in the long run most of what these seem to produce, and which sap and destroy all forms of government that lie across their path.'[40] He moved away from organic historicism in the fifties not, as Anschutz has alleged, because his renewed attachment to the cause of reform made it obligatory for him to believe that 'institutions and forms of government are a matter of choice.'[41] Nowhere in his writing of the forties can we find a condemnation of reform movements so strong as that of 1855, when he told Harriet that he was planning *On Liberty* as virtually an impediment to historical progress because 'almost all the projects of social reformers of these days are really *liberticide* – Comte, particularly so.'[42] The basis of Comte's social philosophy, Mill knew, was precisely, and exclusively, history.

The murder of liberty generally arose, in Mill's view, from the dogma of infallibility. This dogma could be invoked by authority but also by the Comtists and other social reformers who posed as the interpreting agents of predictable historical forces. In fact, it now dawned on Mill, it had thus been invoked in the culminating event of that episode which had captured his youthful imagination and propelled modern Europe into a phase of infinite progression. The Reign of Terror of the French Revolution reappears briefly, in 'Nature,' to be compared, just as it had been in the 1830s, to 'a hurricane and a pestilence,' but the intention behind the comparison has entirely changed. Previously, Mill had used the analogy to explain the Terror as the agent of a historical progression as inevitable and irresistible as a natural disaster. Now he wants to reveal the moral enormity of political murderers who masquerade as the innocent executors of a law of nature: 'Pope's "Shall gravitation cease when you go by?" may be a just rebuke to any one who should be so silly as to expect common human morality from nature. But if the question were between two men, instead of between a man and a natural

38 *Liberty*, 38, 107; cw, x, 396–8
39 *The Improvement of Mankind: The Social and Political Thought of John Stuart Mill* (Toronto 1968), 275
40 'Armand Carrel,' *London and Westminster Review*, xxviii, 1837, 80
41 R.P. Anschutz, *The Philosophy of J.S. Mill* (Oxford 1953), 71–2
42 Letter to Harriet Mill, 15 Jan. 1855, cw, xiv, 294

phenomenon, that triumphant apostrophe would be thought a rare piece of impudence. A man who should persist in hurling stones or firing cannon when another man "goes by," and having killed him should urge a similar plea in exculpation, would very deservedly be found guilty of murder.'[43]

If Mill's mental constitution had been different from what it was, the inner tension which kept him from writing the history of the revolution might have found expression in a work of literary imagination, where the quarrel with oneself can have fruitful issue. The work of the fifties which best expresses Mill's ambivalence about the revolution as an agent of historical progression is not one of his own, but Dickens' *Tale of Two Cities*. This least Dickensian of all Dickens' novels is, by virtue of its indebtedness to Carlyle's *French Revolution*, distantly related to Mill's own early researches into the revolution; but it also resembles Mill in the dual view it offers of the revolution and of history itself. The natural world of the novel is as ferociously malevolent as it is in Mill's essay on nature. The sea at Dover Beach 'did what it liked, and what it liked was destruction.' The French Revolution, according to Mme Defarge, is but an aspect of this irresistible natural destruction: 'Tell me how long it takes to prepare the earthquake? ... I tell thee ... that although it is a long time on the road, it is on the road and coming. I tell thee it never retreats, and never stops. I tell thee it is always advancing.' As agent of this irresistible advance, she is as immune to moral persuasion as the elements are: 'Tell the wind and the fire where to stop; not me!' Dickens himself, to be sure, is attracted to the idea of historical inevitability according to which all the terrible events are sequentially, causally related, and even supernaturally ordained; but also he senses that the law of progression in history is none other than the law of violence and terror.

Like Dickens, Mill never wholly freed himself from the belief that the law of historical progression was a law of improvement. Even as late as 1853 he is capable of writing that the Athenian love of conquest, although 'a blemish, when judged by the universal standard of right,' was yet 'as a fact ... most beneficial to the world,' because without it Athens could not have functioned 'as the organ of progress. There was,' he continues, 'scarcely a possibility of permanent improvement for mankind until intellect had first asserted its superiority, even in a military sense ...' But to the extent that Mill incorporated into his thought an ability, which he had gained from the poets, to imagine the world as always in its beginning, the influence of historicism over his mind receded. During the 1830s he had paid his respects to imagination by celebrating it in literary essays, but later he paid it the higher honour of using it as a check upon what he called the mental habit of historical thought. 'Without [imagination],' he had written, 'nobody knows even his own nature, ... nor the nature of his fellow-creatures' beyond abstraction and generalization. It is

43 CW, X, 384–5

easier, he knew, to countenance the progressive elimination by history of mere abstractions – unprogressive classes, unprogressive nations, unprogressive races – than of fully imagined individuals. Even in *On Liberty* he remarks that it is not really progress that his countrymen object to: 'on the contrary, we flatter ourselves that we are the most progressive people who ever lived. It is individuality that we war against ...'[44] Mill's retreat from the historicist position came from his recognition that man, truly to be free, had to be liberated from the service of history as well as the service of the state, because a principle of progression which assigned to man the role of raw material was unlikely to respect his birth or to deplore his disappearance.[45]

44 'Grote's History of Greece,' 436; 'Bentham,' cw, x, 92; *Liberty*, 128
45 See Hannah Arendt, *The Origins of Totalitarianism* (New York 1951), especially the section on 'Ideology and Terror.'

Rational Animals and Others

JOHN M. ROBSON

Know, man hath all which Nature hath, but more,
And in that more *lie all his hopes of good.*

...

Man must begin, know this, where Nature ends. ...

MATTHEW ARNOLD, 'In Harmony with Nature'

If one believes in and strives for the 'improvement of mankind' as the Mills père et fils did, one must believe that mankind needs improvement and also that mankind can be improved. There is not, in practice, much evidence that people who hold such beliefs also hold, in consequence, that they must analyze their beliefs so that the foundations may be tested descriptively, analytically, or normatively. Most often, concentration on the means of improvement arrogates all effort; it seems better – and perhaps easier – to change mankind than to understand mankind. Applied to the two Mills, this judgment is extreme, for both comment on materials as well as means; however, neither, and especially James Mill, practises for long the endeavour, in John Mill's words, 'in which above all it is necessary that an ethical philosopher should excel' – that of analyzing 'human nature.'[1]

As a result, one cannot with any great confidence assert that either of the Mill's held the view, or developed the view, that mankind or human nature is precisely this, that, and so, to the definite exclusion of this, that, and the other so. Descriptive, analytical, and normative judgments are blended, and the consequences of that blending are manifold. That is, one cannot always discern whether comments apply specifically and restrictively to human nature as it is seen to be, or as it essentially must be, or as it should be; and, furthermore, one cannot always discern whether such comments are intended to apply to individuals, to classes, or to mankind in the abstract. In addition, the degree to which either of them accepted particular traditional views of human nature is not made explicit in their writings.

1 'Remarks on Bentham's Philosophy,' *Collected Works*, x (Toronto 1969), 12

It is very tempting to indulge in some methodological questioning, to try to discover what earthly or heavenly use an endeavour so beset can be. But I have smaller fish to fry. I shall be trying to share what I hope are some insights into the meanings attached by the Mills to 'human nature' and closely related terms, and to see if those putative insights aid in our comprehension of their other views. Once again the younger Mill in an early passage suggests a motto: in criticizing Blakey's *History of Moral Philosophy* he says that Blakey's reader is told 'in what words philosophers have expressed the results of their speculations, but though he may not be made positively to misunderstand, he is not made thoroughly to *feel*, the meaning in the philosopher's own mind, to which the words are but an index, and often a most imperfect one.'[2] That may sound like a hermeneutical blank cheque, but I hope there are some cash reserves.

Even this smaller context needs to be further shrunk. If a writer is not consciously defining terms for specific purposes, and in most cases even when he is, he will be unconsciously accepting and unconsciously adapting current usages. So we have a complex figure/ground problem: Is John Mill's use, for example, of 'the human species' his or his age's? If the former, is his usage constant through his life? If the latter, is it constant? And is it one or many? Regrettably, I cannot here – or perhaps anywhere – answer these questions satisfactorily. But having asked them, I trust I shall avoid the appearance of total idiocy, and I shall make passing reference to some of their implications.

James Mill's most significant comments on human nature occur with reference to its 'laws'; these laws are those of the mind, explicated in his *Analysis of the Phenomena of the Human Mind*. Most attention is paid to the ultimate laws of association, but reference, often more than passing, is made to subsidiary laws, derivative from those basic ones. These laws, it would appear, are universally operative in the species, and are species specific. What is of interest and value in man is the operation of his mind; James Mill seems to accept without question, as who in his age did not, that man is, on the natural level, the rational animal. And for James Mill only the natural level is real.

To say that man is essentially rational is not, of course, to say that all people reason well. Indeed, both Mills, in criticizing their times, refer frequently to the rational deficiencies of their contemporaries. As Swift pointed out, a better definition than 'rational animal' is 'animal capable of reasoning.' Even here, of course, the implication remains that to reason, speaking properly, is to reason well. John Mill's attitude will be glanced at later; James Mill's Socratic faith encompasses an apparent belief – again one commonly held – that clear reasoning induces clearer reasoning, and so *ad infinitum*.

As a result, not being willing to concede differences among human beings in their potential for service to the race, he tried strenuously, both by precept and example, to show that properly devised and conducted education could draw forth the latent powers in all. Initial individual variations are either non-existent or trivial, or else result from physical injury or deficiency. The type then is constant; the impressions, the printed characters we observe, differ because and only because post-natal experiences differ, and those experiences can in large measure be controlled so as to educe beneficial individuals who are, even in their individuality, exemplars of human nature.[3]

In James Mill, as has been often indicated, the Lockean and Helvetian strains are strongly evident, as well as the Hartleyian. Add the Benthamite emphasis on the utility of selfishness, and the picture is approaching complete-ness. The model is economical as well as economic: locate and label the eternal and immutable springs of action, and trigger those that will release beneficent action. Do not worry excessively over benevolence: well enough the results if malevolence is discouraged and remains dormant. The impetus for improve-ment is external and observable. And, to cap all, the scheme is self-explicatory and self-supportive; all rational beings – that is, all human beings – can under-stand and apply it.

Repression of certain elements of human nature is, of course, desirable, though James Mill does not specify, in relevant contexts, which should be repressed. He also seems to have written little in praise or blame of this repres-sion, but his son's sketch in the *Autobiography*[4] suggests what would be per-fectly consonant with his expressed views on a variety of subjects – that re-pression of the anti-social is a praiseworthy activity. Knowing what we do of his admiration of the Classical virtues, and of his eighteenth-century Neo-classical tastes, we should be surprised if control, harmony, and order were not his values. One should also recall, however, that he was a rising son of North Britain and an ex-Presbyterian, and so endorsed, as his son was to do in the Victoria heyday of these qualities, energy and dedication as necessary in applied human nature.

Turning after such an insultingly brief account of the father's view of hu-man nature to the son's, I base my apology to devotees of James Mill not on the weight of John Mill's views, but on the much greater mass of evidence, its applicability to various matters of interest, and its complexity. Furthermore, the son's period is, for the matters I am concerned with, a more interesting one. Or, at the very least, John Mill indicates, sometimes uneasily, attraction

---

3 In one instance, not I believe a significant one for him, though interesting in the history of this idea, James Mill suggests that there are different basic 'tempera-ments.' Such a notion, related to 'humour' theory, is susceptible to explanation by physical or environmental as well as by ontological causes, and Mill, to my knowl-edge, gives no unequivocal explanation. Nor does his son, who also uses the word; the younger Mill hints more strongly, however, at physical and environmental causes.

4 See *Autobiography*, ed. Jack Stillinger (Boston 1969), 29ff.

and reaction to new views, some of which began to be expressed in his father's time. Sir Walter Scott, for example, has been said to have lived at a time of transition from 'the view that human nature is essentially the same in all ages, [to] the view that man and society are a function of history.'[5] Scott was a near-contemporary of James Mill, but the tension here implied is far more obvious in John Mill, who was certainly aware of notions of historical relativity and of the incessant, unwilled flow of cause and effect in human affairs. Put another way, the question as to whether society is the work of man or man is the work of society is much more puzzling to the son than to the father.

Other matters of increasing interest during John Mill's life – matters, it should be noted, that became important mainly after his formative years – that can be seen as influencing but not controlling his views of human nature, include ethnology and its child, anthropology, sociology, eugenics, and, of course, evolutionary theory. More recent developments, especially in genetics, have created a gap between our concepts of human nature and John Mill's, a gap that makes it quite difficult, at least for me, to feel certain that I have grasped his view. Would he understand in the same way that I do, for example, such remarks as Ortega y Gassett's 'man ... has no nature, what he has is ... history'?[6] Mill holds, evidently, that abstract human nature is ahistorical; there is no phylogenetic history. Individuals and groups, however, certainly do have histories for Mill – but he also talks of human nature as manifest in types and classes.

Again, am I right in thinking that the following comment by a psychiatrist in defence of Freud is compatible with John Mill's views? 'Psychoanalytic theory postulates that man's ego, although derived from biological roots, becomes increasingly autonomous from the rigid instincts that rule lower forms, and enables him to create the moral, aesthetic, and intellectual achievements of civilization.'[7]

But this is both to anticipate and to suggest that I shall here deal with more than I can. Let us see just what John Mill has to say. Discussions of his thought, I believe, best start either with the *System of Logic* or the *Autobiography*. Let us choose the *Logic*. There, having rejected his earlier view of Natural Kinds, he argues that 'there are in nature distinctions of Kind; distinctions ... running through the whole nature, through the attributes generally, of the things so distinguished.'[8] A Natural Kind contains things that differ from things in another Natural Kind in more properties 'than can be numbered, more even than we need ever expect to know.' Kinds are of various

5 Alexander Welsh, *Victorian Studies*, xv, 1971, 97
6 *History as a System and Other Essays towards a Philosophy of History* (New York 1961), 217
7 Shelley Orgal, *New York Review of Books*, 30 Nov. 1972, 45
8 cw, viii, 718–19 (iv, vii, 4). See also the Textual Introduction, vii, lxv.

degrees of generality: for example, 'Animal, or living creature,' is a 'real Kind' (Mill uses 'real Kind,' 'Natural Kind,' and 'logical species' as apparent equivalents), but animal kind includes mankind, which is also a real Kind. Indeed, as one proceeds down the ladder of generality, one passes from genera to species to *infima species* – that is, to the one 'proximate (or lowest) Kind to which any individual is referrible' – and mankind is such an *infima species*.[9]

Natural Kinds, which reflect 'radical' and 'specific' distinctions, are 'parted off from one another by an unfathomable chasm, instead of a mere ordinary ditch with a visible bottom ...'[10] This language suggests a belief in the immutability of natural species, though Mill makes it clear that he is using the term 'species' in a logical sense, not as it is used in natural history, where 'organized beings are not usually said to be of different species, if it is supposed that they have descended from the same stock.' So, this latter sense being artificial and for convenience, Mill will not say there are 'different Kinds, or logical species, of man,' such as might be suggested by the 'various races and temperaments, the two sexes, and even the various ages ...' Physiology, furthermore, 'may almost be said' to have 'made out' that such differences indicate only 'classes' that are no more Natural Kinds than are 'Christian, Jew, Mussulman, and Pagan ...'[11]

A few pages earlier in the *Logic*, in discussing the meaning of terms, Mill most frequently illustrates by the word 'man.' If justified merely by the proximity of the discussions, and the common illustration, one might well be accused of philosophic chicanery; however, I believe it is clear that Mill would hold that in both cases 'man' denotes exactly the same individuals, and, if so, may one not argue that in nature and in language there is at least a permanent possibility of identical connotation? Whatever that possibility may be judged to be, the attributes Mill says are connoted by 'man' are interesting. These attributes 'seem to be' – the hesitation may reflect his awareness of the difference here between ideal and common language – 'corporeity, animal life, rationality, and a certain external form, which for distinction we call the human.' All of these are required for any 'existing thing' to be called a man; each of them is an essential property; if one ignores the fourth, to use his example, one would have to call the Houyhnhnms men.[12] Of these attributes,

9 Ibid., 122, 125, 123–4
10 Ibid., 123
11 Ibid., 124–5. There are some interesting minor qualifying variants among editions in this passage. For some comments on Mill's attitude towards female 'nature,' see my 'Mill on Women and Other Poets,' *Victorian Studies Association Newsletter*, no. 12, Nov. 1973, 13–17.
12 Ibid., 31–2. Mill's list is not invariable: in one place he gives 'corporeity, organization, life, rationality, and certain peculiarities of external form' (134; until the 3rd ed., the last attribute was 'a form resembling that of the descendants of Adam'); in another he omits the external form (113); and in another he omits corporeity (James

the final pair, rationality and a particular external form, are specific determinants, marking man off within the genus animal.[13]

Before looking more particularly at specifically human characteristics, however, one must recognize that mankind share some characteristics with other species of animal kind. (To appreciate Mill's view, which is consonant with that taken throughout most of Western history, one must blot out of one's mind the arguments of modern Ethology – a very different science from that Mill foresaw under that title – and also those of the animal liberationists,[14] who, citing Bentham as an ally, have added 'specieist' to that list of opprobrious epithets that include sexist and rascist – and, I increasingly hope, ageist.) Clearly, Mill is not happy about man's animal nature, and would willingly see most of its urgings suppressed.

The contrast between man's humanity and man's animality is most apparent when Mill alludes to – 'discusses' would be too specific – sexual desire. Two contexts are typical: accounts of his relations with Harriet Taylor Mill and arguments against over-population. In the former, one finds the 'sensual relation' described as an 'impulse' of a 'lower character,' distinguished from 'strongest & tenderest' friendships, and capable of being 'put aside when regard for the feelings of others, or even when only prudence & personal dignity require it.'[15] In passages dealing with population, one finds such phrases as 'a degrading slavery to a brute instinct' in men, 'helpless submission to a revolting abuse of power' in women,[16] a 'disproportionate preponderance ... in human life' of the 'animal instinct in question';[17] 'one of the deepest seated and

Mill, *Analysis of the Phenomena of the Human Mind*, 2nd ed., ed. J.S. Mill [London 1869], I, 290n). I shall ignore these variations, as they occur in illustrative and not analytic contexts.

Mere descriptive definitions are of course available for particular purposes. Mill offers these: 'a mammiferous animal, having (by nature) two hands (for the human species answers to this description, and no other animal does): ... an animal who cooks his food: [and] a featherless biped' (*Logic*, CW, VII, 138). The last is Cuvier's; Mill also refers to Linnaeus's 'four incisors in each jaw, tusks solitary, and erect posture.' These characteristics, however, are not connoted 'in common use' by the word 'man' (ibid., 129); corporeity, animal life, rationality, and a particular form are so connoted.

13 See, for example, *Logic*, CW, VII, 128.
14 See, for example, Peter Singer, 'Animal Liberation' (a review of *Animals, Men and Morals*, ed. Stanley and Roslind Godlovitch and John Harris), *New York Review of Books*, 5 April 1973, 17–21
15 *The Early Draft of John Stuart Mill's Autobiography*, ed. Jack Stillinger (Urbana 1961), 171. He refers (only once so far as I know) to the 'natural attraction' of the sexes in a non-pejorative manner; see *The Subjection of Women* (London 1869), 27. Elsewhere (for instance in the *Early Draft* passage just cited) he makes similar remarks, but doesn't use 'natural.'
16 *Principles of Political Economy*, CW, II, 352
17 Ibid., III, 766. The word 'animal' was added in the 3rd ed., 1852.

most pervading evils in the human mind' is the 'perversion of the imagination and feelings' resulting from dwelling on 'the physical relation and its adjuncts ...'[18] These 'impulses' and 'instincts' are in human beings – or at least in male human beings – as part of their animality; and that animality is 'lower.' For example, he makes a comparison between human 'prudence,' 'foresight,' and 'social affections,' on the one hand, and animal 'blind instinct' on the other, when talking of population control,[19] and the poor animal isolated for denigration is the lowly swine who, as we know from *Utilitarianism*, is grossly satisfied.[20] Elsewhere 'a nest of ants or a colony of beavers' is similarly seen as without those qualities (foresight and prudence) that place mankind above them.[21]

The point may be obvious enough, but I should like to cite a few other instances, even though they will again suggest avenues of argument I cannot pursue, to demonstrate that men are animals, that their animality is lower than their humanity, and that their animality can and should be suppressed. In several places, for example, Mill comments on what may induce or foster animal behaviour. Climate and geography – Nature with a capital 'N' – may do so either by niggardliness, so that all energies are necessarily devoted to mere preservation of life, or by over-bounteousness, 'affording a sort of brutish subsistence on too easy terms, with hardly any exertion of the human faculties ...' Both conditions are 'hostile to the spontaneous growth and development of the mind'; both lead to savagery – to the narrowing of man's being to the lower part of his nature.[22]

Social institutions can have similar results, and frequently do for the 'lower classes.' At first glance the indictment appears to be of the individuals composing the class: 'utmost habitual excesses of bodily violence,' 'brutality,' 'mean and savage natures,'[23] 'semi-savage listlessness and recklessness.'[24] But certain 'institutions ... lead naturally [observe that unhappy word] to this de-

---

18 *Autobiography*, 65; here he is referring to his father's views, but there can be little doubt that his are identical.
19 *Principles*, cw, ii, 156–8
20 See cw, x, 210; and compare the previous reference to the *Principles*, where one finds (157) 'propagate like swine.' One must not think of Mill as unusual in these attitudes; see, for example, Queen Victoria's comment to her daughter, the Princess Royal, about the latter's first pregnancy: 'What you say of the pride of giving life to an immortal soul is very fine, dear, but I own I cannot enter into that; I think much more of our being like a cow or a dog at such moments; when our poor nature becomes so very animal and unecstatic' (quoted in Cecil Woodham-Smith, *Queen Victoria* [New York 1972], 403).
21 *Principles*, cw, ii, 358. These qualities for Mill are not, it should be recognized, specifically moral.
22 *Inaugural Address* (London 1867), 4–5
23 *Subjection of Women*, 63–4
24 *Principles*, cw, iii, 768

praved state of the human mind.'[25] The 'bulk of the human race,' Mill says elsewhere, because of poverty, drudge 'from early morning till late at night for bare necessaries ... with all the intellectual and moral deficiencies which that implies – without resources either in mind or feelings – untaught ... selfish ... without interests or sentiments as citizens and members of society, and with a sense of injustice rankling in their minds ...' But 'man is not necessarily a brute';[26] institutions can be changed. Even as things are, the indictment is not by any means total or totally restricted to the lower classes. Mill refers to the 'most naturally [again alas!] brutal and morally uneducated part of the lower classes,'[27] and to the 'brutal part of the population';[28] in the first case there must be another part of the lower classes; in the second there is no suggestion that that part is found only in the lower classes.

Having glanced at the animal in man, let us return to the man in the animal. Man is rational, and has a certain external form. But he also, as a Natural Kind, has other, innumerable other, attributes. Can we gather from John Mill what any of these may be? He most certainly indicates, from time to time, that mankind is marked by certain features. But how can these be classified? If he described them as attributes, or properties, or even elements, one would feel some confidence. But these terms do not appear prominently in appropriate contexts: what one finds instead are such terms as needs, feelings, constituents, capacities, powers, susceptibilities, tendencies, and propensities. A confused and confusing bag: not being identical, the terms cannot be thought to define one category; at the same time, not being always clearly distinct one from another, they cannot be thought to define separate categories. A principle of indeterminancy operates: under examination, co-ordinates are blurred and properties become powers and vice versa, just as needs become tendencies and vice versa. Generally, one may say that the difference between latent and actual is hard to establish, and being and becoming are blended.

With this warning – to myself as much as to anyone else – I feel still justified in uniting Mill's comments on human nature into three fairly clearly marked areas: needs, constituents, and capacities.[29] I shall not be able to cite

25 *Subjection of Women*, 84
26 *Principles*, CW, II, 367. That is, for my argument, man does not necessarily *behave* like a brute; as an animal, he shares attributes with brutes.
27 *Subjection of Women*, 84
28 *Autobiography*, 176–7; *Principles*, CW, III, 765ᵇ. The former refers to the Jamaica case, the latter to mistreatment of wives.
29 Two other interesting areas should be mentioned: tendencies (or propensities) and feelings. Natural tendencies include those to theorize ('Bentham,' CW, X, 102), to abstract and generalize ('Notes on ... The Phaedrus,' *Monthly Repository*, VIII (1834), 416n; Mill's version of Plato, which he translates directly in the text as the ability to apprehend Kinds, and 'which distinguishes man, the rational being, from the mere beasts'!), to interpret the complicated as mysterious (*Utilitarianism*, CW,

every instance in which Mill specifically mentions an aspect of human nature that can be grouped under one or other of these heads, nor can I guarantee anything about the relative weighting he would give them. Let us see what I can do.[30]

First, needs. Concerning the obviously physical, Mill has little to say, although, apparently defining by contrast, he twice says that liberty is our strongest need after means of subsistence.[31] While the need for freedom of thought is most eloquently stressed in *On Liberty*,[32] another need there dealt with, that of choosing one's own mode of life, is more interesting for this discussion. This need, as described by Mill, suggests that this aspect of essential humanness extends to the physical, is part of the physiological consensus, if the need is end-directed; as mere need, it may connoted by all members of the genus animal. To me, at any rate, a passage such as the following has more than analogical weight: 'Let any man call to mind what he himself felt on emerging from boyhood – from the tutelage and control of even loved and affectionate elders – and entering upon the responsibilities of manhood. Was it not like the physical effect of taking off a heavy weight, or releasing

x, 228–9), to anarchy (*Logic*, cw, viii, 922, quoted from 'Coleridge'), to extend the bounds of moral police (*On Liberty* [London 1859], 152), to disparage feelings and mental states of which one is not oneself conscious ('Bentham,' cw, x, 93; in the first version 'spiritual influences' were that of which some are unaware), to intolerance in whatever one really cares about (*On Liberty*, 19), to believe that subjective feelings not otherwise accounted for are revelations of objective reality (*Utilitarianism*, cw, x, 230; actually referred to as a predisposition), and – a sad list – to pugnacity, irascibility, enthusiasm, destructiveness, domination, and cruelty ('Nature,' cw, x, 393; in most of these, given Mill's general view of 'tendencies,' one can detect a sense in which momental as well as initial inertia is a human characteristic). As to feelings (in a somewhat more restricted sense than that of 'states of consciousness'), the following are among those Mill characterizes as natural: of the Infinite (*Auguste Comte and Positivism*, cw, x, 334), of fear ('Nature,' cw, x, 393), of the rightness of the *lex talionis* and its reverse (*Utilitarianism*, cw, x, 253–6), of gratitude to protectors (*Principles*, cw, iii, 760), and to those who, having power, do not use it to crush the weak (*Subjection of Women*, 34); he also refers to social and selfish feelings, and conscientious feelings (for example, *Utilitarianism*, cw, x, 231, 229).

30 In illustrating, I shall choose examples most appropriate to my topic, trusting that they are not simply the most convenient to my case. I omit consideration of the laws of association, fundamental to mental operations, and such matters as the powers of sensory discrimination and the related power of choice. For the first, in relation to human nature, see especially the passage from *An Examination of Sir William Hamilton's Philosophy* quoted in *Analysis*, i, 440–1, where Mill also mentions another matter I shall ignore, expectation (which of course involves foresight; both these powers are essential to the kind of improvement Mill so passionately desires); for examples of the others, see *On Liberty*, 105–6.

31 *Principles*, cw, ii, 208; *Subjection of Women*, 178, where the actual comparison is with 'food and raiment.'

32 See, for instance, 94, 100.

him from obstructive, even if not otherwise painful, bonds? Did he not feel twice as much alive, twice as much a human being, as before?'[33]

The imagery connected with this need, and the closely related need for variety of situations, is more familiar and equally suggestive. Such freedom is opposed to inhuman 'moulds,' 'patterns,' 'compression,' 'stunting and dwarfing,' 'restrictions,' 'restraints.'[34] It favours essentially human 'spontaneity,' 'expansion,' 'unfolding,' 'development,' 'diversity,' 'variety.'[35] In each case, it seems to me, if need is a valid determinant of human nature, man is for Mill only and truly man when he is free to choose among modes of life.

Other needs that Mill mentions, each of them worthy of more extended comment, are the need to pay attention to others' opinions (clearly derivative from man's social nature),[36] the need for sympathizing support and for objects of admiration and reverence,[37] the need for solitude,[38] the need for the internal culture of the individual, the need for the cultivation of feelings, and for the cultivation of both active and passive capacities.[39] Concerning this last group, one should note that the need is for growth and change, and recollect that the diversity, development and so on which Mill sees as resulting from the free choice of one's mode of life are 'co-ordinate' with 'civilization, instruction, education, culture, [and are] ... a necessary part and condition' of them.[40]

Leaving needs, let us turn to the second category, consisting of what I have called the constituents of human nature. (No term is both sufficiently broad and sufficiently narrow, I should again emphasize, but 'constituents' may not

33 *Subjection of Women*, 180–1. (When I wrote this paper I here said that to my knowledge no one had cited this passage in relation to Mill's description of his release from depression in the *Autobiography*. Professor Feuer delivered his paper before I read mine, however, and so I must now say 'to my knowledge only one person [see 100 above] ...')

With such comments one may compare those on activity (*Utilitarianism*, CW, X, 215), and on mental activity ('Bain's Psychology,' *Dissertations and Discussions*, III [London 1867], 119–20).

34 *On Liberty*, 116–17; *Autobiography*, 151; *Subjection of Women*, 188

35 *On Liberty*, 102, 116–17; *Autobiography*, 150; *Principles*, CW, II, 209, where individual utility is stressed. In these passages a physiological element is hinted at. And at times, as when Harriet's 'rich and powerful nature' is mentioned (*Autobiography*, 111), there is more than a hint of a quantitative measure of human nature. See below 155–6.

Connected with these needs is that for variety of situations (*On Liberty*, 103; Mill is quoting von Humboldt, but obviously in agreement – compare my comment on 156 below).

36 For example, *Principles*, CW, II, 206, 370ff

37 'Bentham,' CW, X, 96

38 *Principles*, CW, III, 756, where the justification is on grounds of both social and individual utility.

39 *Autobiography*, 86

40 *On Liberty*, 102

be very misleading.) Obviously, for Mill does not repudiate totally his Benthamite legacy, one must include selfishness. But he does add to that legacy: in two places he offers lists demonstrating how inadequate a limitation of human nature to selfishness is. The first list, in his article on Bentham, includes as powerful constituents of human nature, the love of justice, a sense of honour and personal dignity, the love of beauty, of order, congruity, consistency, and conformity to end, the love of power, of action and of ease, and the love of loving.[41] The second, in *Utilitarianism*, overlaps partly the earlier one, and partly the list of needs: it includes pride, the love of liberty and personal independence, the love of power and of excitement and tranquillity, and a sense of dignity which, Mill adds, is possessed by all in proportion to their higher faculties.[42] As that remark suggests, this list appears in Mill's argument for qualitative differences in pleasures; each of these, and especially the last, the sense of dignity, contributes to a human being's unwillingness to sink to a lower grade of existence.

In a considerably different context, Mill offers yet another list, this time of those constituents that call forth 'energy of character,' which is plainly a good. These are bodily strength and mental energy and cunning, both found in savage states, and the passion for philanthropy, the love of active virtue, and the desire of wealth, all found in civilized states, with only the last being anything like universal.[43] Other important constituents are mentioned in various places: sympathy is often emphasized,[44] a moral sense and conscience are described as 'facts' in human nature,[45] imagination is cited,[46] and important emphasis is given to enthusiasm for the noble (as contrasted with indolence and selfishness) and to high aspirations and intellectual tastes.[47]

Important as needs and constituents are, they pale before a third category, human capacities. In 'Nature' Mill's position is unequivocally stated: 'there is hardly anything valuable in the natural man except capacities – a whole world of possibilities, all of them dependent upon eminently artificial discipline for being realized.'[48] I say unequivocal, because the normative judgment is unqualified; unambiguous it is not, because 'hardly anything' is not very helpful.

41 'Bentham,' cw, x, 95–6
42 *Utilitarianism*, cw, x, 212ff
43 'Civilization,' *Dissertations and Discussions*, 1 (London 1859), 177–8
44 See, for example, 'Nature,' cw, x, 394.
45 'Bentham,' cw, x, 97, 95; the second reference is probably, though somewhat distortedly, to man's 'pursuing spiritual perfection as an end ... desiring, for its own sake, the conformity of his own character to his standard of excellence ...' This passage is dealt with below.
46 *Autobiography*, 68
47 *Utilitarianism*, cw, x, 212ff
48 cw, x, 393

The capacities Mill mentions, unlike the tendencies of human nature,[49] are all laudable, but it is undoubtedly wrong to conclude that he believed mankind to have no capacity for evil, particularly when one considers that the categorizing words most commonly associated with 'capacities' in his accounts are 'powers' and 'susceptibilities.'[50] A more useful assumption is that he turns to capacities in hortatory passages where the improvement of mankind is at issue. In two places in his 'Bentham,' moreover, it should be noted that 'desire' and 'wish' are brought very close to 'capacity' and 'power.' In the first of these he says that Bentham never recognized man as 'a being capable of pursuing spiritual perfection as an end; of desiring, for its own sake, the conformity of his own character to his standard of excellence ...'; in the second, that Bentham's system of ethics recognized 'no such wish as that of self-culture, we may even say no such power, as existing in human nature ...'[51] Other capacities mentioned by Mill are for the cultivation of sensibilities, sacrifice for others, disinterested devotion to one's fellow man and to God, labouring and combining for generous, public, and social purposes, and, most annoyingly to some, as yet another explicit distinction between man and brute, 'acquiring a love of cleanliness.'[52]

As will be evident from some of these examples, we are yet embraced by the tangled vines of language: 'capacity' in most acceptations suggests receptivity, passivity, a property fundamental and original to an entity, but for Mill it evidently involves growth and activity. One passage permits no evasion: 'if, as is my own belief, the moral feelings are not innate, but acquired, they are not for that reason the less natural. It is natural to man to speak, to reason, to build cities, to cultivate the ground, though these are acquired faculties. The moral feelings are not indeed a part of our nature, in the sense of being in any perceptible degree present in all of us ...' Thus far, 'feelings' are in question, though the point is illustrated by 'faculties.' But the passage continues: 'Like the other acquired capacities above referred to, the moral faculty, if not a part of our nature, is a natural outgrowth from it; capable, like them, in a certain small degree, of springing up spontaneously; and susceptible of being brought by cultivation to a high degree of development.'[53] Here the 'acquired faculties,' of course, are also commonly thought of as givens. What can Mill mean in saying that 'to reason' is an acquired capacity? As indicated above, he must mean that to reason correctly is what is acquired. Something there is in our nature, whether physical or moral, that is necessary to such developments, but is not sufficient for beneficial developments.

49 See n29 above.
50 And see the comments on the 'moral faculty,' *Utilitarianism*, cw, x, 230.
51 'Bentham,' cw, x, 95, 98
52 See ibid.; *Utilitarianism*, cw, x, 218; ibid., 228; *Autobiography*, 138; 'Nature,' cw, x, 394.
53 *Utilitarianism*, cw, x, 230

What the primordial elements and organization are matters very little to John Mill; what he is concerned with, especially after the *Logic*, is the beneficial development. But to legitimize the process to himself as well as to others, he must assert that the improvement is based on realities in nature; the development, therefore, must be consistent with the properties of the basic materials. Here it seems needful to venture out on the treacherous quagmire of an analogy. The *tabula rasa*, it may be asserted, is actually impregnated with dyes, the colours of which emerge when the sheet is treated with water, chemicals, or heat.[54] Or, thinking of methods of instruction in the fine arts and architecture, the 'properties' of materials guide the artist in his uses of them, and, interesting though it would be, he need not know the molecular structure of an acrylic paint or a limestone block to determine what he can do with it. What I'm suggesting is that Mill, despite his opinion of his own abilities, is usually operating subsequent to the *Logic*, in passages dealing with human nature, as Artist, not as Scientist, to use his terms.

Like his father, John Mill paid great heed to the external forces of environment and education as shaping development and educing improvement. Unlike his father, however, he stressed, as we have seen, the internal forces that surface in his discussions of the needs, constituents, and capacities of human nature. While arguing that each of these is important, I should like to refer again – impressionistically, perhaps – to a few of them, which appear distinctively important; I must here pass by the others, as well as the external forces, on which much might be said.

But first, a word is appropriate on the distribution of the 'stuff' or 'raw material of human nature.'[55] In part, at least, one must guess as to what is ultimate and original for Mill, as he does not often concentrate his attention on the question, but certain phrases are more than suggestive. Both qualitative and quantitative differences exist at this deep level, normally indicated by one of various pairs of correlative terms. 'Quick,' 'strong,' 'active,' 'energetic,' and 'open,' are frequently attributed to nature, as well as 'slow,' 'weak,' 'passive,' 'susceptible,' and 'close': the contrast is markedly in favour of the former set, even when 'impulsiveness' is seen as a concomitant, or even when the necessity of 'prudence' and 'reserve' is admitted.[56] The qualitative judgment is clear enough here, and surfaces even more evidently when one realizes that they are actually on a scale from little to much (zero is impossible, as the attributes are evidently universal, and infinity is not realizable or even desirable for

54 The image I owe to my friend and wife, who is the inspirer, and in part the author, of all that is best in my writings; were there but a few hearts and intellects like hers, this earth would already become the hoped-for heaven.

55 *On Liberty*, 108

56 See, for example, *Autobiography*, 19–20, 33n, 45, 47, 91; *Principles*, CW, II, 206, 210, 213, 222; 'Thoughts on Poetry and its Varieties,' *Dissertations and Discussions*, I, 93.

separate attributes). That is, quantity curiously becomes a test in kinds of judgment where quality normally reigns. (It is as though a man of many judgments were equivalent to – or better than – a man of much judgment.) Negative assessments come in two well-known passages. In *On Liberty* Mill refers to the 'general average of mankind' as being 'moderate in intellect' and in 'inclinations'; in the *Autobiography* the 'great majority of mankind' are presented as having 'but a moderate degree of sensibility and of capacity for enjoyment ...'[57] The clearest statements of all come in the third chapter of *On Liberty*, where, for example, we find this: 'To say that one person's desires and feelings are stronger and more various than those of another, is merely to say that he has more of the raw material of human nature, and is therefore capable, perhaps of more evil, but certainly of more good.' 'Strong,' 'vivid,' 'powerful': these are the proper modifiers of 'the stuff of which heroes are made ...'[58]

These passages prepare us for the kind of internal forces in human nature that I should like to isolate. Energy, activity, growth: a cluster of words suggesting that essentially mankind *must*, physiologically and psychologically, move and change, and *should* move and change in a particular direction. One should not emphasize very strongly what is quoted from another, but Mill's citing of von Humboldt's desideratum, a harmonious development of human powers to a complete and consistent whole, clearly carries his approval.[59] And harmony and wholeness are consistent with what Mill says in the *Autobiography* and elsewhere about the proper state of an individual. Another cluster of terms suggests more about the process and direction of human growth: enthusiasm, high aspirations, the pursuit of spiritual perfection. (Here, of course, one becomes aware of the gap between father and son.) Finally, and for my purposes most significantly, I would cite two phrases from his 'Bentham': the human desire for conformity of character to a standard of excellence; and the human love of congruity, love of consistency in all things and conformity to their end. These are, whatever their ultimate status, in human nature, and they appear to me to have special importance for Mill.

They could have little but automatic and non-moral force if *individual* human nature could not alter and be altered. What I have said thus far has been, in the main, made to apply to *universal* human nature which, by pre-evolutionary definition, is fixed, ahistorical, given. As I have indicated, Mill's main interest is elsewhere directed, towards that which is changeable, historical, striven for. In the *Logic* he comments that it is peculiar, in a degree, to the sciences of human nature and society 'to be conversant with a subject-

57 *On Liberty*, 124; *Autobiography*, 86
58 *On Liberty*, 108
59 Ibid., 103. To emphasize it strongly would lead to a comparison with Matthew Arnold.

matter whose properties are changeable.' Not 'changeable from day to day, but from age to age; so that not only the qualities of individuals vary, but those of the majority are not the same in one age as in another.' He says again: 'The circumstances in which mankind are placed, operating according to their own laws and to the laws of human nature, form the characters of the human beings; but the human beings, in their turn, mould and shape the circumstances for themselves and for those who come after them.'[60] But one must also recall such other remarks in the *Logic* as this: 'So far as the properties of a thing belong to its own nature, and do not arise from some cause extrinsic to it, they are always the same in the same Kind.'[61]

The two come into most evident conflict when one considers a passage in the *Autobiography* where, praising John Austin, he says: 'He professed great disrespect for what he called "the universal principles of human nature of the political economists," and insisted on the evidence which history and daily experience afford of the "extraordinary pliability of human nature" (a phrase which I have somewhere borrowed from him); nor did he think it possible to set any positive bounds to the moral capabilities which might unfold themselves in mankind, under an enlightened direction of social and educational influences.'[62] As already implied, the solution is that *pliable* human nature is not *universal* human nature, if universal is defined in the *abstract*. That is, when Mill alludes to, comments on, describes, or analyses 'human nature,' normally, and especially when the passages are extensive, he is referring (a) to individual character or type, or (b) to group or class or nation. Such passages provide the bulk of the notes he has bequeathed to us for his unwritten Ethology, both individual and political, and they have very considerable importance for him. His interest lying in modification of behaviour, he looks not at abstract human nature, but at individuals and groups from which action emerges.[63]

60 *Logic*, cw, VIII, 913. Compare the important passage, ibid., 873, where all that cannot be explained by circumstances is assigned to 'congenital predispositions' – about which nothing more is said. It is obvious also that the chapter on liberty and necessity (Bk VI, Chap. ii) is for Mill centrally important to improvement; indeed the whole of Book VI is.

61 Ibid., VII, 584

62 *Autobiography*, 107. Mill adapts Austin's phrase in 'Civilization,' *Dissertations and Discussions*, I, 203.

63 To pursue this question further, one should look at a pattern of usage that appears when one searches for John Stuart Mill's uses of the term 'human nature' or related terms (how useful a concordance would be!). Far from uniformly, but often enough to suggest a mental pattern, he uses a pair of terms that imply a difference, not an overlap. The most common pair is 'human nature and [human] life' (for example, 'Bentham,' cw, x, 89, 89–90, 97 [in the second of these, the study is called a 'wide subject' in 1838, but 'wide subjects' in 1859]; *On Liberty*, 124n; *Autobiography*, 9); others of this sort include 'man's nature and circumstances,' 'man and ... man's

To emphasize the point, let me reiterate: when Mill uses the term 'human nature' (or cognates), he sometimes refers to universal human nature, sometimes to individual human nature, and sometimes to group (class or national) human nature; though a majority of his references are to the latter two, I am mainly concerned in this paper with the former. A few brief comments on individual and group 'nature,' are, however, relevant to my argument. As would be anticipated, both individuals and groups reveal 'better' and 'higher' characteristics, as well as 'worse' and 'lower.' 'Higher' ones are associated with civilization, culture, and development; 'lower' with savagery, brutality, and stagnation. Individuals and societies must, and can, make choices. Furthermore, scientific study can be made of human nature in individuals and groups by observation, by analysis of history and literature, and by imaginative projection and introspection. When one relates these views to what has been outlined of Mill's accounts of basic, elemental human nature, the following conclusion is tenable.

By nature, human kind has certain needs, attributes, and capacities, many of them not now known. Neither by definition nor by necessity are these valuable; that is, the 'natural' may not, and uncontrolled and undeveloped by man's 'art,' probably will not, conduce to individual and social utility. However, among these elements of human nature are certain capacities that will be so conducive when allowed to develop under willed control. What direction they should take can be seen through a study of individuals and groups that are 'higher.' Talking in this way of ends and means, one is moving towards central issues in two of Mill's most-read works, *Utilitarianism* and *On Liberty*. I believe light is thrown by these considerations on a central matter in each of them.

The issue in *Utilitarianism* to which I refer is the quantity-quality crux. Briefly, how is it that Mill could, on his epistemological and psychological beliefs, argue for differences in kind, and not just amount, among pleasures? The issue in *On Liberty* is, similarly briefly, this: Why does Mill attempt to

position in the world' ('Bentham,' cw, x, 90, 89); 'humanity and human affairs' (*Logic*, cw, VIII, 925). One also finds 'human nature and human history' (*Analysis*, I, 405), 'human nature and ... fact' (*Subjection of Women*, 83), and 'human nature and conduct' (*Inaugural Address*, 31). Another group includes 'human nature and [human] society' (for example, ibid., 97; *Logic*, cw, VIII, 943, 950), and 'human and social life' (*Autobiography*, 141).

Of the several lines of approach to his understanding of the term 'human nature' suggested by these pairs, one is methodological. 'Human nature' on the one hand, and 'human life or society or circumstances or affairs or history' on the other, require different methods of examination; one is reminded of James Mill's segregation of knowledge of 'the laws of human nature' from that of the experience of man's behaviour, though of course his son placed much heavier weight on the analysis of the latter.

justify freedom on the grounds of individual development as well as on the grounds of social utility, without strongly connecting the two justifications?

Bringing these questions together, the basis of my answer is as follows: in human nature there are known attributes that are generically animal, and others that are specifically human. The study of individuals and groups shows that those attributes that can be *developed* are the specifically human ones; the animal ones may be so exercised as to dominate thought and behaviour, and may be repressed, but they are and remain what they are. Moreover, those societies where, on an average, social utility has increased are found to be those in which specifically human attributes can be seen to have been developed; this coincidence is not surprising, for among the most important of the specifically human attributes are those of social adhesion, love, sympathy, and co-operation. Another attribute of immense significance is the need to fulfil, to realize, that which is specifically human. So it is that freedom is necessary to mankind: there is a teleological thrust essential to our humanness, the frustration of which is debasing. The double utility of freedom, and the normative judgment of pleasures, are built into such statements as this from his *Inaugural Address,* where Mill proposes to comment on the ways in which the essential departments of general culture 'conduce to the improvement of the individual mind and the benefit of the race; and how they all conspire to the common end, the strengthening, exalting, purifying, and beautifying of our common nature, and the fitting out of mankind with the necessary mental implements for the work they have to perform through life.'[64] On the negative side, there is the danger of regression: 'Deprive human life of all which this system [Communism] would take away from it, & it would be reduced ... to a sort of sentient vegetation, a state not so much superior as may be thought, to the condition of any of the other gregarious animals when they have enough to eat.'[65]

It will be apparent that Mill reveals, as he does also in his acceptance of Natural Kinds, a strong Aristotelian influence, in seeing mankind, like other species or kinds of things, as having a determining excellence that is realized in pursuit of its specific end.[66] Reading *eudamonia,* the human end for Aristotle, as Mill did, in utilitarian terms, one can see the particular importance of the qualitative distinctions he makes between higher and lower pleasures. Indeed, he even sounds at times more like St Thomas or Cardinal Newman in linking virtue and goodness with the fulfilment of the specific ends of man –

64 *Inaugural Address,* 11

65 *Principles,* CW, III, 1023 (cancelled MS passage in Bk II, Chap. i; I believe its cancellation has nothing to do with the view of human nature expressed).

66 The closest approximation I am aware of to the views expressed here is the brief account by Frederick Copleston in his *History of Philosophy,* VIII (London 1966), 31–2.

though of course he would not accept Aquinas's or Newman's definitions of essence and end.

In any case, for John Mill the specifically human, just because it is specifically human, and therefore appropriate, congruent, defining, is 'better' and 'higher'; the animal, though in us all, is 'lower.' There is no genetic history, just a fixed natural inheritance; on it, by art and understanding, a better future will be built by individuals who, knowing themselves, and knowing that those selves are social, strive for the perfection of that which makes man mankind.

Is there much here that is 'inconsistent' with other views that Mill expresses and/or with our experience? Undoubtedly there is some. But is it possible to formulate a consistent model that will not fail the second test – that is, will not disconform to some of our perceptions and conceptions of reality? I do not think so, and I do think that Mill was extremely sensitive to conflicting evidence. And is it possible to include all our conceptions of human nature in a model, descriptive or analytical? Given the strains on language, pressed on one side to express external commonalities of experience, and on the other to express individual conceptions, neither of which it can do, and moulded as language is by its particular culture, time, and utterer, one cannot expect agreement. As John Mill says, 'mankind are much more nearly of one nature, than of one opinion about their own nature ...'[67] I confess that I can hardly conceive what it would mean if all rational men were to agree on a definition, as James Mill thought they eventually would, or if all good men did, as John Mill hoped they eventually might, let alone if all men, irrational, evil, and mixed as we are, knew our species for what it is, was, and may be.[68]

67 'Bentham,' CW, X, 110
68 When this paper was read, this conclusion was taken, by at least one hearer, to imply that I believe the endeavour to know our nature should be abandoned. I believe neither that it will nor should be, and further, hold, like any sane person, that we shall and should continue to use our imperfect knowledge in the attempt to improve our condition. But Mill should have the last word. 'On Saturday night at York,' he writes to Harriet on 17 Feb. 1857, 'I slept little & dreamt much – among the rest a long dream of some speculation on animal nature, ending with my either reading or writing, just before I awoke, this Richterish sentence: "With what prospect then, until a cow is fed on broth, we can expect the truth, the whole truth & nothing but the truth to be unfolded concerning this part of nature, I leave to" &c &c.' (CW, XV, 523)

Contributors

EDWARD ALEXANDER is Professor of English in the University of Washington in Seattle. He is the author of *Matthew Arnold and John Stuart Mill* (1965), *John Morley* (1972), and *Matthew Arnold, John Ruskin and the Modern Temper* (1973), and the editor of *John Stuart Mill: Literary Essays* (1967).

KARL BRITTON was a pupil of Moore and Wittgenstein in Cambridge in the early thirties, and of Whitehead and Sheffer at Harvard. He is Professor of Philosophy in the University of Newcastle upon Tyne and is interested in Hume, Mill, Coleridge, and Arnold. He is the author of *John Stuart Mill: Life and Philosophy* (1953, 1969) and *Philosophy and the Meaning of Life* (1969) and has recently received the degree of D.Litt.(Hon.) from the University of Durham.

J.H. BURNS is Professor of the History of Political Thought in the University of London and General Editor of *The Collected Works of Jeremy Bentham*. Formerly Lecturer in Political Theory at Aberdeen University, he has worked principally in Scottish intellectual history in the fifteenth and sixteenth centuries and in the political ideas of Benthamite utilitarianism.

L.S. FEUER is Professor of Sociology in the University of Toronto. From 1957 to 1966 he was Professor of Philosophy and Chairman of the Social Science Integrated Course at the University of California, Berkeley. His book *Einstein and the Generations of Science* (1974) was nominated for the National Book Award in Science. His latest book is *Ideology and the Ideologists* (1975).

JOSEPH HAMBURGER has taught in the Department of Political Science at Yale University since 1957. He is the editor of a forthcoming edition of James Mill's essays, and his publications include *James Mill and the Art of Revolution* (1963), *Intellectuals in Politics: John Stuart Mill and the Philosophical Radicals* (1965), and *Macaulay and the Whig Tradition* (forthcoming).

SAMUEL HOLLANDER teaches in the Department of Political Economy at the University of Toronto. He studied at the University of London and at Princeton University. His published work includes *The Economics of Adam Smith* (1973) and articles in *Economica, Economic Journal,* and *Oxford Economic Papers.* He is on the advisory board of *History of Political Economy* and is currently engaged on a study of the economics of David Ricardo. He was a Guggenheim Fellow in 1968–9 and a Killam Fellow in 1973–5.

JOHN M. ROBSON is Principal and Professor of English in Victoria College, University of Toronto. He is General and Textual Editor of *The Collected Works of John Stuart Mill,* of which thirteen of a projected twenty-four volumes have been published. Author of *The Improvement of Mankind: The Social and Political Thought of John Stuart Mill* (1968), he has published widely in the field of Victorian literature and thought.

J.B. SCHNEEWIND has taught philosophy in the University of Pittsburgh for the past eleven years, except when he was in England studying and writing about Victorian intellectual history. He has recently completed a book entitled *Sidgwick's Ethics and Victorian Moral Philosophy* which incorporates some material from his Mill Centenary Conference paper.

GEORGE STIGLER has been Walgreen Professor of American Institutions in the University of Chicago since 1958. He has taught at Brown and Columbia universities and at the London School of Economics, and has been a member of the Research Staff of the National Bureau of Economics. His published work includes *The Theory of Price* (1946), *Essays in the History of Economics* (1965), and *The Behavior of Industrial Prices* (1970); he is editor of the *Journal of Political Economy.*